Coping with
Proposition 13

Coping with Proposition 13

Roger L. Kemp

LexingtonBooks
D.C. Heath and Company
Lexington, Massachusetts
Toronto

Library of Congress Cataloging in Publication Data

Kemp, Roger L
  Coping with Proposition 13.

  Bibliography: p.
  1. Finance, Public—California—Oakland. 2. Real property tax—
California. I. Title.
HJ9205.032K45   353.97940072   80-8188
ISBN 0-669-03974-8

Copyright © 1980 by D.C. Heath and Company

Published simultaneously in Canada

Printed in the United States of America

International Standard Book Number: 0-669-03974-8

Library of Congress Catalog Card Number: 80-8188

This book is dedicated to those public officials throughout the country who may have to cope with revenue-reducing mandates similar to California's Proposition 13, and to taxpayers in general so they may gain insight into the difficult process of reducing governmental budgets.

Contents

List of Figures

List of Tables

Preface

The passage of Proposition 13 was historically significant. It is having and will continue to have a great impact on local governments in California for years to come. It has also acted as the impetus to what has commonly been referred to as the "National Taxpayers' Revolt." Many scholarly studies have been completed, planned, or are in progress on the subject of Proposition 13. These deal with the impact of this legislation on specific public services. None seem to treat the political or administrative processes necessary to adapt to such revenue-reducing mandates.

Citizens voted for Proposition 13 in their own self-interests. They calculated the trade-off between the prospective gain from paying fewer taxes to government and the anticipated loss of their public services. Since most citizens stood to realize an immediate financial benefit from the property-tax relief provided by the initiative, they overwhelmingly supported it at the polls. Most people believed that their basic services would not be reduced and, for the most part, this belief has held true, primarily because of the permanent fiscal relief provided by the State of California.

The public sentiments that led to the landslide victory of the Jarvis-Gann Initiative are increasing, both within and outside California's political boundaries. This phenomenon is documented by the fact that, in 1979 alone, twenty-two states reduced property taxes, eighteen states reduced income taxes, fifteen states curtailed the collection of sales taxes on certain products and services, eight states voted spending limits that will result in leaner state- and local-government budgets, and a dozen states repealed or reduced assorted other taxes.

As these sentiments manifest themselves in voting booths throughout the nation, the political arena is bound to become more turbulent. This change in public attitude is likely to lead to a gradual shift in public policy, as politicians and administrators alike are forced to react to this "populist" movement. This is sure to lead to more government belt-tightening, a thorough review and evaluation of existing public programs, and closer scrutiny of new public services. As governmental resources become increasingly scarce, selected public programs and services will have to be reduced in order to balance budgets. The era of unlimited revenues, brought about by ever-higher taxes, is now coming to an end. This is becoming a political fact of life.

Increasingly, the budget-cutting process will be hard-fought as conflicting values are debated and priorities are established. As the purse strings become tighter, special-interest groups will attempt to influence public officials in order to maintain their programs. Public officials cannot merely yield to the pressures brought to bear by these special interests. They must, instead, devise practicable strategies that enable budget reductions to proceed in a logical and defensible manner. This process must take into consideration community-wide interests, as opposed to the narrow concerns of these special-interest groups. If this does not happen, citizens are likely to continue to vent their frustrations at the polls by mandating additional government taxing and spending controls. Nowadays every level of government—local, state, and federal—is under increasing public scrutiny.

The purpose of this book is to lend insight into the political and administrative decision-making process that results from coping with revenue and expenditure constraints. It is hoped that the strategy developed for adjusting governmental budgets may prove useful to public officials in other cities and states who must grapple with revenue-reducing legislation similar to California's Proposition 13. Such strategies must be developed to restore public confidence in government. Citizens must also be aware that any budget-reduction process is a time-consuming and difficult task. The Oakland example clearly illustrates this point.

Acknowledgments

This book underwent many drafts and revisions before reaching its present form. I am particularly thankful to Dr. Randy H. Hamilton, dean of the Graduate School of Public Administration, Golden Gate University, for his guidance, comments, and suggestions on ways to improve upon this study. I am also grateful to Dr. Otto Butz, president of Golden Gate University, for his support and encouragement throughout the entire preparation of the manuscript. Finally, I am indebted to Dr. Victor Jones, professor in the Graduate School of Public Administration, Golden Gate University, for substantially improving upon both the structure and content of this study. The criticisms and suggestions provided by these gentlemen resulted in a much more concise, readable, and scholarly book. All of these individuals took a great amount of time and effort out of their busy schedules to review the manuscript during various phases of its development. These learned gentlemen are responsible for the merits of this work; I alone am responsible for any of its shortcomings.

1 Introduction

The fiscal and operational adjustments local governments will have to make in response to Proposition 13, or similar revenue-reducing legislation, have complicated effects on elected officials, governmental administrators, and citizens. Local governments must assess such legislation to determine its financial impact upon public services, placing emphasis on alternative strategies to cope administratively with such mandates. The fiscal analysis of proposed legislation must be made far in advance of the legislation's scheduled implementation date.

Proposition 13, formally referred to as the Jarvis-Gann Property-Tax Initiative, was passed by California's electorate on 6 June 1978, and became effective on 1 July 1978, only three weeks after its adoption. Needless to say, a local government cannot wait until such legislation is adopted before analyzing its financial and operational ramifications on public services. These implications, and the political and administrative responses used to cope with them, pose a challenge to both local legislators and governmental administrators. These implications, an analysis of the Jarvis-Gann Initiative, including the revenue constraints imposed by this mandate and how they were dealt with by one municipality, are the subject of this study.

The Jarvis-Gann Initiative

The Jarvis-Gann Initiative severely restricts the revenue-generating ability of both state and local governments. One of the major sources of revenues to local governments, the property tax, was the revenue source hit hardest by this initiative. On a statewide basis it is estimated that about $7 billion annually in local property-tax revenues will be taken away from California's local governments. The major provisions of this initiative, which became effective on 1 July 1978, are briefly outlined below.

1. Establishes a ceiling on ad valorem property taxes.
2. Mandates limitations on the full cash-value increases on real property.
3. Prohibits future real property taxes of any kind.
4. Imposes increased requirements on the implementation of new state taxes.
5. Requires a two-thirds voter approval of all new local taxes.

1

6. Prohibits the use of property-tax-supported bond issues in the future.
7. Excludes bond indebtedness having previous voter approval from the provisions of this initiative.

The implications of this initiative are far-reaching. Both state and local governments are restricted from implementing future taxes, regardless of the justifications involved. Prior to 1 July 1978, general obligation bonds required a two-thirds approval by those voters actually casting ballots in an election held for that purpose. The new provision, requiring a two-thirds vote of the qualified electors, may further impose restrictions upon the revenue-generating ability of local governments. It has not yet been determined if the phrase "qualified electors" refers to those individuals registered to vote or to those actually voting in an election. One ramification of this initiative is that local governments, in an effort to offset revenue losses mandated by the Jarvis-Gann Initiative, sought to implement alternative revenue sources prior to 1 July 1978. After this date, the implementation of new taxes at the local level requires voter approval. This provision is bound to adversely affect the revenue-generating capability as well as the delivery of public services by local governments in California in the years ahead. A more comprehensive analysis of Proposition 13, including an analysis of the California Legislature's counterproposal, Senate Bill 1, is contained in chapter 2.

Taxes and Public Services

It appears that most of California's citizens, having felt the financial pressures of increasing property taxes for a number of years, plus the highly publicized fact that large state-surplus revenues had accumulated, were eagerly awaiting the opportunity to express their desires for reduced taxes, whatever the form. This was the basis of the argument used to qualify the Jarvis-Gann Property Tax Initiative for the state ballot. This argument proved successful. Approximately 0.5 million signatures were needed to qualify this initiative for the state ballot; nearly 1.3 million signatures were obtained. Citizens could only perceive the short-term effects of such legislation: the hard-dollar tax savings. The long-run implications, however, are more significant and may involve a substantial reduction in selected public services in the years ahead because of decreased revenues.

The majority of citizens usually only identify themselves with those specific public services they directly utilize. Public services not used directly by the majority, such as those offered in many cultural, recreational, and social programs, are typically considered as the "fat" in government. These programs, however, also have many beneficiaries and cannot be reduced without affecting the lives of many individuals. All public services have their constituents, many of whom comprise only a small minority of a governmental jurisdiction's total population.

By far the most visible of public services offered by local governments appear to be police and fire activities. In fact, the state legislation authorizing the distribution of California's surplus revenues (Senate Bills 154 and 2212), which amounted to $5.1 billion, expressly stated that police and fire services could not be reduced below pre-Jarvis-Gann funding levels, except for economies that could be achieved without disrupting the level of these services.

Of the total state-surplus revenues, $4.2 billion was distributed as financial aid to local governments; the remaining amount, $0.9 billion, was placed in an emergency loan fund for local governments. The purpose of this fund was to act as a "lender of last resort" to purchase local government tax-anticipation notes. The state legislation mandating the distribution of state-surplus revenues is examined in greater detail in chapter 5.

One Government's Response

In the city of Oakland, California, soon after the Jarvis-Gann Initiative qualified for the state's ballot, the city council directed the professional staff of the city to assess the potential financial implications of this measure on the city's revenue base. This financial analysis was presented to the council in January 1978. The revenue loss to the city was determined to be in excess of $35 million.

After reviewing this report, the city council directed the city manager to prepare an alternative city budget, assuming that no replacement revenues would be received to offset the projected revenue losses. At that time, the council felt that if the initiative was passed by the voters, the city should be prepared to implement an alternative budget based on the substantial reduction in revenues and a corresponding decrease in public services. Furthermore, additional revenues were not then certain. Moreover, if the Jarvis-Gann Initiative passed in June, the city's electorate would not want other taxes or nontax revenues to be increased to compensate for the property-tax-revenue loss. Therefore, the council indicated that this budget should provide for a level of public services to meet available, or post-Jarvis-Gann, revenues.

In April 1978 the alternative city budget was presented to the city council. As soon as this budget was prepared, the reductions in public services became apparent. The $35-million-revenue loss meant the closure of fire stations, branch libraries, parks, and recreation centers, and a decrease in police services. This alternative city budget necessitated the elimination of approximately 1,300 positions: about one-third of the city's total labor force. Due to the magnitude of the revenue loss, which amounted to nearly a third of the city's discretionary funds, service reductions could not be made only in selected public-service areas. Instead, public services had to be reduced, by varying degrees, in virtually every city department. Subsequent refinements were made in this budget at the request of the city council. This alternative city budget was approved by the council in early May 1978. A hiring freeze was also imposed by Oakland's city manager during the council's deliberations on the Jarvis-Gann Budget.

In addition to this budget, the city manager prepared a short publication titled "Public Service Impact Statement," describing in detail the public services that would be affected by the passage of the Jarvis-Gann Initiative. This analysis set forth service reductions on a citywide basis, by department. The budget document, along with the "Public Service Impact Statement," was distributed to the city council, the local news media, interested community groups, and concerned citizens. Prior to the election, notices were also placed on those public facilities which would be either closed or reduced under Proposition 13. These signs, titled "Notice of Possible Closure," and "Notice of Potential Reduction of City Services," explained how passage of the Jarvis-Gann Initiative on June 6 would affect public services. These actions enabled the public to relate to specific public-service reductions rather than just to think of "reducing the fat," a term which was frequently heard during the debates on the merits of this initiative. A more insightful perspective of the actual impact of this initiative on public services was gained by the citizens of Oakland as a result of these public-informational efforts.

On 6 June 1978, Proposition 13 passed by nearly a two-to-one margin on a statewide basis. Oakland, however, was one of the few cities in California that voted against this initiative. The statewide vote was approximately 4.2 million in favor, 2.9 million against. The Oakland vote, on the other hand, was 42,060 in favor and 46,118 against. The timely analysis of the impact of this legislation by city officials may have been a decisive factor in this voting pattern. While Oakland still had to cope with the passage of the Jarvis-Gann Initiative, it could do so in a more positive and constructive manner. Rather than merely reducing public services en masse to meet the anticipated level of limited resources imposed by the initiative, selected revenue sources were increased to mitigate estimated revenue losses. Additional revenues were subsequently approved by the city council. These included the use of one-time city savings, elimination of the Convention Center Fund, and increases in the transient-occupancy tax, the business license tax, and the real estate transfer tax. The additional taxes were all approved prior to the 1 July 1978 deadline imposed by the initiative.

The additional revenues, coupled with the city's estimated receipt of the state's surplus revenues and other revenue adjustments, reduced the magnitude of the city's financial deficit from $35 million to slightly over $14 million. The receipt of supplemental revenues from the state enabled the city of Oakland to "spread" its revenue loss under Proposition 13 over a two-year period, thereby minimizing service reductions and reducing the number of city employees to be laid off. Under the original estimate of revenue loss, over 1,300 positions were scheduled to be eliminated. Once additional revenues were mandated and the amount of the state's surplus revenues was determined, only 227 positions were actually cut—only a fraction of the original number. Due to the hiring freeze, all but seventy of these positions were vacant by the beginning of the city's new fiscal year, 1 July 1978.

During July and August, the city council scheduled a series of public workshops to further review departmental budgets. These meetings were designed to explore additional areas for possible future budget reductions. Given the uncertainties surrounding the continued receipt of state-surplus revenues and grant funds under certain federal programs, such as the State and Local Fiscal Assistance Act (revenue sharing) and the Public Works Employment Act (antirecessionary payments), the city faced a future budget deficit in fiscal year 1979–1980. The amount of funds estimated to be received from these sources during fiscal year 1978–1979 was $9.3 million, $5.9 million, and $4.2 million, respectively. These efforts were intended to facilitate future budget reductions which had to be made.

Implications

The short-term implications of Proposition 13, or similar revenue-reducing legislation, are obvious. Government officials must direct their staffs to provide timely analysis of the impact of such legislation on their governmental jurisdiction's financial condition as well as on its public-service levels. This action was taken in Oakland six months in advance of the scheduled implementation date mandated by the Jarvis-Gann Initiative.

Additionally, it is incumbent upon elected officials and appointed administrators alike to educate the citizenry as to the impact such legislation may have upon existing public services. In Oakland, the "Public Service Impact Statement" objectively described such service reductions on a departmental basis. Several public hearings were also conducted by the city council to further review the impact of Proposition 13 on city services. Educating citizens as to the possible service reductions under this type of legislation may prove to be a vital and decisive factor in influencing public sentiments. These actions enabled Oakland's citizens to relate directly to specific public services that would be curtailed or eliminated, rather than merely to identify such legislation with the elimination of the so-called fat in their government. This is not to say, however, that certain economies cannot be achieved without adversely affecting the prevailing level of public services.

In the long run, local governments will have to place greater emphasis on increasing operational productivity; identifying revenues, particularly user fees, with specific public programs; increasing user fees to make as many programs as possible self-sustaining; and analyzing the financial implications of new public services.

Emphasis should be placed, whenever possible, on financing new public programs on a user-fee basis. A public program entirely financed out of the revenues it generates is not likely to be curtailed. On the other hand, citizens increasingly do not like to subsidize many programs they do not directly utilize. This is not to say that all public programs should be financially self-sufficient. It should be kept in mind that many programs exist for the betterment of the health and welfare of the entire community, such as police, fire, public works, and many cultural and recreational programs, to name a few.

Above all, the financial posture of local governments should be austere. Excessive surplus revenues should not be permitted to accumulate. If such revenues exist, taxes should be reduced accordingly. These long-run implications should be the goals of local legislators and administrators alike, regardless of the governmental entity in which they serve. This is the challenge which faces public officials at all levels of government. Only responsible actions in these areas may change prevailing public sentiments and place local governments in a more positive perspective. Until this happens, the taxpayers' revolt is likely to blossom to national proportions.

National Taxpayers' Revolt

The taxpayers' movement is not limited to California. Riding the crest of what many observers have termed a wave of taxpayer revolt, supporters of tax reform have generated numerous proposals in many other states throughout the country. Now that most of the state legislatures have met and adjourned for the year, it is apparent that the trend toward reducing or repealing taxes and imposing spending limits on state and local governments has been a strong and pervasive one. Virtually all states have curtailed revenues or spending, or both, to some extent. The taxpayers' revolt shows no signs of abating. Another round of referendums and initiatives similar to that of the 1978 elections is being planned for next year's elections.

In addition to the reductions and spending limitations authorized last year by state governments and by ballot initiatives, official action so far in 1979 includes the following:

1. Twenty-two states have reduced property taxes with actions ranging from across-the-board rebates for homeowners to limited relief for the elderly and disabled.

2. Eighteen states have reduced income taxes, either through a rollback in rates or by increasing certain deductions and credits.

3. Fifteen states have curtailed, in some fashion, the collection of sales taxes on certain products and services.

4. Eight states have voted spending limits that will result in leaner state and local government budgets in the future.

5. A dozen states have repealed or reduced assorted other taxes. Iowa, for example, is gradually ending its personal-property tax, while Nevada has repealed its tax on household goods.

Scattered through these actions has been specific relief for commercial interests. In Maine, for example, voters approved a sales-tax exemption for farming and fishing equipment, while North Dakota removed sugar-beet-refining machinery from the property-tax rolls. In a number of other states, tax relief was voted for citizens at the lower end of the income scale. Maryland, for example, rolled back property taxes applicable to lower-income homeowners. In Nevada, on the other hand, voters in a special election on 5 June repealed a 3.5-percent sales tax on food.

Overall, it may be said that these state actions were primarily intended to benefit the broad sector of middle-class citizens who have been protesting in recent years about the increasing tax burden. Also commercial interests that have long maintained powerful lobbies in state capitals have capitalized on the middle-class protest against taxes. A listing of tax and spending limitations approved in 1979 is shown in table 1-1.

Reductions have been far more extensive on the income tax, considered to be the most progressive in relation to ability to pay, than on the sales tax, which is regarded as the least progressive. In New York State, the maximum rate on personal-income taxes will be reduced to 10 percent from 12 percent over the next two years. In Delaware, where the general assembly enacted a $21.5 million income-tax cut, the more substantial savings are for the upper-income and middle-income brackets. In Utah, the state legislature voted for a property-tax rebate while rejecting a petition signed by 5 percent of the voters to remove the sales tax on food items.

The middle-class orientation of the tax-relief movement was perhaps best expressed in Texas where the state legislature spent much of the year carrying out a constitutional amendment approved by the voters last November to impose certain tax limits. In addition to increasing homestead exemptions and rolling back property taxes for the elderly, while excluding renters from the relief package, the legislature also exempted from the personal-property tax two cars per family.

The relief extended to business interests stemmed in part from the emphasis that is being placed on private economic development, both by government officials and by other leaders throughout the country. The effort by western states to make the tax picture more favorable to business and industry has spread to the Northeast and Middle West where the older cities have been losing both wealth and population.

Connecticut enacted a property-tax exemption for commercial fishing vessels; Maryland voted to let corporations deduct dividends from foreign subsidiaries; Minnesota voted to end its gross-earnings tax on business over a two-year period; Pennsylvania voted to allow income-tax credit for capital expenditures by beer manufacturers; and Wisconsin exempted commercial farmers from the sales tax on electricity.

The future for tax reductions and spending limitations looks bright. Ballot initiatives scheduled for next year include both the new and the old. In Colorado, for example, a renewed effort is being mounted to make spending limits on the state budget, now statutory, a part of the constitution. In Ohio an initiative will go on the ballot next June to give homeowners broad-based property-tax relief, to increase the personal-income tax for those earning more than $30,000 annually, and to repeal several business taxes. In Florida, where property owners were granted $375 million in tax relief this year, a proposal will be on the ballot to increase homestead exemptions from $5,000 to $25,000. In Washington an initiative will be on the ballot this November to impose a statutory limit on state-revenue increases pegged to the rate of growth in personal income.

This list will continue to grow as citizens become angered by increasing taxes and high levels of government spending. The taxpayers' revolt appears to be spreading throughout the country. In those states where legislation has mandated revenue or spending limitations on state and local governments, these public entities will be forced to place priorities on their respective public services. The least desirable programs will have to be cut in order to balance state and municipal budgets. This phenomenon has already occurred in many cities in California as a result of the passage of Proposition 13. The experience and insights gained in this process can benefit elected officials, governmental administrators, and citizens in other cities and states undergoing the same arduous process.

State and local governments are not the only targets of the tax-revolt movement. The budget of the federal government is under an increasing level of scrutiny. Twenty-eight states have already petitioned Congress to call for a constitutional convention for the purpose of amending the U.S. Constitution to provide for a balanced federal budget. Only six more states are needed to require this convention. As additional cities and states are

Table 1–1
National Survey, Tax and Spending Limitation Reductions Approved in 1979

Property-tax reductions

Arkansas	Massachusetts	Ohio
Florida	Minnesota	Oregon
Idaho	Missouri	South Dakota
Iowa	Montana	Tennessee
Kansas	Nevada	Utah
Kentucky	New Mexico	Washington
Maryland	North Dakota	Wisconsin
		Wyoming

Income-tax reductions

Arizona	Minnesota	Oklahoma
Colorado	Mississippi	Oregon
Delaware	Montana	Rhode Island
Indiana	New Mexico	Vermont
Iowa	New York	Virginia
Kansas	North Carolina	Wisconsin

Sales-tax reductions

Kansas	Minnesota	Tennessee
Kentucky	Mississippi	Virginia
Maine	Nevada	Washington
Maryland	New York	West Virginia
Michigan	South Dakota	Wisconsin

Spending limitations

Florida	Nebraska	South Carolina
Massachusetts	Oregon	Utah
Montana	Rhode Island	

Property assessment limitations

Arizona	Iowa	Maryland
		Oregon

Note: Survey conducted by the National Conference of State Legislatures and the Coalition of American Public Employees, Washington, D.C., June 1979.

forced to reduce their taxes and spending, attention will increasingly be focused upon the level of government with the largest budget—the federal government.

Purpose of the Study

The passage of Proposition 13 is historically significant. It is having, and will continue to have, a great impact on California cities for years to come.

Many scholarly studies are presently planned or in progress on the subject of Proposition 13. These deal with the impact of this legislation on specific public services. None seems to treat the political or administrative processes used to adapt to such revenue-reducing mandates.

This study will set forth and analyze the administrative and political processes undertaken in the city of Oakland, California, to cope successfully with the passage of the Jarvis-Gann Initiative. It will result in a paradigm, or model, which, it is hoped, can be used by elected and appointed officials in other cities and states which will have to grapple with similar revenue-reducing mandates. This study will also record for historical purposes the political, administrative, and operational impact of Proposition 13 on one California municipality. Since Oakland faces many of the political, economic, and social problems prevalent in other cities, the strategy used in Oakland should be applied in other cities with equal success.

Most cities in California waited until the passage of this initiative before implementing measures to counteract its adverse impact. Oakland was one of the few that strategically planned far in advance of the passage of this initiative for its potential ramifications. Also it was one of the few cities in California that voted against the Jarvis-Gann Initiative. Some observers say that the process used to adapt to the impending revenue constraints imposed by this mandate was a decisive factor in this voting pattern.

Chapter 2 examines the many property-tax-relief proposals facing California's voters in the June 1978 election. The next three chapters describe and analyze the political and administrative decision-making processes in the city of Oakland, California, to cope with Proposition 13. For analytical purposes, the sequence of events occurring in Oakland in response to Proposition 13 has been broken down into three phases: advanced planning, anticipated impact, and actual impact. These categories are the titles for chapters 3, 4, and 5, respectively. Included in the discussion of the actual impact of Proposition 13 is an analysis of its continuing effect on Oakland's city government. Each chapter concludes with a commentary, which sets forth possible improvements in Oakland's response to this revenue-reducing mandate. Chapter 6 describes the statewide impact of Proposition 13. Chapter 7, the conclusion, proposes a comprehensive methodology for reducing public services.

2 Property-Tax Relief

Introduction

On 6 June 1978, California voters approved a constitutional amendment which drastically altered the system of local government finance. The property-tax loss to local governments (counties, cities, schools, and special districts) is estimated to be about $7 billion.[1] In addition to reducing property taxes, the passage of Proposition 13 brought national attention to what has been termed the "taxpayers' revolt." Although signs of the revolt had surfaced many times before in California, taking the form of proposals to limit government spending and reduce taxation, it seldom enjoyed much success. The tax revolt in California, however, seemed to gather momentum as the referendum date drew closer. Many areas of the state had experienced meteoric increases in property taxes, primarily due to skyrocketing assessed valuations. Additionally, the state found itself with a massive amount of surplus revenues. The knowledge of the existence of this "booty" outraged many taxpayers since the legislature had made no efforts to return the surplus to the taxpayers.

This chapter examines the intricacies of the Jarvis-Gann Property-Tax Initiative, subsequently labeled Proposition 13; Senate Bill 1, the state legislature's response to the widespread popularity of the property-tax relief movement; and Proposition 8, the vehicle used to implement the legislature's property-tax-relief proposal.

There was a maze of property-tax legislation in California during the spring of 1978. The various tax-reduction proposals were complex and often confusing to the voters who ultimately had to decide upon the form the reduction would take. The following pages will sort out the many often-conflicting property-tax-reduction proposals on California's June 1978 ballot. The California Supreme Court's decision on the constitutionality of Proposition 13 is also examined.[2]

Proposition 13

In 1968 a proposal to limit property taxes to 1 percent of value was placed on the state ballot under the sponsorship of Phillip Watson, then assessor of

11

Los Angeles County. It was defeated by a margin of two to one. Watson tried again with a somewhat different proposal four years later. It too was defeated by a vote of almost two to one. Howard Jarvis, chairman, United Organization of Taxpayers, and Paul Gann, president, Peoples Advocate, had each tried previously to qualify tax measures for the state ballot but had not been successful. They pooled their resources in 1977 and managed to obtain enough signatures to qualify their property-tax-relief proposal for the state ballot.[3]

Jarvis, a resident of Los Angeles County, coordinated the campaign for the Jarvis-Gann Initiative in southern California. Gann, who resides in Sacramento County, coordinated the property-tax-relief effort in northern California. Initiative measures affecting the state constitution must, by law, acquire the signatures of 8 percent of the votes cast in the last gubernatorial election.[4] Approximately 0.5 million signatures were needed to qualify this initiative for the state ballot.[5] The combined efforts of Jarvis and Gann produced nearly 1.3 million signatures. The signatures were verified by the secretary of state. On 29 December 1977, the Jarvis-Gann Initiative qualified to be included on the state ballot for the 6 June 1978 elections.[6]

The Jarvis-Gann Initiative, Proposition 13 on the state ballot, was designed to add article 13 A to the state constitution. While this constitutional amendment was reportedly poorly drafted, it was relatively simple and straightforward. The complete amendment, barely more than a page long, is reproduced in figure 2–1.[7]

Proposition 13 was intended to reduce the level of ad valorem property taxes and impose limitations on future property-tax increases. The measure was also designed to limit the powers of the state and local governments to impose future taxes. A summary of the provisions of the Jarvis-Gann Initiative is provided below.

Property-Tax Relief. Mandated limits on real property taxes to 1 percent of "full cash value." This 1 percent will be collected by the counties and apportioned "according to law" to the political subdivisions within each county. The maximum allowable property-tax rate was established at $4 per $100 of assessed valuation, excluding voter-approved bond indebtedness passed prior to the effective date of the initiative.[8]

Property Values. Property values were frozen to the full cash value listed on the county assessor's 1975–1976 valuation of real property. These valuations were established by respective county assessors on 1 March 1975. Thereafter, the maximum increase in the assessed valuations of real property is limited to 2 percent per year. Assessment increases are permitted to the current value upon the sale or new construction of property after the effective date of the initiative.[9]

Adds Article XIII A to the California Constitution

Section 1

(a) The maximum amount of any ad valorem tax on real property shall not exceed one percent (1%) of the full cash value of such property. The one percent (1%) tax [sic] to be collected by the counties and apportioned according to law to the districts within the counties.

(b) The limitation provided for in subdivision (a) shall not apply to ad valorem taxes or special assessments to pay the interest and redemption charges of any indebtedness approved by the voters prior to the time this section becomes effective.

Section 2

(a) The full cash value means the County Assessors valuation of real property as shown on the 1975–76 tax bill under "full cash value," or thereafter, the appraised value of real property when purchased, newly constructed, or a change in ownership has occurred after the 1975 assessment. All real property not already assessed up to the 1975–76 tax levels may be reassessed to reflect that valuation.

(b) The fair market value base may reflect from year to year the inflationary rate not to exceed two percent (2%) for any given year or reduction as shown in the consumer price index or comparable data for the area under taxing jurisdiction.

Section 3

From and after the effective date of this article, any changes in state taxes enacted for the purpose of increasing revenues collected pursuant thereto whether by increased rates or changes in methods of computation must be imposed by an Act passed by not less than two-thirds of all members elected to each of the two houses of the legislature, except that no new ad valorem taxes on real property, or sales or transaction taxes on the sales of real property may be imposed.

Section 4

Cities, counties and special districts, by a two-thirds vote of the qualified electors of such district, may impose special taxes on such district, except ad valorem taxes on real property or a transaction tax on the sale of real property within such city, county or special district.

Section 5

This article shall take effect for the tax year beginning on July 1 following the passage of this Amendment, except Section 3 which shall become effective upon the passage of this article.

Section 6

If any section, part, clause, or phrase hereof is for any reason held to be invalid or unconstitutional, the remaining sections shall not be affected but will remain in full force and effect.

Figure 2–1. Jarvis-Gann Property-Tax Initiative Constitutional Amendment

New Property Taxes. Prohibits the state and local governments from levying any type of property tax or property-transfer tax. Any other increases in
property taxes, including voter-approved tax increases, are prohibited.[10]

State Taxes. All future state taxes, regardless of their form, must receive a
two-thirds vote of the state legislature before being implemented. The state
legislature previously required a simple majority to approve taxes. This
provision was effective upon the passage of the initiative.[11]

Local Taxes. All future local taxes, regardless of their form, must receive a
two-thirds vote of the qualified electors to become effective. Most local
governments previously required a simple majority vote of their elected
representatives to implement new taxes. This requirement became effective
with the beginning of the new fiscal year: 1 July 1978.[12]

Implementation. All provisions of the initiative became effective on 1 July
1978, with the exception of the two-thirds vote requirement placed upon the
state legislature, which became effective upon the passage of the initiative
on 6 June 1978. The initiative also contained a severability clause whereby if
any portion of the measure were to be declared unconstitutional, the
remaining sections would remain in effect.[13]

    One of the most controversial problems surrounding the implementa-
tion of the initiative was the issue of property values. Assessors in one-half
of California's counties, arguing that real property assessments are not
updated each year, increased the 1975–1976 valuations to reflect the then-
current market values. This action, which generated much public outrage,
was immediately challenged in the courts. In Alameda County, in which
Oakland exists, a suit was decided by the superior court in favor of property
owners. A few months later, the state legislature adopted Senate Bill 17
which mandated a statewide refund of all overassessments and forced the
country assessors to use the 1975–1976 property valuations listed on assessment records. Other problems relating to the implementation of the initiative are discussed in chapter 6.

Senate Bill 1

The state's politicians, along with the tens of thousands of people who work
for local governments, feared Proposition 13 as they have feared nothing
else in many years. The estimates vary somewhat, but local governments
(counties, cities and towns, schools, and fire districts) stood to lose as much
as $7 billion in revenues if the Jarvis-Gann Initiative passed. Statewide, this

averages out to 57 percent of their revenues, though the figures for individual agencies vary depending on how dependent they are on the property tax for their income.[14]

Whether or not Proposition 13 would be approved by the electors on 6 June 1978, the possibility of its passage accomplished one important objective. It not only prompted the state legislature to act on much-needed property-tax relief, but also influenced the design of the measure which was finally approved. To a large extent, Senate Bill 1, sponsored by Senator Peter Behr of Marin County, reflected the legislature's attempt to produce a competitive alternative to Proposition 13.[15] Senate Bill 1 was the only viable alternative to the Jarvis-Gann Initiative.

On 3 March 1978, Governor Jerry Brown signed Senate Bill 1 into law. This was the final action of a fourteen-month effort by the state legislature to come up with a substantive property-tax-relief program. It provided something for everyone: homeowners, renters, and senior citizens alike. It did all this without increasing either state or local taxes. The state's surplus revenues, estimated to be slightly over $5 billion, were to be used as the revenue-replacement vehicle for local governments. Local governments were to be reimbursed dollar for dollar for all property-tax-revenue reductions. Furthermore, Senate Bill 1 provided additional tax relief by placing revenue limits on cities, counties, and special districts. This provision alone was calculated to save all taxpayers as much as a billion dollars a year by the mid-1980s.[16]

Senate Bill 1, unlike Proposition 13, was a very complex piece of legislation. It contained twenty-seven pages of fine print written in legal terminology that was difficult for the average citizen to understand. One source indicated that it was "one of the most complex pieces of legislation to emerge from the legislature in many years."[17] Unlike the Jarvis-Gann Initiative, which simply added an article to the state constitution, senate Bill 1 amended sections of the California Government Code, the Revenue and Taxation Code, and the Welfare and Institutions Code.[18] A discussion of the most important aspects of Senate Bill 1 is provided below.[19]

Property-Tax Relief. Provided for an across-the-board total reduction of 30 percent in property-tax bills for all owner-occupied dwellings in California effective for the 1978–1979 property-tax year. This reduction was to come in the form of a deduction from the tax bill, as opposed to a reimbursement for taxes paid. This form of relief would have been in addition to the current homeowner property-tax exemption of $1,750 per year.[20]

Social Progams. Currently, the property-tax rate paid by homeowners includes costs for the state's Medi-Cal Program, Aid to Families with Dependent Children, Supplementary Security Income, and the State Supplementary Program. Senate Bill 1 required the state to assume the costs of these welfare programs.[21]

Renter's Relief. Mandated an increase in the level of the renter's credit program from $37 to $75 per year, effective with the 1978 income year. It also extended the credit to persons receiving public assistance. This increase provided property-tax relief to renters in proportion to the relief provided to homeowners.[22]

Senior Citizen Relief. Additional tax relief for senior citizen renters and homeowners was made available. The income limit provided to senior citizen homeowners (over 62 years of age) was increased from $12,000 per year to $13,000 per year. The percentage of tax relief equivalent for senior citizen renters was increased from $220 to $250 annually. Also the income limit for renters was increased from $5,000 to $13,000 per year.[23]

Local Taxes. Imposed a limit on city, county, and special district property-tax-revenue growth on owner-occupied homes effective with the 1978–1979 property-tax year. Revenue increases could be no greater than the percentage increase in the gross national product (GNP) deflator plus new construction. The GNP deflator is an index which reflects the costs of governmental goods and services. This index was to be replaced in two years by a California index, which is currently being developed by the California Department of Industrial Relations. This limit on local property-tax-revenue growth included state-assessed property, newly annexed property, and redevelopment agency property.[24]

State Taxes. Imposed a limit on the annual increases in major state revenues (95 percent of all revenues) at a rate no greater than the percentage increase in California personal income, multiplied by a 1.2 revenue elasticity factor.[25]

Excess Revenue Fund. Established an excess revenue fund into which state revenues above the state revenue limit would be deposited. Moneys in this fund could be allocated, upon a two-thirds vote of the legislature, for additional state property-tax relief, a reduction of state taxes, maintenance of a prudent state surplus (3 percent of total state revenues), officially declared state emergencies, or the funding of a state revenue-sharing program with local governments.[26]

Implementation. Senate Bill 1 would have become effective on 3 March 1978. It could only become operational, however, upon the passage of Proposition 8 and the defeat of Proposition 13 on the state's June ballot.[27]

Proposition 8

Proposition 8 was as simple as Senate Bill 1 was complex. It would have amended the California Constitution to permit the state legislature to lower property-tax rates for owner-occupied dwellings.[28] This measure did not describe how much lower the tax rates on owner-occupied dwellings could be. However, the proposition prohibited any increase in the tax rates on other types of property as a result of lowering the tax rates on owner-occupied dwellings.[29] The complete one-paragraph narrative of this amendment to the state constitution is shown in figure 2-2.[30] Presently, the state constitution requires all property, including homes, apartments, and commercial and industrial buildings, to be assessed for tax purposes at the same percentage of market value. With few exceptions, all property within the same taxing area is taxed at the same rate.[31]

Proponents of Proposition 8 referred to Proposition 13 as the "meatax" approach to cutting property taxes and reducing government spending. One writer referred to the Jarvis-Gann Initiative "as something like the old farmer's 2 × 4—the one he had to smack his mule between the eyes to get his attention. It worked very well."[32] Opponents of Proposition 8, on the other hand, compared the measure "to a scalpel in the hands of a surgeon."[33] They saw it as just the right thing to get the job done "without damaging any of the body politic's vital organs."[34] Jarvis-Gann Initiative supporters saw Proposition 8 as a legislative sellout, perfectly designed to preserve the fat in the public payroll.

The sponsors of Proposition 8, including Governor Brown, maintained that homeowners had become overburdened in recent years because home values had risen much faster than the market prices of other types of properties. As a result, homeowners had been saddled with a larger share of the property-tax burden. The governor claimed that this injustice could be cured by allowing home-tax rates to drop as assessments rose, while leaving

---

Adds Article XIII, Section 9.5, to the
California Constitution

Section 9.5

The legislature may provide for the taxation of owner-occupied dwellings, as defined by the legislature, or any fraction of the value thereof, at a rate lower than that levied on other property. In no event may the tax rate levied on other property be increased as a result of lowering the tax rate levied on owner-occupied dwellings.

Figure 2-2. Proposition 8—Legislative Constitutional Amendment
Number 6

the rates on other classes of properties as they were. The sponsors emphasized that this measure would provide reductions in home taxes without
increasing taxes on rentals, businesses, and farms.[35] As previously
indicated, the revenue loss to local governments would be financed out of
state-surplus revenues. This measure was basically the legislature's response
to property-tax relief without affecting the revenue base of local governments.

It is important to note that this proposition only authorized the legislature to act. It did not require it to do so. Consequently, the proposition,
by itself, would have had no direct fiscal effect on either the state or its local
governments.[36] Supporters of Proposition 13 recognized this weakness. A
typical criticism of this measure was that it "would be permissive, not man-
datory—that it would only permit a lower assessment rate on residential
property, not require it."[37] Additionally, critics frequently noted that
Senate Bill 1 could easily be overturned by a simple majority vote in the
legislature. Nevertheless, this proposition would have given the green light
to Senate Bill 1. A more comprehensive analysis of Proposition 13 and
Senate Bill 1 is provided below.

Analysis of Proposition 13 and Senate Bill 1

Proposition 13 provided immediate property-tax relief to homeowners at
the expense of local governments. Senate Bill 1 also provided property tax
relief, though to a lesser degree, with no reduction in revenues to local
governments. State-surplus revenues would have been allocated to local
governments in sums equivalent to the amount of tax dollars lost. Because
voters identify with their own pocketbooks before they relate to the revenue
loss of local government, the saving to taxpayers was the dominant issue on
the method of property-tax relief. A sample property-tax bill, calculated
under normal assessment and taxation practices, the Senate Bill 1 mandate,
and the Proposition 13 mandate is illustrated in table 2–1.[38]

Under normal property assessment and taxation practices, the owner of
a house valued at $80,000 would pay $2,117 in annual property taxes,
assuming the homeowners' exemption was taken. Under the requirements
of Senate Bill 1, the same homeowner would pay $1,482 in annual property
taxes, a saving of $635. Under the provisions of Proposition 13, this home-
owner would pay only $748 in annual property taxes, accruing savings of
$1,369. It should be noted, however, that any reduction in property taxes
increases a family's taxable income. These savings are subject to both state
and federal income taxes.

For example, under Senate Bill 1 the homeowner would lose $190 of the
savings to income taxes: $152 to the federal government and $38 to the state

Table 2–1
Sample Property Tax Bill: Normal/Senate Bill 1/Proposition 13,
Average California City, Fiscal Year 1978–1979

	Normal	Senate Bill 1	Proposition 13
Market value	$80,000	$80,000	$70,000[a]
Assessed valuation	20,000	20,000	17,500
Homeowner's exemption	1,750	1,750	1,750
Net assessed valuation	18,250	18,250	15,750
Composite tax rate	11.600	8.120[b]	4.075[c]
Property taxes	$2,117	$1,482	$748
Savings	—	$635	$1,369

[a] Assumes a market value of $70,000 in fiscal year 1975–1976.
[b] Assumes a tax-rate reduction of 30 percent over previous year.
[c] Assumes maximum allowable tax rate plus municipal bond rate of $0.075.

government. This leaves new annual property-tax savings of $445. The same homeowner, under Proposition 13, would stand to lose $411. Of this amount, $329 would go to pay federal income taxes; $82 would go to pay state income taxes. This leaves a net annual property tax reduction of $958. Even after taxes, the property-tax savings under Proposition 13 were twice as much as those provided under Senate Bill 1. The above tax "bite" assumes the average family of four with an adjusted annual gross income of $17,400.[39]

Proposition 13 could reduce homeowners' savings in other ways as well. Since this mandate limits property taxes without limiting government spending, counties, cities, and special districts could compensate for their revenue loss by increasing nonproperty-tax-revenue sources. For example, user fees and charges for services could be raised. Since Senate Bill 1 would not affect local government revenues, this situation would not be likely to happen.

It has been estimated that renters comprise 45 percent of all California households. Property taxes represent from 17 to 23 percent of rental payments.[40] While Proposition 13 includes residential-rental properties under its tax limitation and assessment freeze, it does not require landlords to pass on reduced property taxes through lower rents. Senate Bill 1, on the other hand, provided immediate relief by increasing the renter's income-tax credit from $37 to $75 per year. This was one of the distinct advantages of Senate Bill 1.

Another major issue was that of placing spending limitations on state and local governments. Proposition 13 established a two-thirds vote requirement upon the state legislature to implement new taxes. At the local governmental level all new taxes must receive approval of two-thirds of the qualified electorate. These requirements were effective on 6 June 1978 and 1 July 1978, respectively. Senate Bill 1, while imposing limitations on state and local government spending, was not nearly so severe. The estimated growth in expenditures at the state level was 12 percent, while the growth rate at the local level was estimated to be 8 percent.[41] Proposition 13 imposed considerable "growth" restraints on governmental spending, while Senate Bill 1 was more lenient.

The effect of Proposition 13 on local governments, including schools, could be tremendous, depending upon the individual unit of government's dependence on the property tax. While property taxes generally constitute 50 percent of total school-operating revenues, they may provide anywhere from 20 to 90 percent of school funds. Similarly, counties typically rely on property taxes for about 35 percent of their funds, but their dependence ranges between 24 and 49 percent. Cities average 23 percent but may use from 0 to 60 percent, while special districts may use property taxes for 0 to 100 percent of their budgets.[42] While the Proposition 13 property-tax limit would not directly affect the twelve California cities which do not levy a property tax,[43] it would have a considerable impact on other counties, cities, and special districts throughout the state which depend heavily on the property tax as a major revenue source. It should be noted that in some cities that do not receive property taxes, residents depend upon special districts for certain public services.

The drastic reduction in revenues predicted for California's many local governments did not become a reality, at least not during the first two years of the Proposition 13 mandate. The state legislature approved Senate Bill 154 and Assembly Bill 8, signed into law by the governor in June 1978 and July 1979, respectively. The provisions of these mandates which authorized the distribution of the state's surplus revenues are discussed more fully in chapters 5 and 6.

A side-by-side comparison of the requirements of Proposition 13 and Senate Bill 1 is provided in table 2-2.[44] This comparison illustrates the provisions mandated by each of these measures. Upon reviewing this comparison, one thing becomes apparent: Proposition 13 favored all property owners while Senate Bill 1 concentrated on providing relief primarily to homeowners, senior citizens, and renters. Senate Bill 1 could do this without raising taxes because of the existence of the state's surplus revenues. The continued distribution of these revenues to local governments, however, was dependent upon maintaining the high taxes that created the surplus in the first place. In essence, the state government was receiving much more revenue than it actually needed to provide the services it rendered. Because of the vast media coverage of the various property-tax-relief proposals, citizens were aware of what each measure purported to accomp-

Table 2–2

Comparison of Proposition 13 and Senate Bill 1 Provisions

Proposition 13	Senate Bill 1
Homeowner relief	
Statewide property taxes would be reduced by about 57 percent. The tax rate would be based on about 1.25 percent of value (1 percent plus funds for retirement of bonds).	Statewide, the average property-tax relief would be 32 percent in the first year and about 35 percent in four years.
Other property owners	
The 57-percent cut would apply to factories, apartment houses, farms, and other classes of property.	No direct relief.
Renters	
No direct relief. (Landlords could, however, pass on their savings in property taxes to tenants through lower rents.)	The income-tax credit for renters would be increased from $37 to $75 per year.
Senior citizens	
Nothing beyond general homeowner relief.	Homeowners over 62 with incomes below $13,000 a year would be eligible for additional property-tax exemptions. Renters over 62 also would get improved benefits. These senior-citizen benefits work on a sliding scale based on income.
Assessment features	
Rates would remain the same for all classes of property.	For the first time, rates could be reduced for owner-occupied homes, while rates remained at a higher level for other classes of property.
Government spending	
Establishes two-thirds vote requirement for increases in state taxes and for voter approval of new local taxes.	Places limits on increases in state and local governmental spending. The maximum annual income increase under this provision has been estimated at 8 percent for local government and 12 percent for the state. But these figures could vary significantly with an overall change in economic conditions.
Other taxes	
Californians would pay about $2 billion of their tax-relief money in higher-income taxes. They might have to pay additional state and local taxes to make up for the loss from the property-tax base.	The entire program would be financed from current state-surplus funds. There would be a $400 million increase in state and federal income-tax collections through loss of property-tax deductions.
Bonding capacity	
General obligation and other bonds will become more costly and much more difficult to finance.	General obligation and other bonds will still be available for financing capital improvements. General obligation bonds will continue to require a two-thirds voter approval.

Table 2–2 continued

Proposition 13	Senate Bill 1
Redevelopment agencies	
57-percent revenue reductions and 2-percent per year assessed valuation growth limits will make tax-increment financing infeasible.	Gradual rate reductions resulting from revenue limits will reduce receipts slightly. Assessed valuation growth is not controlled, and improvements within redevelopment areas are excluded from computations for establishing revenue limits.
Implementation	
Became effective 1 July 1978, except for two-thirds legislative voting requirement, which becomes effective immediately.	Became effective 3 March 1978; affects local and state revenues starting 1 July 1978; will be repealed unless Proposition 8 is approved and Proposition 13 is defeated or declared unconstitutional.

lish. It should also be noted that Proposition 13 was much easier to understand than Senate Bill 1. Additionally, the implementation of Senate Bill 1 was contingent upon the passage of Proposition 8, which further confused matters. Senate Bill 1 could only become law if Proposition 13 was defeated and Proposition 8 passed. Proposition 13, on the other hand, was not linked to the passage of any other measures. It stood by itself. The final decision on the form property-tax relief would ultimately take was made by voters in California's primary election held on 6 June 1978.

The Voters' Decision

Because the state legislature had adopted Senate Bill 1, California voters faced more than a simple yes-or-no choice on property-tax relief. There were several possible alternatives in the battle over property-tax relief. The possible options and the ramifications of each are briefly examined below.

Both Proposition 8 and Proposition 13 could have been defeated. If this had happened, there would have been no property-tax relief until the state legislature considered the matter at a later date.

Proposition 8 could have been adopted and Proposition 13 defeated. In this case, the provisions of Senate Bill 1 would have been automatically implemented.

If Proposition 13 had passed and had been declared unconstitutional by the California Supreme Court, there would have been no immediate property-tax relief.

If Proposition 13 had been adopted by the voters and upheld by the California Supreme Court and no additional taxes had been mandated at the local level before the 1 July 1978 deadline, the popular intent of the mandate would have prevailed.

If Proposition 13 had passed and had been upheld by the California Supreme Court and if additional replacement revenues had been implemented by local governments, property owners would have had to pay unknown amounts of unknown new taxes. This action would have been interpreted by many as negating the intent of the mandate.

As complex as the property-tax-relief measures were, California voters turned out at the polls in record numbers. As the returns came in, the pattern became quite clear. Proposition 13 was to be the winner, Proposition 8 the loser. The final vote for Propostion 13 was 65 percent in favor, 35 percent against: a victorious margin of nearly two to one. The final vote on Proposition 8 was 47 percent in favor, 53 percent against.[45] The legislature's property-tax-relief proposal lost. The complete tabulation of the votes on these two measures is presented in table 2-3.[46]

The only major opposition to the Jarvis-Gann Initiative came from metropolitan core cities and from the agricultural counties of California's Central Valley, which had not suffered from the skyrocketing tax assessments experienced by most California property owners. Only three counties voted against Proposition 13: San Francisco County, which is comprised of many renters, minorities, and government workers; Kern County, which has traditionally had low-property-tax assessments; and Yolo County, which contains many college students and government workers and has relatively low taxes. In metropolitan areas, cities with high populations of minorities, renters, government workers, and college students provided the only significant opposition to the revolt against property taxes. The voters favored Proposition 13 by margins of more than three to one in suburban cities where most voters are homeowners.[47]

Even though the Jarvis-Gann Initiative was poorly drafted and had the potential for creating many legal problems, voters overwhelmingly approved the form of property-tax relief it provided. Because Propositon 8

Table 2-3
Final Vote, Proposition 13/Proposition 8 Primary Election, 6 June, 1978

Measure	No Vote	Yes Vote
Proposition 13	2,326,167	4,280,689
Proposition 8	3,345,622	2,972,424

met with defeat, Senate Bill 1 became moot. Many supporters of Proposition 8 eagerly awaited the California Supreme Court's decision on the constitutionality of Proposition 13.

The Supreme Court Ruling

On 6 June 1978, the people of California had spoken, loud and clear. The governor, state legislature, and local elected officials throughout the state had been developing various plans to cope with the Proposition 13 mandate. The real outcome of the Jarvis-Gann Initiative, however, would not be known until a decision on its constitutionality had been made by the California Supreme Court. This would be the ultimate test of the legality of the initiative.

After *The Godfather* became a best-seller, Mario Puzo wrote that he would have spent a little more time polishing the manuscript if he had known that the book would be so popular. Howard Jarvis and Paul Gann found themselves in the same position. Had these gentlemen known that their initiative was going to become law, they undoubtedly would have arranged to have lawyers specializing in government law and taxation put the measure into decent shape. Presumably, this will be done as differing versions of the initiative are presented to citizens in other states. The initiative sold to the voters of California, however, is proving to be a legal nightmare. Some of the major legal issues which have emerged from the initiative are discussed in the following paragraphs.

Constitutionality. The California Constitution provides that "an initiative embracing more than one subject may not be submitted to the electors or have any effect." Does the initiative cover more than one subject (that is, property-tax limits, assessment practices, and requirements for new taxes at the state and local level)?[48]

Revenue-Distribution System. How are property-tax revenues to be distributed under the initiative? The measure says "according to law" and there was no law in existence.[49] State legislation was subsequently approved to resolve this issue.

Assessment Inequities. The rationale for going to 1975–1976 assessments was to lower current assessed valuations. Many assessed valuations, however, were carried over from previous years, since all property is not assessed on an annual basis. Additionally, what happens to properties that have had a decline in assessed value since 1975–1976? It is obvious that many of these potential inequities will have to be ironed out in the courts.[50]

Voting Requirements. Under the California Election Code, an elector is any American citizen over eighteen who has resided in the district for twenty-nine days. It can be construed that a qualified elector need not even be a registered voter. Even if registered voter is intended in the initiative, the adoption of any special tax would be difficult because any nonvote becomes a "no" vote under the provisions of the initiative.[51]

New Taxes. What is the precise definition of the term *special taxes*? Does it apply to increases in existing taxes? This question is critical because if lost property-tax revenues are to be partly replaced, cities must have the ability to raise alternative revenue sources.[52]

Definitional Problems. Although the reassessment of newly constructed property is required, it is not defined. How will remodeling, reconstruction, and other forms of structural modifications or additions be treated? Some definition of what the term *new construction* applies to will have to be set forth to make the initiative workable.[53]

Taxation Formula. The initiative's taxation formula mandates 1975–1976 as the base year for assessment purposes and limits annual increases to 2 percent. The initiative also allows higher assessments for properties transferred or newly constructed since the base year. Does the initiative violate the equal-protection clause of the federal constitution?[54]

Tax-Increment Financing. The initiative does not affect voter-approved bonded indebtedness prior to 1 July 1978. It does, however, impact tax-increment bonds issued by redevelopment agencies. Because of the effects of property-tax-rate reductions and minimal increases of assessed valuation, many current contractual obligations of redevelopment agencies may be immediately jeopardized. Redevelopment agencies, in the past, have depended upon increases in assessed valuations to generate revenue to pay outstanding debt service. The debt service on such contracts will have to be financed from other revenue sources.[55] The state legislature recognized this problem and established a local agency emergency loan fund (Senate Bill 154) to act as a "lender of last resort" to local governments.

The California Supreme Court upheld the legality of Proposition 13 in *Amador Valley Joint Union High School et al.* v. *State Board of Equalization et al.*[56] The petitioners in this case raised four issues: was the ballot measure an illegal revision of the California Constitution rather than a simple amendment? Did the measure cover more than one subject, which is prohibited by the California Constitution? Did the measure violate the equal-protection clause of the U.S. Constitution because it based property assessments on 1975 values except for those persons buying property after that time? Did Proposition 13 impair contractual obligations between public-employee organizations and public agencies?[57]

The sixty-two-page opinion of the California Supreme Court was released on 22 September 1978. The court ruled unanimously that Proposition 13—now officially article 13 A of the California Constitution—"survived each of the substantial challenges raised by the petitioners."[58] The legal decision, written by Associate Justice Frank Richardson, avoided the last issue, dealing with the impairment of contractual obligations, on the grounds that a case of alleged impairment had not been brought before the supreme court. The court recognized some of the imperfections contained in the Jarvis-Gann Initiative. The decision stated that "as with other provisions of the Constitution, [the measure] would necessarily require [additional] judicial, legislative and administrative construction, and it was already being implemented by extensive legislation and regulations that, if judicially challenged, could be dealt with on a case-by-case basis."[59] Since the petitioners only raised a few of the legal questions involved, subsequent litigation will be needed to clarify the many legal issues previously discussed. One of these issues, the distribution of property-tax revenues, has already been decided by state legislation in Senate Bills 154 and 2212.[60]

So far, the California Supreme Court has dealt with Proposition 13 only in terms of broad concepts. In the years to come, the courts will have to deal with a plethora of specific issues involving individuals and organizations who feel they have been damaged unfairly by the initiative and its implementation. Already the contractual obligations of employers (that is, local governments) to employees have been held violated by Senate Bill 154. The court also left a variety of issues open for future discussion. Additionally, there is also the possibility that the equal-protection issue will be appealed to the U.S. Supreme Court. Because of the California Supreme Court's ruling, however, state and local government officials are free to implement the provisions of the initiative without the uncertainty of its constitutionality hanging over their heads. The implementation and impact of Proposition 13 on one municipality are discussed in the following chapters.[61]

Notes

1. Richard P. Simpson, "Spotlight on Proposition 13," *Western City Magazine* 53 (April 1978):9.
2. *Amador Valley Joint Union High School District et al* v. *State Board of Equalization et al.*, 22 Cal., 3d series (1978), p. 208.
3. "California Journal Ballot Proposition Analysis," *California Journal* 9 (May 1978):6.
4. California Constitution, art. 2, sec. 8(b).

5. March Fong Eu, *Statement of Vote: Primary Election, June 6, 1978* (Sacramento, Calif.: Office of Secretary of State, July 1978), p. vi.

6. John G. Goode, *Jarvis-Gann: Implications for Holders of State of California Municipal Issues* (San Francisco: Davis, Skaggs & Co., March 8, 1978), p. 1.

7. People's Advocate and United Organization of Taxpayers, *State-wide: People's Petition to Control Taxation* (Los Angeles: People's Advocate and United Organization of Taxpayers, 1977), p. 1.

8. California, Assembly, Revenue and Taxation Committee, Willie L. Brown, Jr., chairman, *Facts about Proposition 13: The Jarvis-Gann Initiative* (Sacramento, 15 February 1978), p. 2.

9. Ibid.

10. Ibid.

11. "California Journal," p. 6.

12. Ibid.

13. Ibid.

14. Juan Hovey, "Hottest Election Items—Jarvis-Gann, Behr Bill," *Oakland Tribune,* 25 May 1978, sec. B, p. 21.

15. Simpson, "Spotlight on Proposition 13," p. 9.

16. Ibid.

17. Hovey, "Hottest Election Items," p. 21.

18. California, Senate, *Senate Bill 1* (Sacramento, 3 March 1978), p. 1.

19. Ibid.

20. "Special Bulletin Regarding Property Tax Relief," *Legislative Bulletin,* (3 March 1978):1–2.

21. Ibid., p. 2.

22. Ibid.

23. "Analysis of SB 1 (Behr) Property Tax Relief and Proposition 8," Oakland Director of Finance, to Oakland City Manager, 10 March 1978, files of Office of Budget and Management Services, Oakland, Calif.

24. "Special Bulletin," p. 2.

25. Ibid.

26. Ibid.

27. Ibid.

28. March Fong Eu and William G. Hamm, *California Voters Pamphlet: Primary Election, June 6, 1978* (Sacramento, Calif.: Office of Secretary of State, June 1978), p. 36.

29. Ibid.

30. Ibid., p. 37.

31. Ibid., p. 36.

32. Hovey, "Hottest Election Items," p. 21.

33. Ibid.

34. Ibid.

35. "California Journal," p. 4.

36. Eu and Hamm, *California Voters Pamphlet,* p. 36.

37. Hovey, "Hottest Election Items," p. 21.

38. The average city-tax rate of $11.60 was taken from League of California Cities, *Summary Analysis of "Jarvis" Initiative* (Sacramento: League of California Cities, January 1978), p. 2.

39. Shirley Cool, CPA, Greenstein, DeMarta & Rogoff, Certified Public Accountants, Fremont, Calif., interview held 12 December 1978. Calculation assumes that 24 percent of increased income would be taken by federal taxes; 6 percent by state taxes.

40. Simpson, "Spotlight on Proposition 13," p. 10.

41. "California Journal," p. 7.

42. Simpson, "Spotlight on Proposition 13," p. 10.

43. Ibid.

44. This analysis was taken from "California Journal," p. 7, and Simpson, "Spotlight on Proposition 13," p. 11.

45. Eu, *Statement of Vote,* pp. 37, 39.

46. Ibid.

47. Fred Garretson, "Bay's Core Cities Voted 'No' on Proposition 13," *Oakland Tribune,* 18 June 1978, sec. A, p. 9.

48. California, Assembly, *Facts about Proposition 13,* p. 5.

49. Simpson, "Spotlight on Proposition 13," p. 10.

50. Don Benninghoven, *Proposed Jarvis/Gann Constitutional Amendment on June 6, 1978 Ballot* (Sacramento: League of California Cities, 15 February 1978), p. 5.

51. Simpson, "Spotlight on Proposition 13," p. 12.

52. Benninghoven, *Jarvis/Gann Constitutional Amendment,* p. 3.

53. Ibid., p. 2.

54. Ed Salzman, "Jarvis in the High Court: How Much (if any) Will Survive?" *California Journal* 9 (July 1978):212.

55. Benninghoven, *Jarvis/Gann Constitutional Amendment,* p. 4.

56. *Amador Valley* v. *State Board of Equalization,* p. 208.

57. Ed Salzman, "The Court Ruling: Constitutional on All Counts," *Tax Revolt Digest* 1 (November 1978):2.

58. Kenneth Hall and Edward R. Gerber, "Supreme Court Upholds Complete Text of Prop. 13," *Prop. 13 Impact Reporter,* no. 6 (26 September 1978):13.

59. *Amador Valley* v. *State Board of Equalization,* p. 210.

60. California, Senate, Senate Bill 154 and Senate Bill 2212 (Sacramento, passed 24 June 1978, and 30 June 1978, respectively).

61. For additional information on Oakland's financial structure refer to Arnold J. Meltsner, *The Politics of City Revenue* (Berkeley: University of California Press, 1971).

3 Advanced Planning

Introduction

Soon after the Jarvis-Gann Property-Tax Initiative qualified for the state's June ballot, city officials in Oakland began analyzing its potential financial, legal, and operational implications on their municipal government. The reaction of Oakland's newspapers during this period ranged from one of mere apathy to one of avid exploitation. While press coverage at the beginning of the property-tax-relief campaign was almost nonexistent, interest continually increased to that of a frenzied pace during the closing days of the battle for property-tax relief.

Citizen reaction to the Jarvis-Gann Initiative developed slowly. The tempo of activity, both within and outside the city of Oakland, increased rapidly as the 6 June 1978 election drew closer. After the election, the pace was frantic as the elected officials of municipal governments throughout the state attempted to grapple with the revenue constraints imposed by the Proposition 13 mandate. Oakland was no exception. The Oakland City Council held several special public meetings immediately prior to the 1 July 1978 deadline for the imposition of new taxes to mitigate the financial impact of the initiative. These revenues are examined in detail in chapter 5.

This chapter examines the initial anticipatory efforts by Oakland officials to predict the ramifications of the passage of Proposition 13 on city finances and public services. The major studies undertaken during this initial planning phase were, in sequence of their preparation, a preliminary financial analysis, a legal interpretation of the initiative, a concluding financial analysis, and a report on the anticipated effects of Senate Bill 1. The financial reports and the analysis of Senate Bill 1 were prepared by the city's office of finance. The legal opinion was prepared by the office of the city attorney. Armed with information provided by these staff reports, the city council directed the city manager to prepare an alternative city budget assuming passage of the Jarvis-Gann Initiative. Soon thereafter, Oakland's City Council officially adopted a resolution formally announcing its opposition to Proposition 13.

Preliminary Financial Analysis

The first official city document dealing with Proposition 13 was a preliminary financial analysis prepared by the office of finance at the direction of
the city manager.[1] This report informed the city council that the initiative
had recently qualified for the state's June ballot and, if approved by the
voters, would "have a profound and far-reaching impact on local governments."[2] This study, which was fairly general in nature, outlined the major
provisions of the Jarvis-Gann Initiative and briefly discussed the anticipated impact of the initiative on the city of Oakland. This impact was
described as follows.

Property Taxes. The city would face a 71 percent decrease in its property-
tax revenues for fiscal year 1978–1979. This meant a potential revenue loss
of about $27 million, assuming Oakland retained its proportionate share of
the composite county property-tax rate. It was also noted that if cities were
not considered as "districts" within counties, then Oakland's total property-tax revenues for the upcoming fiscal year, nearly $38 million, could be
lost entirely.[3]

Revenue-Sharing Funds. The city's receipt of funds from the federal government's State and Local Fiscal Assistance Act (more commonly referred
to as the Revenue-Sharing Program) could be diminished, since funding
allocations are determined, in part, on the basis of local-taxing effort. Since
Oakland's discretionary funds stood to be reduced by over one-third, this
impact could be substantial. The Office of Revenue Sharing, U.S. Department of the Treasury, indicated that it could not determine the specific
impact of the Jarvis-Gann Initiative on the distribution of revenue-sharing
funds.[4] Oakland was scheduled to receive nearly $5.9 million in such funds
for fiscal year 1978–1979.[5]

Replacement Revenues. Replacement revenues, the report indicated, would
have to come from additional state or local taxes. Local control would be a
major issue in the determination of what governmental level provided
replacement revenues.[6] The revenue constraints imposed by the initiative on
state and local governments were not discussed.[7]

Operational Impact. The potential loss of from $27 million to $38 million
in city revenues was equivalent to eliminating the city's entire police department or the office of public works and the fire department or the office of
public works, office of general services, office of parks and recreation,
library department, and museum department. In short, the potential reve-

nue loss from the initiative would eliminate about one-third of the city's operations.[8]

Bonding Capacity. It was noted that the city's bonding capacity, though not of immediate concern, could be affected by the slower growth of the assessed valuation.[9] It should be noted that Oakland has a fairly low rate of bond indebtedness (1 percent). Its last municipal bond, the Public Museum Bond, was passed by voters in 1961 to help finance the city's museum complex.[10]

Tax-Increment Financing. The report indicated that only tax-increment financing would be impaired. The income flow from the city's tax-increment projects would be decreased. Voter approval would be required for future projects financed with the use of tax-increment funds.[11] The specific financial impact of the initiative on the city's many tax-increment projects was not examined.

This preliminary financial analysis also stated that "the initiative was vague and poorly drafted."[12] The office of finance explained that "several provisions of the initiative would require court interpretation and further constitutional amendments."[13] The concluding portion of the report took a political stand by stating that "it is not clear who will really benefit from approval of the Jarvis-Gann Initiative, since the determination of replacement revenues and/or service reductions are unknown."[14] The report also cited a recent newspaper article and indicated that "Jarvis and Gann have threatened to launch another initiative drive for the November ballot on a measure which would freeze income and sales taxes."[15]

This report also forwarded several different analyses of the potential impact of the Jarvis-Gann Initiative on local governments. These reports included information compiled by the League of California Cities,[16] Oakland's "Sacramento representative,"[17] the California Senate Office of Research,[18] the Assembly Revenue and Taxation Committee,[19] and a copy of the initiative itself, which had been circulated by People's Advocate and the United Organization of Taxpayers.[20] The city's Sacramento representative is a paid lobbyist retained by the city to advance its political efforts in the state capital.

The report was presented to the city council on 24 January 1978, less than one month after the Jarvis-Gann Initiative had qualified for the state ballot. At this time, one of the council members suggested that a special-council-work session be held on this matter. The city manager noted that the report was only preliminary and that a more comprehensive analysis of the subject would be submitted to the council in about two weeks. The city manager recommended that the special-council hearing be held after the subsequent report had been prepared. The city council agreed. At this time, the mayor directed the city attorney to prepare a report evaluating the legal implications of the initiative.[21]

Legal Analysis

The city attorney's legal interpretation of the Jarvis-Gann Initiative, consisting of eleven pages of carefully worded text, analyzed each of the provisions of the initiative.[22] The report commenced by noting that the initiative was "vague and ambiguous in many respects."[23] It went on to state that "if adopted by the electorate, [the measure's] effect on the city's operations would range from mildly disastrous to absolutely catastrophic, depending upon the ultimate interpretations which will be given the initiative by the courts."[24] The city attorney's analysis examined many of the legal issues previously discussed in chapter 2.

In addition to pointing out the many ambiguities contained in the measure, the report set forth various interpretations relative to the impact of the initiative on the city of Oakland. These points, which were not available when the preliminary financial analysis was prepared, are discussed in the following paragraphs.

Property-Tax Relief. The city attorney recommended that the term *districts,* as contained in section 1 of the initiative, be interpreted to include cities. This assumption would mean that Oakland would collect its proportional share of the property taxes collected by the county. This assumption had to be made prior to projecting the fiscal impact of the initiative on the city. The report indicated that while revenue bonds were not directly covered by the initiative, it would be difficult for cities to raise revenues by this means since financial institutions would hesitate to purchase bonds of municipalities whose fiscal affairs would be in a state of flux for years to come. Oakland's Redevelopment Agency, the report stated, would be adversely affected by the initiative since the financing of tax-increment projects is paid out of the increases in assessed valuations on such properties. Due to the fact that increases in assessed valuations would be limited, the city would have to pay the difference out of its General Fund.[25]

Property Values. While the initiative would freeze assessed valuations as the value contained on the 1975-1976 county assessor's tax bill, many properties are not assessed by counties. Oakland's position should be that utilities, common carriers, and other properties not assessed by the county should not be subject to this limitation. Because the term *newly constructed real property* is not specifically defined, the city could interpret this term to mean all additions or renovations to existing structures. It was also noted that the court could make a stricter interpretation of this phrase, making it applicable to only entirely newly constructed properties. It was also noted that Oakland could argue that the 2-percent annual-assessment adjustment, tied to the consumer price index, is not an accurate gauge of the rise and fall in the fair-market value of real property.[26]

State Taxes. The report stated that the two-thirds vote requirement imposed upon the state legislature for the implementation of new taxes, excluding real property taxes of any kind, contradicted the California Constitution,[27] which allows the state to levy property taxes up to the extent of 25 percent of its annual budget. Section 3 of the initiative would supersede this section of the constitution.[28]

Local Taxes. The initiative states that cities, counties, and special districts, by a two-thirds vote may impose special taxes, except ad valorem taxes on real property or a transaction tax on the sale of real property. It was noted that the terms *such districts* and *special taxes* were not defined in the initiative. The city's position was that such districts should refer to cities, counties, and special districts. The city could assume that the term special taxes was all inclusive, encompassing all kinds of taxes, except those specifically prohibited by the initiative. It was the opinion of the city attorney that Oakland's present real estate transfer tax would be declared invalid if the initiative was adopted. It was also stated that the two-thirds vote requirement for imposing taxes would not be construed to apply to taxes the city had in existence as of 6 June 1978. The court could rule that the term *imposing taxes* is analogous to levying taxes. If this were the case, any tax levied by the city would be subject to the mandated voting requirement. The report indicated that the city should argue that the term qualified electors refers to those registered voters who actually vote in an election. Otherwise, 100 percent of the voters in an election could approve a tax and it could not be legally implemented unless this 100 percent represented two-thirds of the registered voters. This would make it virtually impossible for any local government to implement any form of new taxes.[29]

Implementation. This provision of the initiative was quite clear. The city attorney noted, however, the impracticality and oppressiveness of the effective date of the measure. Cities, counties, and special districts would have less than one month following passage of the initiative to rearrange their budgets and procedures in accordance with the requirements mandated by the initiative. The report predicted that local governments would be in such fiscal turmoil that a long period of time would be required to adjust to all of the provisions of the Jarvis-Gann Initiative.[30]

The city attorney qualified his report by stating that it contained legal interpretations at which the courts could reasonably arrive. In the event that the initiative became law, however, the city attorney would attempt to construe the various sections of the initiative in a manner most beneficial to the city until such time as the courts had ruled on the various legal issues involved.[31] This report, presented to the city council on 28 February 1978, was for informational purposes only. No council action was required. While the city has not pursued legal action to clarify any provisions of the initiative, the report did provide some valuable assumptions from which to calculate the city's potential revenue loss. These assumptions were incorporated in the follow-up financial analysis discussed below.

Final Financial Analysis

The subsequent financial analysis of the impact of the Jarvis-Gann Initiative,[32] dated 28 February 1978, was much more comprehensive than the original report of 24 January 1978. This report, in addition to expanding upon the issues identified in the initial report, presented the city council with a more detailed analysis of the impact of the initiative on the city's revenues. It also expanded upon the impact of the initiative on tax-increment financing. Additionally, it provided the council with possible revenue options and policy alternatives to enable the city to cope successfully with the fiscal constraints imposed by the initiative.

The specific city-revenue losses examined included its property taxes, revenue-sharing funds, real estate transfer tax, and user charges. It was assumed, as in the city attorney's legal analysis of the initiative, that the city would continue to receive its proportional share of the county's composite-property-tax rate. The policy options examined included differing budget-reduction strategies and several city and state revenue alternatives to mitigate the expected financial loss. The specific areas addressed in the report (revenue losses and policy alternatives) are discussed in greater detail below.

Revenue Losses

Property Taxes. The property-tax-revenue loss was estimated to be $28 million, $1 million more than the original estimate contained in the 24 January 1978 report. It was also pointed out that the city's growth in assessed valuation would be limited to 2 percent annually under the provisions of the initiative. This was contrasted with the city's average growth rate in assessed valuations of 8.1 percent annually over the past three years. The impact of the initiative on the city's receipt of property-tax-subvention revenues from the state was also quantified. City revenues from this source would be reduced by $3.3 million in fiscal year 1978–1979. State subventions include the homeowner's property-tax exemption, business inventory exemption, cargo container exemption, aircraft exemption, and documented vessel exemption.[33]

Revenue-Sharing Funds. The information relative to revenue-sharing funds in the initial financial report was incorrect. No loss of revenue is expected during the remaining two years of the Revenue-Sharing Program. Although such funds are partially affected by local tax effort, the Jarvis-Gann Initiative will have no impact on city-funding levels until fiscal year 1978–1979. The city's final revenue-sharing allotment is based on the local tax effort for fiscal year 1977–1978. The State and Local Fiscal Assistance Act, under which revenue-sharing payments are made, is presently scheduled to terminate in September 1980.[34]

Tax-Increment Financing. It was determined, in contrast to the original financial report, that the initiative would have a profound effect on the city's use of tax-increment financing as a redevelopment tool. The revenue loss during the first year was calculated to be $4.7 million. This revenue loss was based on the limits imposed by the initiative on the growth rate of assessed valuations. The current city-council policy is to use 50 percent of its available tax-increment funds.[35] The remaining funds are distributed to the other taxing agencies in Alameda County based on their proportional share of the county's composite-property-tax rate. The loss from this revenue source assumed that the city council would alter its present policy to use 100 percent of available tax-increment funds. It was noted that the city had advanced funds from its Community Development Block Grant to commence work on selected capital projects. These projects were in the community development district. The repayment of these moneys from tax-increment funds would be delayed for several years. It was also noted that the use of tax-increment financing and tax-increment bonding was planned as an integral part of the financing program to develop the city's central business district. These efforts would be postponed indefinitely.[36]

Other Revenues. Based on the information provided in the city attorney's report, it was determined that the city's real estate transfer tax would be invalidated. The revenue loss during the next fiscal year was estimated to be $4.3 million. It was noted that the city could lose other revenues, basically from user charges, from any decreases in city services resulting from the passage of the initiative. This potential revenue loss could not be calculated until specific service reductions were known.[37]

Bonding Capacity. The information provided in the original financial analysis was reiterated. Basically, because the city's three outstanding municipal bonds were all voter-approved, the initiative would not affect their status. It was noted that the initiative prohibits the use of general obligation bonds after 1 July 1978.[38]

Policy Alternatives

Service Reductions. The office of finance presented two alternative service-reduction options, both of which would achieve a total dollar reduction of $39 million in fiscal year 1978–1979. This was the most conservative estimate of revenue loss under the initiative. Option 1 represented a 35-percent across-the-board reduction in all general-funded city services. This reduction would eliminate 1,197 city positions. Option 2 set forth an 87-percent across-the-board service reduction in all general-funded city services, excluding the police and fire departments. It should be noted that the police and fire departments comprise about 54 percent of the city's total nonrestricted-fund budget.[39] This alternative would require the elimination of 1,599 city positions. Both these service reductions were very general in nature and were basically designed to illustrate the magnitude of the impact of the revenue loss on city operations. The report indicated that the potential staff reduction would be much greater than presented because of the impact of the elimination of General Fund positions in the city's Comprehensive Employment and Training Act (CETA) program. Federal regulations require that fund recipients eliminate all CETA positions first if reductions are made in similar job classifications for any reason.[40]

Revenue Alternatives. A number of revenue options were presented for the city council's consideration. Due to the magnitude of the potential revenue loss under the Jarvis-Gann Initiative, only major city and state revenue sources were considered as replacement revenues. Additional city revenues included a number of different rate increases in its business license tax, ranging from 328 to 1,628 percent. One possible new revenue source, the city's employee license fee, was also discussed. Varying levies were given, ranging from 0.7 to 3.6 percent. The various rates presented for both revenue sources would generate between $10 million and $50 million. The business license tax would be based on the gross receipts of businesses within the city. It would be applied to the annual income of all employees working in Oakland, with an exemption given for the first $6,500 of income. Increases were also presented for three state taxes: the sales tax, the bank and corporation tax, and the personal-income tax. Possible increases in the sales tax ranged from 0.85 to 6.05 percent. Increases in the bank and corporation tax ranged from 4.2 to 25.5 percent. Increases in the state's personal-income tax were from 18 to 109 percent. The ranges presented for each revenue source would generate between $1 billion and $6 billion in state revenues.[41] Although the city does not control state revenues, options were presented to illustrate how the state could generate sufficient moneys to offset the revenue losses suffered by local governments under the Jarvis-Gann Initiative. How the city could effect increases in these state revenues was not explained.

The report, like previous city documents on this matter, stated that "uncertainties and necessary interpretations of the initiative prevent a precise determination of its impact on the city."[42] The potential impact of the initiative on the city was described as "far-reaching."[43] In closing, the report indicated that the city could expect to lose local revenues ranging from approximately $39 million to $50 million in fiscal year 1978–1979. The report made no recommendations; it only set forth and examined general and somewhat limited policy alternatives. This document did, however, point out the severity of the impact of the Jarvis-Gann Initiative on city revenues. It also acted as an impetus to motivate the city council to direct the city manager to prepare an alternative city budget. The council ultimately held a special meeting to consider the information contained in this report and a subsequent staff report prepared on the impact of Senate Bill 1. This latter report is discussed briefly in the following paragraphs.

Senate Bill 1 Analysis

The staff report on Senate Bill 1, also prepared by the office of finance, was fairly simple and straightforward.[44] It indicated that the governor, on 3 March 1978, signed this legislation into law. This ended a fourteen-month effort by the state legislature to come up with a property-tax-relief program. It was also noted that the Behr Bill, named after its sponsor Senator Peter Behr (Marin County), was the only alternative to the Jarvis-Gann Initiative on the state's 6 June 1978 ballot. The report indicated that Senate Bill 1 was a more conservative measure that provided direct property-tax relief to home-owners without increasing state or local taxes. The widespread appeal of this legislation to local governments was that all property-tax savings were completely financed out of the state's surplus revenues which, at the time, were estimated to be about $3 billion.[45]

This report provided a brief summary of the major provisions of Senate Bill 1. It included a listing of the benefits of this legislation to homeowners, renters, and senior citizens. It also discussed the advantages of this legislation for local governments. Since this legislation had no immediate revenue impact on local governments, including Oakland, the report could only offer insights into its various legal provisions.

While this legislation did not impose any immediate financial constraints, it did place controls on the growth of property-tax revenues at the local level. Senate Bill 1, it was noted, would limit Oakland's property-tax-revenue growth to the percentage increase in the gross national product (GNP) deflator plus new construction. As indicated in chapter 2, the GNP deflator is an index which measures changes in the costs of governmental goods and services. The report indicated that Oakland's property-tax revenues had increased by an average of 6.7 percent over the last three years.[46] Given the present rate of inflation, this constraint would have no impact on Oakland's estimated property-tax-revenue growth in fiscal year 1978–1979.

The report concluded by reiterating that Oakland, along with other local governments, would be completely reimbursed for all property-tax revenues lost as a result of Senate Bill 1. It was also noted that Senate Bill 1 would not become effective unless Proposition 8 was approved and Proposition 13 was defeated.[47] This document, along with the final financial analysis of the Jarvis-Gann Initiative, was presented to the city council on 14 March 1978. Because of the nature of Senate Bill 1, the staff report was for information purposes only. No council action was required. The council, at its March 14 special session on the Jarvis-Gann Initiative, ultimately decided the financial strategy the city would adopt to cope with the property-tax-relief legislation.

City-Council-Budget Mandate

The Oakland City Council held its first public meeting on the Jarvis-Gann Initiative on 14 March 1978. The two staff reports previously discussed (the financial analysis of Proposition 13 and the report on Senate Bill 1) had been distributed to the council in advance of the meeting. The city manager briefly summarized the contents of these reports for the elected officials. The attention of the city council seemed to focus on the magnitude of the budget reductions set forth in the financial analysis. As indicated earlier, two budget-reduction alternatives were presented for illustrative purposes. One consisted of an across-the-board 35-percent budget reduction, which required the elimination of nearly 1,200 city positions. The other encompassed an 87-percent budget reduction in all city departments, except the police and fire departments. This option necessitated the elimination of almost 1,600 city positions.

After some discussion on the potential impact of Proposition 13, the city manager suggested to the council that it might wish to consider three alternative city budgets.[48] These three budget-reduction plans were outlined as follows.

1. A city budget which would assume no replacement revenues.
2. A city budget which would incorporate new taxes which could be enacted by the city council to compensate for the anticipated revenue losses.
3. A city budget which would show some sort of balance between replacement revenues and reduced service levels.

After these financial options had been presented and examined by the city council, a motion was made to direct staff to provide the three alternative budgets suggested by the city manager. This motion, however, failed for lack of a second. The mayor at this time indicated that "the city council must make philosophical decisions and determine the approach [the elected officials] wished to take in making decisions involving possible budget reductions."[49] After additional debate on this matter, and lacking such philosophical direction, a motion was made to direct staff to prepare an alternative city budget which would place priority on public safety (police and fire) services. Such a budget would involve making service reductions in other areas of the city budget. The mayor, upon hearing this motion, said that he felt budget reductions should "be something closer to across-the-board."[50] After additional discussion by the city council, the motion to give priority to police and fire services was disapproved unanimously.[51]

The debate on what action the city council should take suddenly began to change. One council member stated that "if people vote for the Jarvis-Gann Initiative, it is because they do not want to pay taxes and the city council should not look for new sources of revenue."[52] After additional discussion, the motion was made that the council not attempt to seek replacement revenues to mitigate the financial loss mandated by Proposition 13. This motion, upon receiving a second endorsement, was put to a vote. It barely passed with five "yes" and four "no" votes. This action served to limit the number of financial options available to cope with the expected revenue loss.

Soon after this motion was adopted, a second motion was approved to direct city staff to prepare two alternative city budgets. One budget would include an across-the-board reduction throughout all city departments. The other budget, described as "strictly staff originated,"[53] would outline areas in which staff felt reductions could best be made. The mayor stated that "if the people are going to pass 'Jarvis,' they don't have a right to expect full fire and police services."[54] This budget strategy was approved unanimously by the city council. The council also suggested that staff inform the public of the potential impact of Proposition 13 by preparing and posting notices on each city facility that would be either closed or operated on a limited basis.[55]

Throughout the entire meeting only seven citizens spoke concerning the impact of Proposition 13 on city services. A few citizens expressed disbelief that all the service reductions and employee terminations could happen. One citizen indicated that if Proposition 13 was adopted, the state legislature would provide supplementary funds to local governments.[56] The mayor quickly indicated that he disagreed, describing such wishful thinking as "pie in the sky."[57] The mayor stated that he had recently talked with top state legislative leaders and they showed no inclination whatsoever for bailing out local governments. City-council members, during public discussion, described Proposition 13 as "[providing] an instant depression as soon as unemployment benefits ran out" and "[an] invitation to chaos and anarchy."[58] It was obvious that the staff reports had a dramatic impact on the city council.

After nearly two hours of somewhat heated discussion on the potential impact of Proposition 13, including the magnitude of service reductions and employee terminations, the council directed the city attorney to prepare a resolution declaring its opposition to Proposition 13. At the close of this meeting, the city manager indicated that the alternative budgets requested would be prepared and submitted to the city council within thirty days. The city manager also suggested that another special meeting should be scheduled to consider the impact of these budgets on city services.[59]

The following morning, after meeting with the city manager, the director, office of budget and management services (OBMS), prepared and distributed a budget directive to all city-department managers informing them of the city council's action.[60] To present the city's elected officials with an orderly format for making programmatic service reductions, a relatively simple scheme was developed for departmental use when preparing budget cuts. This format is illustrated in table 3–1.[61]

All department managers were given a predetermined budget-reduction "target" figure, representing approximately 35 percent of their discretionary fund budget. Department managers were given the latitude of reducing their budgets as they deemed most appropriate. They were also told to keep in mind that under existing CETA regulations whenever a general-funded employee is terminated or laid off, all CETA-funded employees within the same classification in the affected department must be terminated. Naturally, it behooved department managers to minimize their CETA personnel reductions since most, if not all, of the salaries of such employees are paid out of federal funds.[62] Proposed budget reductions were to be returned to the OBMS no later than 29 March 1978.[63] Once this information was prepared, the potential impact of Proposition 13 on city services became apparent. The impact of proposed service reductions will be examined in

Table 3–1
Oakland Budget Reduction Format, Jarvis-Gann Contingency Budget,
Fiscal Year 1978–1979

Schedule of Proposed Program Reductions

Organizational information
 Office name
 Department name

Program information
 Priority number
 Name of program
 Fiscal year 1978–1979 cost
 Proposed reduction
 Staff reduction (number and title)
 CETA positions lost (number and title)
 Description of reduction

---

chapter 4. In the meantime, the city attorney had prepared the council's
resolution opposing Proposition 13.

City Council Opposes Proposition 13

For over two months the city council had been receiving information from
city-staff reports concerning the potential impact of Proposition 13. These
reports contained nothing positive about the initiative. The finance director
had referred to the initiative as "vague and poorly drafted,"[64] "requiring
court interpretation and further constitutional amendments,"[65] and "having a profound and far-reaching impact on local governments."[66] He also
stated that "it is not clear who will really benefit from [its] approval."[67] The
city attorney said the initiative "is vague and ambiguous in many
respects"[68] and "if adopted by the electorate, its effect on the city's operations would range from mildly disastrous to absolutely catastrophic."[69] The
final report indicated that the potential revenue loss, about one-third of the
city's discretionary funds ($35 million out of a total of $113 million), would
require massive service reductions and employee terminations. The anticipated revenue loss was nearly unbelievable; the loss of jobs would be devastating to a city with an already high-unemployment rate.

The city council officially declared its opposition to Proposition 13 on
28 March 1978. The resolution opposing the initiative contained much of
the information presented in city-staff documents. The council listed several
reasons for its opposition.

1. A potential revenue loss of nearly $40 million.
2. No replacement revenues would be provided.
3. Limits would be placed on the ability of state and local governments to provide alternative revenues.
4. A substantial curtailment of city services, including police and fire services.
5. A dramatic increase in unemployment.
6. The ambiguous nature of the initiative.
7. The uncertainties and confusion in financial planning it would create for local governments.

They felt so strongly about Proposition 13 that the concluding phrase of their resolution stated "Proposition 13 will not be in the public interest as it will severely limit the services available to the citizens of Oakland, it will create substantial unemployment, and it will cause confusion in local governmental activities."[70] The full text of this resolution is presented in figure 3-1.[71] While this resolution did not pass unanimously, it did receive substantial approval: eight votes in favor, one abstention. The council member abstaining did so without explanation.[72]

Prior to approval of the resolution, several speakers expressed their concern that Proposition 13's passage could be a special threat to poor and minority citizens of Oakland.[73] One speaker said, "It [the initiative] will hinder the little folks."[74] Another citizen expressed concern over the magnitude of the loss of city jobs and the fact that many minorities who were the most recently hired would be the first fired. This speaker concluded his statement by saying, "We [the citizens] could end up with a city run by old white men."[75] Based on the information available at the time, most of these statements were accurate reflections of what could become a reality if Proposition 13 were adopted. The anticipated and actual impact of Proposition 13, however, turned out to be significantly different, perhaps adding to a further loss in the credibility of government as perceived by citizens. These topics and the events that substantially reduced the anticipated impact provide the subjects for the following two chapters.

Commentary

The efforts of Oakland officials to predict the potential impact of Proposition 13 on city finances and public services were fairly comprehensive. Due to the urgency to predict this impact as soon as possible, however, the pattern of staff reports was somewhat disjointed and incremental in nature. For example, the preliminary financial analysis was prepared without the advantage of first having a legal interpretation of the provisions of the ini-

---

Oakland City Council Resolution No. 57101 C.M.S.[a]

Resolution Declaring the Opposition of the City Council of Oakland to Proposition 13 (Jarvis-Gann Amendment)

Whereas, the City Council of Oakland after careful consideration of the impact on the City of Oakland of the passage of Proposition 13, known as the Jarvis-Gann Amendment, finds that its passage would drastically reduce revenues to the City of Oakland in the approximate amount of $40,000,000 for Fiscal Year 1978–79, with proportionate losses in subsequent years; and

Whereas, Proposition 13 makes no provision for replacement revenues and substantially limits the ability of the State and City of Oakland to raise replacement revenues; and

Whereas, such a drastic reduction on the City of Oakland's revenues would result in a severe curtailment of services that the City of Oakland can offer to its citizens; including among other things substantially less police and fire protection, the closure of libraries, parks, the Zoo and the Museum; and

Whereas, the passage of Proposition 13 will result in a dramatic increase in unemployment in City government positions, the elimination of nearly all CETA positions, and a resulting general increase in unemployment throughout the City; and

Whereas, Proposition 13 is so ambiguously drafted that its passage will result in uncertainty and confusion for local governments' planning their budgetary activities for many years; now, therefore, be it

Resolved: That the City Council of Oakland has determined that the passage of Proposition 13 will not be in the public interest as it will severely limit the services available to the citizens of Oakland, it will create substantial unemployment, and it will cause confusion in local governmental activities; and be it

Further Resolved: That the City Council of Oakland declares its opposition to Proposition 13.

---

[a] Adopted by the city council on 28 March 1978.

Figure 3–1. Oakland Resolution Opposing Proposition 13 (Jarvis-Gann Initiative)

tiative. Thus, the first financial report was incorrect in a number of its revenue assumptions and projections. Additionally, some of the staff reports contained misleading or inaccurate information and blatantly subjective statements concerning Proposition 13. The shortcomings of the city-staff reports are discussed below.

Because of the hasty preparation of the initial financial analysis, the report did not address the impact of the initiative on a number of important city-revenue sources. The impact on the city's tax-increment funds, real estate transfer tax, and state subventions was entirely omitted in this report. Because these factors were not addressed, the projected revenue loss to the city was underestimated by some $12.3 million. Additionally, the effect of Proposition 13 on the city's receipt of revenue-sharing funds was not thoroughly analyzed. The original report indicated that revenue-sharing funds "may be diminished, since allocations are determined partially by local tax effort." The final report, on the other hand, stated that "no loss of revenue is expected over the final two years of the Revenue Sharing [Program]." This latter statement was based on the fact that city funds under this program are based on the previous tax year. This fact was readily ascertainable from federal revenue-sharing regulations and should have been indicated in the initial financial analysis.

The initial financial report also stated that "revenues to replace . . . losses must come from additional state and/or local taxes." The initiative, however, placed clear limitations on the ability of state and local governments to raise offsetting revenues to mitigate the fiscal impact of Proposition 13. This information was readily obtainable from the wording of the initiative itself, yet it was not contained in this first staff report. The initial financial analysis also contained legal opinions. The report referred to the initiative as "vague and poorly drafted." It also said Proposition 13 would "require court interpretations and further constitutional amendments." While the first two assumptions may hold true, the latter assumption never became a reality. In any event, these statements should appropriately have been contained in the city attorney's legal interpretation, not in the finance director's fiscal analysis.

It is obvious that the legal interpretation should have been completed before the financial analysis was undertaken. The incomplete and inaccurate information contained in the first financial report lends credence to this statement. Many of the revenue assumptions in the original report proved to be either incorrect or less than comprehensive relative to the anticipated effect of the initiative on city revenues. The subsequent legal analysis provided many important interpretations and assumptions upon which to base the city's projected revenue loss. These factors were ultimately included in the city's concluding fiscal report.

The final financial report set forth several state taxes which could be increased to offset the fiscal impact of the initiative, yet the initiative itself specifically prohibited the state from levying any new taxes after 6 June 1978, without approval of two-thirds of the legislature. In any event, the city has no control over state revenues, and it was an improper assumption that such revenues would be available to bail out local governments. Additionally, the final financial report did not mention the 1 July 1978 deadline for adopting new taxes at the local level to mitigate the anticipated revenue loss. This deadline, as will be shown later, was crucial in the city's response to the passage of Proposition 13.

Incorrect revenue projections, misleading information, and lack of pertinent information were only part of the problem. Staff reports frequently included subjective opinions about the initiative itself. The initial financial report stated, "It is not clear who will really benefit from approval of the Jarvis-Gann Initiative" and "Jarvis and Gann have threatened to launch another initiative drive for the November ballot on a measure which would freeze income and sales taxes." This latter prediction, which never materialized, was based solely on a single newspaper article. It was not pertinent to the subject of the report.

The city attorney's legal analysis also contained several subjective statements. The report referred to the financial impact of the initiative on city operations as "ranging from mildly disastrous to absolutely catastrophic." This statement involved more than a legal analysis and was a subjective assessment of the impact of the initiative on the city's public services, which had not yet been fully determined. It was also not pertinent to the subject of the report. The city attorney also indicated he would, in the event the initiative became law, "attempt to construe the various sections [of the initiative] in a manner most reasonably beneficial to the city." This action could ultimately serve to undermine the intent of the initiative itself and in turn the will of the people. Additionally, the city attorney referred to the effective date of the initiative, 1 July 1978, as "impractical" and "oppressive," yet local governments had several months advance knowledge (that is, 29 December 1977 to 30 June 1978) to prepare for its passage. This should have allowed local governments sufficient time to prepare alternative city budgets in anticipation of the initiative's financial impact.

With the exception of the initial financial report, all of the city's documents were comprehensive and highly informational. The legal analysis, the report on Senate Bill 1, and the concluding financial report were all prepared in a timely manner, notwithstanding severe time constraints. These reports were an integral part of the city's attempt to anticipate the impact of Proposition 13 on city revenues and prevailing public services. To this end, they served their purpose in a professional manner.

The city's advanced planning process, in retrospect, served three important purposes. This effort helped to alert the city's elected officials to the possible fiscal, legal, and operational impacts of Proposition 13 on the city. The information contained in these reports also acted as an impetus to motivate the city council to direct the staff to prepare an alternative city budget. Additionally, this process served to educate Oakland citizens as to the possible impact of the initiative on public services. It should be noted that the anticipated financial impact of Proposition 13, though later substantially reduced, was accurate, based on the information available at the time.

Notes

1 ."Jarvis-Gann Initiative," Oakland Director of Finance, to Oakland City Manager, 24 January 1978, files of Office of Budget and Management Services, Oakland, Calif.

2. Ibid.

3. Ibid.

4. Ibid.

5. City Manager, *City of Oakland Adopted Budget: Fiscal Year 1978–79* (Oakland, Calif.: Office of City Manager, November 1978), p. A-5.

6. "Jarvis-Gann Initiative," Director of Finance, 24 January 1978.

7. People's Advocate and United Organization of Taxpayers, *Statewide: People's Petition to Control Taxation* (Los Angeles: People's Advocate and United Organization of Taxpayers, 1977), secs. 3 and 4, p. 1.

8. "Jarvis-Gann Initiative," Director of Finance, 24 January 1978.

9. Ibid.

10. City Manager, *City of Oakland Adopted Budget,* p. B-64.

11. "Jarvis-Gann Initiative," Director of Finance, 24 January 1978.

12. Ibid.

13. Ibid.

14. Ibid.

15. Ibid. The newspaper article referred to appeared in the *Oakland Tribune,* 21 January 1978, sec. A, p. 3.

16. League of California Cities, *Summary Analysis of "Jarvis" Initiative* (Sacramento: League of California Cities, January 1978).

17. Lynn M. Suter, *The Jarvis-Gann Initiative* (Sacramento, Calif.: Office of Lynn Suter, legislative consultant, January 1978).

18. Martin Helmke, *Jarvis-Gann Initiative* (Sacramento: California Senate Office of Research, 13 December 1977).

19. California, Assembly, Revenue and Taxation Committee, Willie L. Brown, Jr., chairman, *A Brief Analysis of a Proposed Initiative Relating to Property Taxation and Legislative Voting Requirements of Certain Bills by People's Advocate and United Organization of Taxpayers,* (Sacramento, 6 December 1977).

20. People's Advocate and United Organization of Taxpayers, *Petition to Control Taxation.*

21. City Clerk, *City Council Meeting Minutes* (Oakland, Calif.: Office of City Clerk, 24 January 1978).

22. "Jarvis-Gann Initiative," Oakland City Attorney, to Oakland City Council, 23 February 1978, files of Office of Budget and Management Services, Oakland, Calif.

23. Ibid., p. 1.

24. Ibid.

25. Ibid., pp. 2–3.

26. Ibid., pp. 4–5.

27. California Constitution, art. 13, sec. 22.

28. "Jarvis-Gann Initiative," City Attorney, p. 6.

29. Ibid., pp. 8–10.

30. Ibid., p. 11.

31. Ibid., p. 1.

32. "Jarvis-Gann Initiative," Oakland Director of Finance, to Oakland City Manager, 28 February 1978, files of Office of Budget and Management Services, Oakland, Calif.

33. Ibid., pp. 1–2 of letter, pp. 1–2 of Attachment A.

34. Ibid., p. 2 of letter, p. 2 of Attachment A.

35. Ibid., p. 2 of letter, pp. 2–3 of Attachment A.

36. Ibid.

37. Ibid., pp. 2–3 of letter, p. 4 of Attachment A.

38. Ibid., p. 2 of letter, p. 4 of Attachment A.

39. City Manager, *Oakland Adopted Budget,* p. A–3.

40. "Jarvis-Gann Initiative," Director of Finance, 28 February 1978, p. 3 of letter, p. 1 of Attachment C.

41. Ibid., p. 3 of letter, p. 1 of Attachment D.

42. Ibid., p. 1.

43. Ibid., p. 3.

44. "Analysis of SB 1 (Behr) Property Tax Relief and Proposition 8," Oakland Director of Finance, to Oakland City Manager, 10 March 1978, files of Office of Budget and Management Services, Oakland, Calif.

45. Ibid., p. 1.

46. Ibid., p. 2.

47. Ibid., p. 3.

48. City Clerk, *City Council Meeting Minutes* (Oakland, Calif.: Office of City Clerk, 14 March 1978), p. 1.

49. Ibid.

50. Ibid.

51. Ibid.

52. Ibid., p. 2.

53. Ibid.

54. Sue Soennichsen, "Prop. 13 Warning—Council: 'They'll Get What They Vote for,'" *The Montclarion,* 22 March 1978, p. 1.

55. City Clerk, *City Council Meeting Minutes,* 14 March 1978, p. 2.

56. Soennichsen, "Prop. 13 Warning," p. 1.

57. Ibid.

58. Ibid.

59. City Clerk, *City Council Meeting Minutes,* 14 March 1978, p. 2.

60. "Jarvis-Gann Budget Reductions," Oakland Director of Budget and Management Services, to Oakland Department Managers, 15 March 1978, files of Office of Budget and Management Services, Oakland, Calif.

61. Ibid., p. 2.

62. Ibid., p. 1.

63. Ibid.

64. "Jarvis-Gann Initiative," Director of Finance, 24 January 1978, p. 2.

65. Ibid.

66. Ibid., p. 1.

67. Ibid., p. 2.

68. "Jarvis-Gann Initiative," City Attorney, p. 1.

69. Ibid.

71. City Council, *Resolution 57101 C.M.S.,* Oakland City Council, Oakland, Calif., 28 March 1978.

71. Ibid.

72. Sue Soennichsen, "City Run by Old Whites if Prop. 13 Passes?" *The Montclarion,* 5 April 1978, p. 7.

73. Ibid.

74. Ibid.

75. Ibid.

4 Anticipated Impact

Introduction

This chapter examines the preparation of the city's alternative budgets designed to counteract the revenue loss anticipated by the passage of Proposition 13. The city council had decided upon the most conservative estimate of revenue loss (nearly $40 million) as a basis for this alternative budget. Of this amount, nearly $3.7 million was attributable to the city's projected loss of tax-increment funds. This fiscal impact on the city's operating and capital budgets was slightly over $35 million. Therefore, departmental-budget reductions had to equal this amount. Departmental-budget reductions were determined in the initial letter sent to departments by the director, office of budget and management services (OBMS).[1] These figures were arrived at by calculating 35 percent of each department's total non-restricted-fund budget.

This action served to fulfill the city council's directive for an across-the-board budget reduction, later referred to as Jarvis-Gann Contingency Budget A. Staff recommendations concerning budget reductions, also requested by the city's elected officials, were determined in meetings between the staffs of the city manager's office and the OBMS. Departmental input was not solicited for this alternative city budget, ultimately called Jarvis-Gann Contingency Budget B. The budget resulting from this effort fulfilled the city council's request for a strictly staff-originated budget.

The two budgets were subsequently prepared in a nearly 300-page document and submitted to the city council for its consideration. The council was not entirely satisfied with either alternative budget. This led to the preparation of two additional budgets, which placed different priorities on selected public services. These alternative budgets were also reviewed by the council before it agreed upon what was considered at the time to be the final Proposition 13 budget.

The public hearings on these alternative budgets were often heated, with both the public and the city council wanting to give preference to specific public services. This was a difficult task since the projected amount of limited resources placed severe constraints on all public services. The final Proposition 13 budget reflected much debate concerning various levels of public services. During these discussions, great concern was expressed over whether to give the city's police and fire services priority over cultural and recreational programs. The deliberations over "hard" versus "soft" services consumed many hours of public debate. The city's Proposition 13 budget incorporated something of a trade-off, placing public priorities on police and fire services while not drastically reducing cultural and recreational programs. This was accomplished by the use of one-time savings from a number of different sources. The city council adopted its Jarvis-Gann Budget in early May 1978.

As soon as the alternative budget had been prepared, the reductions in public services became apparent. The $35-million-revenue loss meant the closure of fire stations, branch libraries, many park and recreational centers, and a decrease in police services. This alternative city budget necessitated the elimination of over 1,300 jobs—about one-third of the city's total labor force. Due to the magnitude of the revenue loss, service reductions could not be made in only selected public service areas. Instead, public services had to be reduced, by varying degrees, in virtually every city department.

Upon the adoption of the city's Proposition 13 budget, the city council directed the city manager to place notices on all city facilities that would be either eliminated or reduced if the alternative budget were to be implemented. This action was very controversial. Some members of the public accused the city of officially campaigning against the passage of Proposition 13. The city attorney, however, held that this effort was informational only and that the city was obligated to inform the public of the anticipated impact of Proposition 13 on public services.

The above events are examined in detail in this chapter. The topics discussed in this chapter include the preparation of the city's alternative Jarvis-Gann budgets, the public-hearing process held by Oakland officials to review these budgets, the city council's adoption of what was thought to be the final Proposition 13 budget, and the anticipated financial and operational impact of this budget on prevailing public services. The efforts of the city's elected and appointed officials to inform Oakland citizens of these anticipated service reductions are also discussed. As will be shown in the subsequent chapter, the city's "final" Proposition 13 budget underwent substantial revisions before being actually implemented. These changes included substantial revenue increases to offset the magnitude of projected service reductions.

Alternative City Budgets

City departments, upon receiving the budget-reduction-plan directive, began the painful task of analyzing their respective operations in an effort to determine appropriate budget reductions. As previously indicated, city departments were allowed complete discretion in proposing these reductions. The only criterion that had to be followed was that proposed budget reductions had to equal the previously determined target-reduction figure. For the most part, departments "did their own thing." Only a few inquiries were received by the staff of the OBMS. Almost all these inquiries questioned the amount of a department's total budget reduction. No reduction figures were revised. With the exception of answering these few inquiries, the staff of the OBMS waited for the 29 March 1978 deadline to approach.

In the interim, the OBMS staff recalculated the estimated amount of the city's budget reduction under Proposition 13. The estimated revenue loss, excluding the loss from tax-increment funds, amounted to $35.4 million. This was attributable to a revenue loss from three revenue sources: property taxes ($27.8 million), state taxes and subventions ($3.3 million), and the real estate transfer tax ($4.3 million). A comparison of the city's anticipated normal revenues versus its projected revenues under Proposition 13 is illustrated in table 4-1.[2] Tax-increment funds are processed outside the city's normal budgetary cycle since these funds are not used to finance regular city operations. Rather, tax-increment funds are allocated by the city council annually to various tax-increment projects. The estimated revenue loss from this source, $3.7 million,[3] is still substantial. The reduction does not, however, impact prevailing public services. For this reason, this revenue source will be treated separately from the city's normal operating and capital budget.

These revenue estimates were combined with the expected fund

Table 4-1
Oakland City Revenue Position, Normal Revenues versus Jarvis-Gann Revenues, Fiscal Year 1978-1979

	Normal Revenues (millions of dollars)	Jarvis-Gann Revenues (million of dollars)
Property taxes	37.2	9.4
In-lieu taxes and subventions	4.8	1.5
Real-estate transfer tax	4.3	—
General revenue sharing	5.9	5.9
Public Works Employment Act	4.3	4.3
Other revenues	50.4	50.4
Total revenues	106.9	71.5
Revenue loss	—	35.4

Note: Discretionary funds, excluding tax-increment and bond funds.

balances to determine the city's total resources for fiscal year 1978–1979. Fund balances represent the portion of budgeted funds not used during the previous fiscal year on a citywide basis. The estimated fund balance to be carried over into fiscal year 1978–1979 was $6.6 million. Total resources determine the ceiling figure for the city's operating and capital budget. A comparison of the city's alternative budget projections, including its normal budget, Jarvis-Gann Contingency Budget A, and Jarvis-Gann Contingency Budget B, is set forth in table 4–2.[4] The $0.3 million listed under Contingency Budget A represents the anticipated savings from the city's capital projects from the previous fiscal year. The $2.2 million indicated in Contingency Budget B reflects the use of one-time city savings, discussed more fully in the preparation of the city manager's budget recommendations. This information reveals that Contingency Budget A required a reduction of $35.2 million, while Contingency Budget B necessitated a reduction totaling $33 million.

As the 29 March deadline approached, proposed budget reductions came pouring into the OBMS. These reductions, after being reviewed by the budget director, were channeled to each department's respective budget analyst. Each analyst, because of time constraints to meet the council's one-month deadline, only checked departmental-budget reductions for reasonableness and accuracy. During the first two weeks of April, the staff sorted through 220 proposed program reductions submitted by nineteen city departments. These reductions, in the aggregate, included a total city-budget reduction of $35.2 million and required the elimination of 1,485 city positions. The reductions eliminated $17.5 million in public-safety services and $5.4 million in cultural and recreational programs.[5] This amounted to 50 percent and 15 percent, respectively, of the total budget reduction. The remaining 35 percent of the budget reduction was allocated to other city departments. This series of budget reductions completed the across-the-board reduction requested by the city council. A departmental listing of these reductions, including the number of programs involved and the city positions eliminated, is presented in table 4–3.[6]

Upon the completion of Jarvis-Gann Contingency Budget A, representatives of the city manager's office and the OBMS met to determine the additional alternative to fulfill the city council's request for a staff-originated budget. The city manager determined that this budget should increase reductions in other city departments in order to mitigate the magnitude of the proposed reductions in the city's police and fire departments. Additionally, it was decided that the amount of the reduction would be lowered by $1.8 million by utilizing one-time savings available in the city's Convention Center Fund ($1.4 million) and the City Council Emergency Contingency Fund ($0.4 million).[7] Even with the use of these resources, additional budget reductions had to be solicited from selected city departments. When

Table 4–2
Oakland City Financial Position, Normal Budget versus Jarvis-Gann
Contingency Budgets, Fiscal Year 1978–1979

Category	Normal Budget (millions of $)	Contingency Budget A (millions of $)	Contingency Budget B (millions of $)
Estimated fund balances (7/1/78)	6.6	6.6	6.6
Estimated revenues (FY 1978–1979)	106.9	71.5	71.5
Other resources	—	0.3	2.2
Total resources (FY 1978–1979)	113.5	78.4	80.3
Fiscal year 1978–1979 budget	113.0	77.8	80.0
Estimated fund balances (7/1/79)	0.5	0.6	0.3

Note: Discretionary funds, excluding tax-increment and bond funds.

Table 4–3
Oakland City Budget Reduction, Jarvis-Gann Contingency Budget A,
Fiscal Year 1978–1979

Departments	Amount (millions of $)	Percent	Programs [a]	Positions
Police	10.3	28	45	371
Fire	7.2	27	19	226
Public works	3.8	33	18	202
General services	3.9	57	20	117
Parks and recreation	3.2	37	63	281
Library	1.3	35	12	106
Museum	.9	36	15	64
General government	2.5	35	21	118
Nondepartmental	2.1	24	7	—
Total reduction	35.2	31	220	1,485

Note: Discretionary funds, excluding tax-increment and bond funds.
[a] Includes programs reduced or eliminated.

this second alternative budget was completed, the portion of the total reduction attributable to public safety amounted to 33 percent. In comparison, the amount of the reduction in cultural and recreational programs totaled 23 percent. Contingency Budget B decreased the magnitude of the reduction in public-safety services by one-third, while increasing the amount of the reduction in cultural and recreational services by about one-third. The balance of this budget reduction was allocated among the remaining city departments. This alternative budget consisted of 244 program reductions in nineteen city departments. A departmental listing of these reductions, including the number of programs involved and the city positions eliminated, is presented in table 4-4.[8]

Both alternative city budgets were assembled into a voluminous document which was presented to the city council for its special public meeting to discuss Oakland's Proposition 13 budget. This document, which summarized program reductions in all city departments, was appropriately labeled *Jarvis-Gann Emergency Budget: FY 1978-79.*[9] It served as a focal point for much public discussion, often heated debate, before the city's final Proposition 13 budget would be decided upon. The public hearings held on these alternative city budgets are discussed below.

Proposition 13 Budget Hearings

The Oakland City Council held three public meetings prior to the June election on the city's Proposition 13 budget, on 18 April, 27 April, and 9 May. No one perceived at the time that many additional meetings would be held after the passage of Proposition 13 to mitigate its financial impact on the city. This section examines the first two budget hearings held by city officials. The third meeting, at which the final version of the Proposition 13 budget was officially adopted, is discussed in the following section of this chapter.

On 18 April 1978, the first meeting was held at Oakland City Hall to publicly discuss these alternative budgets. The city manager briefly set forth the assumptions under which each of these budgets had been prepared, explaining the extent of each reduction on public services, including the number of programs involved and city jobs eliminated. He indicated that these budgets were "starting points for discussion and not firm staff recommendations."[10] The city manager went on to state, "It is essential that staff get a speedy decision from council as to the course of action it desires."[11] The city manager concluded his presentation by saying,

> The impact of these service reductions upon the ongoing operations of the city would be catastrophic. Such reductions, if implemented, would drastically alter the quality of life within the city of Oakland. Additionally, Oakland's already high unemployment rate would be further aggravated. Those individuals who lose their jobs may find it difficult to obtain other employment, since other governmental jurisdictions are being forced to implement similar service reductions.[12]

Table 4–4
Oakland City Budget Reduction, Jarvis-Gann Contingency Budget B,
Fiscal Year 1978–1979

Departments	Amount (millions of $)	Percent	Programs[a]	Positions
Police	6.3	17	37	254
Fire	3.6	14	12	114
Public works	4.6	40	24	229
General services	3.8	56	22	156
Parks and recreation	3.8	44	73	342
Library	2.3	62	13	132
Museum	1.5	60	34	89
General government	3.1	43	21	162
Nondepartmental	4.0	45	8	—
Total reduction	33.0	29	244	1,478

Note: Discretionary funds, excluding tax-increment and bond funds.
[a]Includes programs reduced or eliminated.

The council then responded to these proposals. Because of the time involved in analyzing the alternative budgets, the mayor deferred public discussion to the following budget hearing—one week away. The city council was incredulous over the magnitude of the services reduced in the across-the-board budget reduction, which included closing down nine of the city's twenty-seven fire stations and eliminating 223 sworn fire personnel.[13] The council was alarmed at the possible cuts in the police department where approximately one-third of the city's police officers would be laid off.[14] The chiefs of these two departments, who were requested to be present at this meeting by the city manager, were asked to describe the impact of this alternative budget on their respective operations. The police chief indicated that the impact of this reduction on the city's crime rate would be disastrous and that minorities hired in recent years would be the first to be fired under the civil-service regulations (last hired, first fired).[15] The fire chief stated that the proposed reductions would create an increase in response time to fires and an increase in fire-insurance rates for city property owners.[16] This alternative budget was viewed as clearly restricting the city's fire-fighting capability and precipitating an increase in the city's already high-crime rate. For these reasons, the city council voted unanimously to reject Jarvis-Gann Contingency Budget A.[17]

Council members were equally repulsed by Jarvis-Gann Contingency Budget B, which restored police and fire services at the expense of "deeper" reductions in the city's cultural and recreational programs. The impact of these additional cuts was severe. Under this alternative, the office of parks and recreation was forced to close fifteen parks and recreational facilities. The library department had to eliminate six branch libraries and drastically curtail services at its main library. The museum department suffered an extreme reduction in the number of programs it offered to the public. The mayor emphatically stated that "parks and recreation are not just fun places, but are critical."[18] He also expressed concern over the need for cultural and recreational programs given the "problems of unemployment and unoccupied youth."[19] One council member responded that the problem of "people on the streets" would be significant and that "libraries, the museum and parks will be hard, essential services."[20] Because of the drastic impact of this alternative budget on cultural and recreational facilities, the city council flatly rejected this financial option.[21]

Upon the defeat of both contingency budgets, and after additional discussion, the city council adopted a motion to direct staff to prepare a modified version of Jarvis-Gann Contingency Budget B.[22] The council directed the city manager to make additional reductions in the police and fire departments and, with these funds, to restore services in the city's cultural and recreational programs.[23] A subsequent meeting was scheduled for 27 April 1978 to consider what would be referred to as Jarvis-Gann Contingency Budget C.

It was back to the drawing board. The budget director and the city manager met the next morning to determine how to fulfill the council's request. Additional budget reductions, amounting to $3.8 million, were ultimately made in police and fire services. In the police department, misdemeanor investigation, burglary/grand theft investigation, narcotics offense investigation, and two walking patrols were eliminated. In the fire department, the fire-prevention bureau was drastically reduced, one truck company eliminated, and two engine companies closed. About half of this amount was used to restore cultural and recreational programs. In the office of parks and recreation, additional playgrounds and recreation areas were restored. Six branch libraries were added back in the library department. Funds were restored in the museum department, enabling the museum to retain most of its programs. The city manager also determined that the $2.1 million in one-time savings should not be used since the status of the city's antirecessionary payments under the Public Works Employment Act was unknown.[24] These changes formed the basis for what was referred to as Jarvis-Gann Contingency Budget C. A departmental listing of these revised reductions, including the number of programs involved and the city jobs eliminated, is set forth in table 4–5.[25] This budget was assembled and presented to the city council for its next public meeting.

On 27 April 1978, Oakland's elected officials met again to consider the

Table 4–5
Oakland City Budget Reduction, Jarvis-Gann Contingency Budget C,
Fiscal Year 1978–1979

Departments	Amount (millions of $)	Percent	Programs [a]	Positions
Police	8.3	22	42	315
Fire	5.4	20	16	170
Public works	4.6	40	24	234
General services	4.4	65	22	133
Parks and recreation	3.4	40	57	231
Library	1.7	46	12	121
Museum	1.2	48	26	52
General government	2.9	40	21	141
Nondepartmental	3.1	35	7	—
Total reduction	35.0	31	227	1,397

Note: Discretionary funds, excluding tax-increment and bond funds.
[a] Includes programs reduced or eliminated.

third version of the city's Proposition 13 budget. The city manager summarized the city council's budget preferences from the previous public meeting. The reallocation of funds from the police and fire departments to other departments, basically those offering cultural and recreational programs, formed the basis for Jarvis-Gann Contingency Budget C. The city manager highlighted the additional reductions in police and fire services and summarized the program additions in the office of parks and recreation, museum department, and library department. This version of the city's Proposition 13 budget cut an additional 117 sworn personnel: 61 police officers and 56 fire fighters.[26] The funds made available from this action enabled 102 city positions to be added back in cultural and recreational programs.[27] The city manager also expressed his preference for retaining the $2.1 million in one-time savings. He concluded his opening remarks by saying, "The complexity of the additional material is as painful as the proposed reduction itself. I believe that this [alternative budget] will provide a basis for you to complete your development of the city's contingency budget in the event of the passage of the Jarvis-Gann Initiative."[28]

Although the city council was relatively satisfied with this budget proposal, it wanted one additional alteration. Council members were not entirely satisfied with the additional reductions made in police and fire services. After further discussion, the council voted unanimously to use the $2.1 million in one-time savings to add back the reductions made in public-safety services. The city council voted to allocate $1.5 million to the police department and the remainder, $0.6 million, to the fire department.[29] This action served to complete the allocation of the city's anticipated resources under Proposition 13 to city departments for the upcoming fiscal year.

The city manager also recommended that the council utilize 100 percent of the city's available tax-increment funds in fiscal year 1978–1979. Previous council policy had been to use only 50 percent of these funds, allowing the remaining amount to be allocated among other taxing jurisdictions in the county based on their proportional share of the composite-property-tax rate. The elected officials unanimously approved this recommendation with little discussion.[30] It should be noted that while previous contingency budgets eliminated all local support for capital improvement projects, Jarvis-Gann Contingency Budget C restored $0.7 million for this purpose. This funding level was approved by the council to enable the city to obtain leverage by qualifying for federal matching funds. The council also voted to eliminate the city's Convention Center Fund and to transfer all transient-occupancy-tax revenues, which were normally deposited into this fund, into the General Fund to finance regular city operations.[31]

The city council also decided that it was important to inform the public of the anticipated impact of Proposition 13 on city services. To achieve this goal, the council directed the city manager to immediately place appropriate signs on city facilities that would be affected upon the passage of the Jarvis-Gann Initiative.[32] The extensive efforts of city officials to inform Oakland's citizens of the anticipated impact of Proposition 13 on city services are explained in detail in a subsequent section of this chapter.

Throughout the entire meeting, only one citizen requested to speak concerning the impact of Proposition 13 on city services. This individual accused the council of disseminating "scare materials" on the effect of the initiative on public services. He stated that the city had a duty to find out if the state legislature was going to support local governments with its surplus revenues.

The mayor replied that there was no way of telling if or how much outside help the city might obtain from the state, and it would be irresponsible to count on help of which no one was sure.[33] The mayor refused to allow this individual to speak on the merits of the Jarvis-Gann Initiative, insisting that the speaker address only the issue on the agenda: the budget. The speaker made no additional comments. While several other citizens were present at this meeting, none of them requested to speak on the issue.

Oakland's council members, prior to the close of the meeting, unanimously adopted a motion to direct the city manager to finalize the city's Proposition 13 budget based on the criteria previously set forth by the city council.[34] The last public hearing on this final alternative budget was scheduled for the council's regular agenda at its 9 May 1978 meeting.

The revisions that had to be made for the city's final Proposition 13 budget were relatively simple. The budget director, in adding back the $2.1 million to the police and fire departments, restored thirty-nine sworn positions in the police department and eighteen sworn positions in the fire department.[35] The programs to which these additional funds were added were those proposed for reduction in Contingency Budget C. Upon the completion of this budget, the city attorney prepared a resolution which would enable the city council to adopt the city's Jarvis-Gann Emergency Budget as the official financial plan for the city in the event of the passage of Proposition 13. The final version of the budget, as well as the resolution formally adopting this financial plan, were reviewed and approved by the city manager and forwarded to the city council for its 9 May 1978 meeting. This was the last public meeting held prior to the passage of Proposition 13. It is discussed below.

City Council Adopts Proposition 13 Budget

The date scheduled for the adoption of the city's final Proposition 13 budget was 9 May 1978. This was the first item on the council's agenda. The city manager began by explaining the previous budget modifications requested by the city council, stating that the city's budget, under the financial constraints mandated by Proposition 13, would include operating and capital expenditures of $80.1 million.[36] The city's normal budget, on the other hand, was expected to be $113 million. The final version of the Jarvis-Gann Emergency Budget required a reduction in public services amounting to $32.9 million, encompassing 220 programs in nineteen city departments and involving the elimination of 1,330 city positions. A departmental listing of these reductions is illustrated in table 4-6.[37]

After this brief presentation, the mayor declared the meeting open for public discussion. Only two individuals spoke concerning the city's Proposition 13 budget: one public-employee union representative and a local minister. The union representative urged city council members to "do more" to help educate the public on the local effects of the Jarvis-Gann Initiative. He also criticized the local press for not providing adequate coverage of the impact of Proposition 13 on public services.[38] The minister accused the council of using scare tactics by describing the drastic reductions in city services under Proposition 13. This speaker told the city's elected officials to direct their efforts toward educating the poor regarding the impact of the initiative on services they receive.[39] One council member

Table 4-6
Oakland City Budget Reduction, Adopted Jarvis-Gann Budget, Fiscal Year 1978-1979

Departments	Amount (millions of $)	Percent	Programs[a]	Positions
Police	6.8	18	37	267
Fire	4.8	18	14	151
Public works	4.6	40	24	234
General services	4.4	65	22	133
Parks and recreation	3.4	40	57	231
Library	1.7	46	12	121
Museum	1.2	48	26	52
General government	2.9	40	21	141
Nondepartmental	3.1	35	7	—
Total reduction	32.9	29	220	1,330

Note: Discretionary funds, excluding tax-increment and bond funds.
[a] Includes programs reduced or eliminated.

quickly responded that "the public claim of scare tactics . . . is inaccurate" and "the council had been realistic in reducing the city's operating budget."[40] This member of the council also criticized the media for "not fulfilling its responsibility in spelling out the effects of Proposition 13 and disseminating information to the public." He concluded by stating that "the media has to look at the facts and start printing them."[41] The mayor also accused the press of being irresponsible and angrily stated that the press "refuses to face the facts. And when we present the facts, they call it scare tactics."[42]

After this often heated exchange, one council member introduced a motion to approve the resolution adopting the city's Proposition 13 budget. With little discussion, this resolution was approved unanimously.[43] The council officially adopted the city's Jarvis-Gann Emergency Budget for the next fiscal year, contingent, of course, upon the passage of Proposition 13 on 6 June 1978. This legislation served to implement the various fund changes and departmental appropriations previously agreed upon by the city council. This resolution also authorized the use of 100 percent of the city's available tax-increment funds. A copy of the complete text of this resolution is set forth in figure 4-1.[44]

At the close of this meeting, the city manager indicated that, should implementation of the city's Jarvis-Gann Emergency Budget become necessary, some fine-tune adjustments would have to be made.[45] The term fine-tune adjustments proved to be a gross understatement. The actual adjustments made to this budget, which reduced the magnitude of the city's financial deficit from $32.9 million to $14.3 million, and personnel reductions from 1,330 positions to 227 positions, are examined in chapter 5. It is now appropriate to discuss the anticipated financial and operational impact of Oakland's adopted Proposition 13 budget.

Anticipated Financial Impact

The city's normal discretionary fund budget for fiscal year 1978–1979 amounted to $113 million. This budget authorized funding for over 3,800 city positions, including Comprehensive Employment and Training Act (CETA) funded personnel. The adopted Jarvis-Gann Budget, on the other hand, totaled $80.1 million and provided funding for nearly 2,500 city jobs, including CETA-funded personnel. This latter financial plan involved a budget reduction of $32.9 million and the elimination of 1,330 city positions. The adopted Jarvis-Gann budget eliminated about one-third of the city's discretionary funds and, in so doing, abolished slightly over one-third of the city's total work force. The financial impact of the council-approved Proposition 13 budget on specific city departments is discussed below.[46]

Police Department. This department's normal budget was $37.4 million, which authorized 684 sworn personnel and 359 civilian personnel. The Proposition 13 budget allocated $30.6 million, 513 sworn personnel, and 263 civilian personnel. This involved a reduction of $6.8 million and 267 positions, 171 of which were sworn. This department would be operated at slightly over three-fourths of its normal funding and staffing level.

Fire Department. This department's regular budget included $26.4 million, which financed 597 positions: 579 sworn positions and 18 civilian positions. The adopted Jarvis-Gann budget authorized $21.6 million, 432 sworn positions and 14 civilian positions. This reduction amounted to $4.8 million and eliminated 147 sworn positions and 4 civilian positions. This department would be operated at approximately three-fourths of its normal funding and staffing level.

Office of Public Works. This department's normal funding and staffing level involved $11.5 million and 537 city positions. The Proposition 13 budget included $6.9 million and 303 personnel. This involved a reduction of $4.6 million and 234 city positions. Public works would be forced to operate at about 60 percent of its regular funding and staffing levels.

Oakland City Council Resolution No. 57201 C.M.S.[a]

Resolution Adopting the Jarvis-Gann Emergency Budget, in Event of the Passage of Proposition 13 on June 6, 1978, as the Financial Plan for Use of Unrestricted Funds for Conducting the Affairs of the City for Fiscal Year 1978–79 and Appropriating Certain Moneys to Provide for the Expenditures Proposed by Said Budget.

Whereas, the Jarvis-Gann Initiative has qualified for the State of California's June primary ballot; and

Whereas, the City of Oakland would lose approximately $39,000,000 in nonrestricted fund revenues during Fiscal Year 1978–79 if this initiative is implemented; and

Whereas, the City Council has given careful consideration to the adoption of an alternative budget utilizing unrestricted funds for the Fiscal Year 1978–79, in event of the passage of Proposition 13 on June 6, 1978, hereinafter referred to as the Jarvis-Gann Emergency Budget; now, therefore, be it

Resolved: That Resolution No. 52810 C.M.S., adopted November 28, 1972, establishing the Convention Center Fund, is hereby repealed. Effective July 1, 1978, all Transient Occupancy Tax revenues will be deposited directly into the General Fund to finance other City of Oakland operations; and be it

Further Resolved: That the remaining fund balances in the Convention Center Fund, effective July 1, 1978, are hereby transferred to the General Fund balances; and be it

Further Resolved: That the project balances in excess of $1,000,000 in the City Council's Emergency Contingency Project No. 87300, effective July 1, 1978, are hereby transferred to the General Fund balances; and be it

Further Resolved: That the unencumbered balances in the project appropriation accounts on June 30, 1978, are hereby reappropriated for Fiscal Year 1978–79 for the same purposes for which the projects were originally established; and be it

Further Resolved: That all unencumbered balances existing in operating nonproject appropriation accounts hereby lapse on June 30, 1978, to the fund balances of the funds from which the appropriations were originally made; and be it

Further Resolved: That the City Manager may transfer operating expenditure appropriations between departments and activity programs during the budget year, except that $1,000,000 maintained in the Emergency Contingency Project may not be transferred and expended without City Council authorization, and except that Capital Improvement Project appropriation balances necessary for accomplishment of the purposes for which the original appropriations were made may not be transferred without City Council authorization; and be it

[a]Adopted by the city council on 9 May 1978.

Figure 4–1. Oakland Budget Resolution, Adopted Jarvis-Gann Budget, Fiscal Year 1978–1979

Further Resolved: That the sum of $5,911,000 appropriated from the Revenue Sharing Fund (211) is hereby specifically allocated to the Police Department for the purpose of funding police services; and be it

Further Resolved: That the City Manager is hereby authorized to expend in accordance with the laws of the State of California and the City of Oakland on behalf of the City Council $81,072,000 in nonrestricted funds from new appropriations for the departments and activity programs shown below:

Jarvis-Gann Emergency Budget

Operating Expenditures	Amount
0100 Mayor/Council	$270,000
0200 City Manager	395,000
0300 City Clerk	210,000
0400 City Attorney	398,000
0500 Personnel	254,000
0600 City Planning	224,000
0700 City Auditor	89,000
0800 City Physician	39,000
0900 Retirement Administration	87,000
1000 Finance	1,106,000
2100 Police	20,180,000
2200 Fire	12,794,000
3000 Public Works	6,941,000
4000 General Services	2,441,000
5000 Parks and Recreation	5,172,000
6100 Library	1,974,000
6200 Museum	1,304,000
6300 Paramount Theatre	176,000
7300 Community Development	274,000
8100 Employee Benefits	713,000
8200 Insurance and Liability Claims	928,000
8300 Debt Service	1,020,000
8400 Miscellaneous	3,619,000
8600 Coliseum Support	750,000
8720 Police and Fire Retirement	19,172,000
9000 Budget and Management Services	843,000
9300 Central Service Overhead	(940,000)
Subtotal, Operating Expenditures	$80,433,000

Capital Improvements	
3000 Public Works	$639,000
Subtotal, Capital Improvements	$639,000
Grand Total	$81,072,000

and be it

Further Resolved: That the sums hereinafter set forth are appropriated for the Fiscal Year 1978-79 from the following designated unrestricted funds:

Figure 4-1 continued

101 General Purpose Fund	$70,351,000
211 Revenue Sharing Fund	5,911,000
226 Public Works Employment Act Fund	4,314,000
291 City Street Fund	421,000
293 Select System Fund	75,000
Total	$81,072,000

and be it

Further Resolved: That the sum of $2,691,000 is made available for tax increment purposes from available tax increments, effective July 1, 1978, for Fiscal Year 1978–79. This represents 100% of available tax increments; and be it

Further Resolved: That this resolution shall only be effective upon the passage of Proposition 13 on the State's June 6, 1978, ballot.

Figure 4–1 continued

Office of General Services. This department's regular budget allocated $6.8 million and 404 personnel. The Jarvis-Gann budget authorized $2.4 million and 271 positions. This reduction totaled $4.4 million and 133 positions. General services would be operated at one-third of its normal funding level and two-thirds of its regular staffing level.

Office of Parks and Recreation. This department's normal budget and staffing amounted to $8.6 million and 505 personnel. The Proposition 13 budget allocated $5.2 million and 274 positions. This mandated a reduction of $3.4 million and 231 positions. This department's operations would be financed at 60 percent of its regular funding level. Staffing was reduced by almost one-half.

Library Department. This department's regular budget authorized $3.7 million and 207 city positions. The final Jarvis-Gann budget included $2 million and funded eighty-six positions. The reduction amounted to $1.7 million and eliminated 121 personnel. The library would be operated at slightly over one-half of its normal funding level with about 40 percent of its regular staff.

Museum Department. This department's normal budget included $2.5 million and 132 personnel. The Proposition 13 budget, on the other hand, authorized $1.3 million and eighty positions. This involved a reduction of $1.2 million and fifty-two positions. The museum would be operated with about one-half of its regular funding and 60 percent of its authorized staff.

General Government. This area of the city budget encompasses city-staff departments. These include mayor, council, city manager, city clerk, city attorney, personnel, city planning, city auditor, city physician, retirement administration, finance, budget and management services, and housing conservation. The normal budget for these departments was $7.2 million and authorized 394 positions. The adopted Jarvis-Gann budget allocated $4.3 million and 253 positions. This reduction amounted to $2.9 million and 141 positions. The General Government departments would be operated at about 60 percent of their regular funding and staffing levels.

Nondepartmental. This portion of the budget includes functions outside the city's regular operations. These budgets include miscellaneous expenditures, community promotion, insurance and liability claims, employee benefits, capital improvements, and central service overhead. This last budget is merely a cost center used to capture overhead costs charged to federal grant programs. No staffing is necessary for these budgets because of their unique nature. The regular budget for these activities amounted to $8.9 million. The Proposition 13 budget authorized $5.8 million; this mandated a reduction of $3.1 million. These activities would be maintained at about two-thirds of their normal funding level.

Tax-Increment Projects. Tax-increment funds are administered by the Oakland Redevelopment Agency and authorized by the city council. These funds are used to finance various capital projects in the city's redevelopment area. The normal tax-increment-fund budget was expected to be $6.4 million. The anticipated amount of these funds under Propostion 13 was $2.7 million. This funding source would be reduced by $3.7 million, nearly 60 percent of the normal funding level.

A departmental comparison of Oakland's normal budget and Jarvis-Gann budget is illustrated in table 4–7.[47] This table sets forth the magnitude of the dollar and staffing reduction in each area of city government. The anticipated impact of these reductions on city operations is explained below.

Anticipated Public-Service Impact

The operational impact of these budgetary reductions was unbelievable. Eliminating over one-third of the city's discretionary funds and abolishing one-third of its work force had a drastic effect on prevailing public services. This cut, under normal circumstances, would have been unthinkable. This alternative budget, however, was predicated on the assumption that no offsetting revenues would be available for the city to counteract an expected financial deficit created by Proposition 13. The conditional tense is used to describe these service reductions, since they were prospective in nature— dependent upon the passage of Proposition 13 on 6 June 1978. This was less than one month after Oakland's elected officials adopted the Jarvis-Gann Emergency Budget. The impact of the anticipated budget reductions is described below.[48]

Police Department. Within the criminal investigative division, the following programs would be affected.

1. Investigative programs concentrating on arson, auto theft, fraud, consumer fraud, and forgery/credit offenses would be eliminated entirely. Misdemeanor and burglary/grand theft offenses would be substantially reduced.

2. The investigative services unit, which enhances the evidence-gathering ability of the department, the inspectional services unit, which facilitates the recovery of stolen property, and the field investigation unit, which conducts follow-up investigations on reported complaints, would be abolished.

In the vice control division, the prostitution/gambling investigation unit would be totally eliminated and the narcotics offense investigation unit would be reduced by one-half. Investigative efforts involving prostitution, gambling, and bookmaking would virtually cease.

The intelligence division, which gathers, analyzes, and reports information about organized criminal activity and terrorism, would be discontinued. Critical information relative to potential threats to public safety would not be available.

The Community Services Program would be abolished. This would eliminate the Home Alert Program, Spanish Language Assistance Program, residential and commercial building security, and other police-community cooperation programs. The community and its citizens would have an increased vulnerability to crime as a result of the eliminiation of these programs.

Youth services would be substantially reduced. Bicycle licensing, the missing persons unit, traffic-safety unit, and youth services field activity, which involves juvenile-oriented community-relations programs, would be eliminated entirely.

The Fugitive Apprehension Program would be virtually eliminated. Criminals apprehended outside the city would only be returned on a selective basis, determined by the seriousness of their offense. Only the most serious offenders would be returned for prosecution.

The patrol division would eliminate night-walking patrols in the downtown and Jack London Square areas and the daytime East Oakland walking

Table 4–7
Comparison of Oakland City Budgets, Normal Budget versus Adopted Jarvis-Gann Budget, Fiscal Year 1978–1979

	Normal		Jarvis-Gann		Reduction	
Departments	Budget (millions of $)	Staffing	Budget (millions of $)	Staffing	Budget (millions of $)	Staffing
Police	37.4	1,043	30.6	776	6.8	267
Fire	26.4	597	21.6	446	4.8	151
Public works	11.5	537	6.9	303	4.6	234
General services	6.8	404	2.4	271	4.4	133
Parks and recreation	8.6	505	5.2	274	3.4	231
Library	3.7	207	2.0	86	1.7	121
Museum	2.5	132	1.3	80	1.2	52
General government	7.2	394	4.3	253	2.9	141
Nondepartmental	8.9	—	5.8	—	3.1	—
Totals	113.0	3,819	80.1	2,489	32.9	1,330

Note: Discretionary funds, exluding tax-increment and bond funds.

patrol. Crime in these areas of the city might increase accordingly, and loss of personal contact between walking officers and residents and business people in the area would degrade police-community relationships.

Within the traffic division, traffic-accident investigation, drivers'-license investigation, and commercial-vehicle control would be eliminated. The screening of public vehicles and public-vehicle operators would cease, possibly increasing the risk of injury and accidents to citizens who use public forms of transportation.

The Animal Control Program would be eliminated. This program would discountinue the enforcement of animal-control ordinances and state humane laws and the removal and disposal of dead animals. The Animal Shelter would also be closed.

Fire Department. Eight fire-suppression companies would be eliminated, which would have the following effects on those fire stations indicated.

1. Six fire stations would be permanently closed. These stations are listed in table 4–8.

2. Fire-suppression services at two fire stations (Number 3 at 7th and Pine Streets and Number 23 at 7100 Foothill Boulevard) would be reduced.

Fire-prevention services would be cut in about half with the elimination

Table 4-8
Closed Oakland City Facilities, Adopted Jarvis-Gann Budget, Fiscal Year 1978–1979

Facility	Address
Police	
Animal Control Facility	3065 Ford Street
Emergency Services	
Planning Facility	3304 Joaquin Miller Road
Fire	
Fire Station No. 2	29 Jack London Square
Fire Station No. 7	1027 60th Street
Fire Station No. 12	822 Alice Street
Fire Station No. 14	3459 Champion Street
Fire Station No. 21	13150 Skyline Boulevard
Fire Station No. 29	1016 66th Street
Public works	
District 1	
Maintenance Yard	3455 Ettie Street
District 4	
Maintenance Yard	5921 Shepherd Canyon Road
Parks and recreation	
Knowland Park Zoo	98th Avenue and Mountain Boulevard
Lockhaven Recreation Center	1327 65th Avenue
Redwood Heights Recreation Center	3731 Redwood Road
Studio II, Arroyo Viejo	
Recreation Center	7701 Krause Avenue
DeFremery Swimming Pool	1651 Adeline Street
Lions Swimming Pool	3860 Hanley Road
Temescal Swimming Pool	371 45th Street
Feather River Camp	Quincy, California
Kamp Kidd	Quincy, California
Camp Sierra	Quincy, California
Greenhouse (Nursery	
Complex), Lakeside Park	Grand and Bellevue Avenues
Morcom Rose Garden	Jean and Olive Streets
Putting Greens, Lakeside Park	Grand and Bellevue Avenues
Putting Greens, Snow Park	20th and Harrison Streets
Ranger Station	3540 Joaquin Miller Road
Library	
Main library facility	125 14th Street
California Room	
Jack London Room	
Youth Room	
Two Bookmobile Vans	
Cityline Offices	1421 Washington Street
Branch library facilities	
Melrose	4805 Foothill Boulevard
Rockridge	5701 College Avenue
North Oakland	3134 San Pablo Avenue
Park Boulevard	1934 Park Boulevard

Table 4-8 continued

Facility	Address
Glenview	4231 Park Boulevard
Baymont	10617 MacArthur Boulevard
Laurel	3625 MacArthur Boulevard
Museum	
Special Exhibits	Oakland Museum
Aquarium Exhibit	1000 Oak Street
Outdoor Fish Pond	
Oakes Observatory Gallery	

of eight sworn and one civilian positions. Fire-prevention code enforcement would be drastically reduced, bringing about the curtailment of fire-inspection and plan-checking services and public fire-safety programs.

Office of Public Works. The most immediate and noticeable effect would be the accumulation of litter on city streets, since street sweeping would be reduced by two-thirds. The downtown area would be swept twice a week, major arterial streets once a week, and residential areas once every three months.

Numerous street maintenance programs would be reduced or eliminated. As a result, streets would deteriorate faster and public complaints would increase. It is expected that about half of all reported potholes would not be filled in a timely manner.

Approximately half of the traffic signs would be allowed to deteriorate and eventually be removed. In the future, such signs could only be erected and maintained on major streets.

The capacity to conduct traffic-control studies would be greatly reduced. Response to public requests for new stop signs and review of traffic problems would be significantly delayed.

The Sidewalk Repair and Weed Abatement programs would be virtually eliminated. The remaining staff would attempt to deal with only the most serious sidewalk hazards and the most pressing weed-abatement problems. The curtailment of the Weed Abatement Program would result in the accumulation of weeds on many parcels of vacant land throughout the city, contributing to potential fire hazards.

There would be a significant reduction in the department's ability to answer citizen requests for information, process subdivision proposals and review building permits, provide up-to-date financial and accounting information, and respond to public complaints.

The following facilities would be closed: (1) District 1 Maintenance Yard, 3455 Ettie Street, and (2) District 4 Maintenance Yard, 5921 Shepherd Canyon Road.

Office of General Services. Maintenance of electrical facilities would be severely restricted and nearly one-half of the city's traffic signals would be shut off. A 40-to-50-percent drop in the citywide purchase of equipment, supplies, and material would occur, and processing and handling time would be greatly increased.

City buildings would be cleaned at a minimum required to meet health standards, heat and lights would be substantially reduced, and structural and mechanical repairs would be made only on an emergency basis. All fire alarms and police call boxes would be turned off and eventually removed. The appearance of city vehicles would show deterioration because maintenance would be solely directed toward keeping vehicles roadworthy.

Office of Parks and Recreation. Knowland Park, located at 98th Avenue and Mountain Boulevard, would no longer be maintained. The Knowland Park Zoo could not be kept as a city zoo. Three recreation centers, three municipal swimming pools, and three campgrounds would be closed. A listing of these centers, pools, and campgrounds is provided in table 4–8.

The following facilities would also be closed: (1) Greenhouse (Nursery Complex), Lakeside Park, Grand and Bellevue Avenues; (2) Morcom Rose Garden, Jean and Olive Streets; (3) Putting Greens, Lakeside Park, Grand and Bellevue Avenues; (4) Putting Greens, Snow Park, 20th and Harrison Streets; and (5) Ranger Station, 3540 Joaquin Miller Road.

Reductions in the parks services department would result in minimal maintenance and litter control in city parks, in play areas, and around city buildings. The increased litter and degraded vegetation would affect both functional and aesthetic appeal as well as pose health, safety, and security risks.

The Park Ranger Force would be virtually eliminated. This action would reduce safety for citizens who use Lakeside Park and Joaquin Miller Park. Patrolling activities at parks, playgrounds, and recreation centers would be eliminated. Trail maintenance and preservation would cease in Joaquin Miller Park, which reduces fire-prevention effectiveness in the city's "hill" area.

Library Department. The main library would be open only 37.5 hours per week, instead of the 62 hours per week it is normally open to the public. Three rooms at the main library would be closed. Eight branch-library facilities would be closed. The names of the rooms and the names and addresses of these libraries are listed in table 4–8.

The following branch libraries would be open on a half-time basis only: Piedmont Branch Library, 160 41st Street; Temescal Branch Library, 5205 Telegraph Avenue; Golden Gate Branch Library, 5606 San Pablo Avenue; West Oakland Branch Library, 1801 Adeline Street; Elmhurst Branch

Library, 1427 88th Street; and Brookfield Community Branch Library, 501 Jones Avenue.

The Asian Community Branch Library would be relocated to the Lakeview Branch Library Auditorium, located at 550 El Embarcadero.

Additional library services eliminated include two bookmobile vans; and "cityline" and "nightline" library services.

Museum Department. The number of weekly hours the museum would be open to the public would be reduced by thirteen. The museum would be open to the public five days a week (Wednesday through Sunday), for a total of only thirty-five hours. Under normal conditions, the museum is open six days a week (Tuesday through Sunday) for a total of forty-eight hours.

Museum Outreach programs, conducted through the museum-on-wheels and special community festivals, would be eliminated. These programs are specially designed for patrons who are in educational and health-care institutions and the handicapped.

The permanent aquarium exhibit in the Natural Science Gallery would be closed. The outdoor fish pond in the museum's main entryway would be drained and closed. This would terminate the exhibition of a major aspect of California's ecology. The multimedia presentation in the Oakes Observatory, which is a specialized educational facility, would be terminated.

General Government. City-staff departments include mayor, council, city manager, city clerk, city attorney, personnel, city planning, city auditor, city physician, retirement administration, finance, budget and management services, and housing conservation. The public and staff services available from these departments would be reduced by about 40 percent.

Nondepartmental. The Convention Center Fund would be abolished. All transient-occupancy-tax revenues would be transferred into the city's General Fund to finance regular city operations. This means Oakland would have to postpone indefinitely its planned Convention Center. Support to the Oakland Chamber of Commerce's Convention and Visitors Bureau would be eliminated.

Because of the vast reduction in available tax-increment funds created by the Jarvis-Gann Initiative, the previous council policy of utilizing only 50 percent of tax increments has been increased to 100 percent, so that the $2.7 million available for tax increment proposed in fiscal year 1978–1979 would be used to fund only very limited redevelopment activities in the central business district.

General-Fund support for capital improvements would be reduced. A minimal level of funding would be maintained in order for the city to qualify for federal matching funds. All funding for community organizations from the Community Promotion Program would be entirely eliminated.

Other reductions, for the most part, directly relate to the decrease in the number of city positions. Personnel reductions affect miscellaneous expenditures, insurance and liability claims, employee benefits, and central service overhead.

These service reductions include the closure of many city facilities. These facilities would no longer be needed if the proposed elimination of public services was actually implemented. The police department would be forced to close its Animal Control Shelter and Emergency Services Planning Facility. The fire department would eliminate six fire stations. Public works would abolish two maintenance yards. Many recreational and cultural facilities would also be permanently closed. The office of parks and recreation would close the city zoo, three recreation centers, three municipal swimming pools, three public camps, its ranger station, and several other smaller recreational centers. The library department would seal off portions of the city's main library and close several branch libraries. The museum department would close sections of the museum complex. A complete listing of those city facilities proposed to be closed under the city's adopted Jarvis-Gann Emergency Budget is set forth in table 4-8.[49]

The description of the anticipated impact of Proposition 13 on city services was assembled by the staff of the OBMS. Department managers had previously been requested to prepare and submit a narrative description of the effect on their respective operations of the expected revenue loss under Proposition 13. While the anticipated service reductions seemed severe, they were based on the assumptions contained in the council-approved Jarvis-Gann Emergency Budget. These reports were reviewed, edited, and compiled in a short publication titled *Public Service Impact Statement—Jarvis-Gann Emergency Budget—Fiscal Year 1978-79*. This document set forth service reductions on a citywide basis by department. This publication was part of the effort of Oakland city officials to inform the public of the predicted impact of the passage of Proposition 13. This public-informational effort, which was fairly extensive, proved to be very controversial.

Informing the Public

The *Public Service Impact Statement* was distributed to the city council, local news media, interested community groups, and concerned citizens. Oakland's elected officials and members of the local news media were presented copies of this document at the 9 May 1978 meeting of the council.

Citizens and community groups were furnished copies upon request. Copies were made available in the mayor's office, city manager's office, city clerk's office, and the OBMS. The anticipated impact of proposed service reductions made the front page of the local newspaper the next day.[50] From this point forward, members of the city council and individual department managers freely discussed the anticipated effect of Proposition 13 on the city's operations.

The first newspaper article on the city's adopted Jarvis-Gann budget, appearing in the *Oakland Tribune,* said "Oakland, following the Jarvis-Gann mandate, is preparing to face the long, hot summer by firing almost a quarter of its employees and closing six fire stations, three recreation centers, three swimming pools, and seven branch libraries."[51] This article also explained that "about a quarter of the city's police and firemen will be laid off."[52] The story went on to discuss the expected impact of Proposition 13 on the city's Affirmative Action program, stating that 'the last-hired, first-fired' effect [of Proposition 13] on Oakland's minority hiring program—which has only become effective in the past few years is being assessed but is bound to be severe."[53]

The city's personnel director, when questioned about the influence of the initiative on minority hiring, indicated "it knocks the hell out of it, no question about it."[54] The police chief stated his deparment "would lose 46 percent of its sworn minority members and all 17 of its policewomen, whose category was eliminated."[55] The fire chief announced that "about 100 persons would be laid off, with about 40 of these minority fire fighters."[56] This article concluded by setting forth the complete listing of proposed departmental-service reductions contained in the *Public Service Impact Statement.*

Throughout the many public meetings held by Oakland city officials, only a few citizens expressed concern over the city's Proposition 13 budget. Most citizens were apparently apathetic during the early months of the city's effort to plan for the possible adoption of the Jarvis-Gann Initiative. The low citizen turnout at public meetings on Proposition 13 reflected this mood. After the city's Proposition 13 budget was adopted and its impact on public services described and printed in the press, thousands of Oakland residents became more aware of the possible effect of the initiative on their local government. They were specifically aware of the many public programs that would be curtailed.

The city council, at its 27 April 1978 meeting, directed the city manager to post notices on those city facilities affected by the passage of the Proposition 13. These notices, more like signs because of their large size, were prepared and printed by the city's office of general services. These signs were carefully worded and reviewed by the city attorney before being made available to department managers. They were appropriately titled "Notice

of Possible Closure" and "Notice of Potential Reduction of City Services."
Copies of these signs are illustrated in figure 4–2.

The city manager, during his next meeting with department managers, distributed these signs for posting on all city facilities that would be either closed or reduced if Proposition 13 was adopted. After this meeting, a directive was sent by the city manager to all department managers informing them how to describe their respective service reductions.[57] Department managers were instructed to describe service reductions "in terms relating to the level of services to be reduced and not in a percentage of numbers of personnel to be eliminated."[58] This description was to be "in block lettering as large as the type on the poster,"[59] which was about one inch in height.

Nearly a thousand of these signs were placed on public facilities throughout the city: fire stations, recreation centers, swimming pools, parks, branch libraries, and the museum. They informed Oakland citizens using these public facilities of the potential reduction or elimination of services created by the passage of Proposition 13. The city manager, on 1 June 1978, sent another directive to department managers instructing them to remove these notices at the close of the workday on 5 June 1978—one day before the election.[60]

Posting these notices on city facilities proved to be very controversial. Some citizens accused the city of using public money to influence the outcome of the election. The city attorney, when presented with this allegation, responded that "the city's legal staff had researched the question whether the signs would be legal, and concluded that case law—if not statutory law—appears to demand that public officials inform the citizenry when they intend significant changes in public services."[61] The city attorney concluded his statement by indicating that the signs made no statement either for or against the initiative, but merely described the service reductions contained in the city's adopted Proposition 13 Emergency Budget.[62]

In addition to the above efforts to inform the public, a few of the city's elected officials made public speeches concerning Proposition 13. The mayor referred to Proposition 13 as "having a devastating effect on local governments" and noted that "if the citizens want better police and fire protection, they better not pass the Jarvis-Gann Initiative."[63] The mayor also stated that passage of Proposition 13 had "racial overtones, would bring chaos to the state, hamper the schools that are trying to improve education for minorities, and flood the streets with unemployed minorities."[64] The mayor also urged other elected officials to be "aware of the problems caused by the measure and to fight it."[65]

One council member attacked Proposition 13 with equal vehemence. This official alleged that the initiative had elements of "racism" and was "against a city like Oakland with its high population of seniors, racial minority members, and poor and renters."[66] "Services to these residents,"

Notice of Possible Closure

If Proposition 13 (Jarvis-Gann) is adopted at the June 6, 1978 election, the Oakland City budget will require that this facility be closed.

                City of Oakland

**Notice of Potential
Reduction of City Services**

If Proposition 13 (Jarvis-Gann) is adopted at the June 6, 1978 election, the Oakland City budget will require the following reduction in services at this facility:

                City of Oakland

Note: Actual size approximately 1½′ by 3′.

Figure 4–2. Copies of Notices Posted on Oakland Public Facilities, Adopted Jarvis-Gann Budget

he said, "would be among those cut or sharply cut back if Jarvis-Gann passes."[67] This initiative was referred to as the meat-ax approach that would "bring death to the things that make a city viable."[68] This council member also characterized the initiative as a "fraud" and "a windfall for people who own apartment houses, for people who own businesses, but not renters."[69]

Oakland, in retrospect, conducted an extensive effort to plan for and inform its citizens of the potential impact of Proposition 13. Although sometimes reactionary, the point was quite clear. Passage of the Jarvis-Gann Initiative would severely reduce revenues and, in so doing, force drastic reductions in public services. The many public hearings, the notices posted on city facilities, the speeches by city officials, and the press coverage, all served their purpose. These actions enabled the citizens of Oakland to relate to specific service reductions, rather than merely to think of "reducing the fat," a term frequently used during the campaign on the merits of the initiative.

The anticipated impact of Proposition 13, based upon the assumption that the city would not receive replacement revenues, proved to be erroneous. The actual effect of the passage of Proposition 13 was substantially less than what had been predicted by city officials. The anticipated

revenue loss and expected massive employee terminations never materialized. The events that reduced the impact of Proposition 13 on Oakland, as
well as the actual effect of this measure on city revenues and public services
are examined in chapter 5.

Commentary

The evolution of Oakland's Proposition 13 budget reflected much political
compromise with respect to the relative value of public services. Three
alternative city budgets had to be prepared before the city council adopted
the final Jarvis-Gann Emergency Budget. This entire process was very time-
consuming and created a great amount of paperwork for all parties
concerned. Hundreds of hours of staff time went into the preparation of
these budgets. In fact, almost all other budgetary and analytical work
normally undertaken in the OBMS came to a standstill because staff
resources had to be directed to this effort. While Oakland was one of the
few cities in California to officially adopt an alternative Jarvis-Gann
budget,[70] the budgetary process used contained several unique characteris-
tics which are worth exploring in further detail. These are examined in the
following paragraphs.

The preparation of the city's Jarvis-Gann budget definitely lacked
political leadership. The mayor, during one of the first public hearings on
Proposition 13, stated that the city council must make philosophical decisions regarding the priorities of the city's public services. Such direction was
never given. Instead, the city manager was directed to prepare an across-
the-board budget reduction. This instruction was very political since it side-
stepped the issue of sorting out public-service priorities in advance. Such a
budgetary strategy, upon closer examination, possesses inherent shortcomings.

A simple analogy reveals the problems contained in this approach to
reducing expenditures. If a family were cutting its household budget by 35
percent, all expenditures could not be reduced by equal amounts. Basic
expenses, such as those for medical and dental services, food, and shelter,
for example, possibly could not be reduced at all. Other expenses, such as
those for nonessential items like entertainment and travel, could be
eliminated entirely. Certainly hard public services should have been reduced
by a different criterion than the city's soft public services. This course of
action, however, is highly political and involves much public discussion and
debate on the relative value of specific public services. The latter approach,
in an era of rising public expectations, may have undesireable political
ramifications. Additionally, in a city like Oakland with a heterogeneous
population, such a consensus on the relative value of public services would

have been difficult, if not impossible, to obtain. In any event, many of the problems encountered in preparing Oakland's Jarvis-Gann budget might have been eliminated if public priorities had been set initially.

As previously indicated, department managers proposed their own budget reductions. The OBMS did not rigorously analyze these reductions, it simply reviewed them for reasonableness and accuracy. Consequently, many of the proposed program reductions were really pieces of programs, portions of line-item budget expenditures and, in some cases, a simple reduction in capital outlay purchases. The OBMS could have assumed a more positive role. If additional time had been available and if the city manager had so directed, proposed budget reductions could have been thoroughly reviewed, analyzed, screened, and possibly even rejected. City departments, in some cases, would have been forced to submit other budget reductions. The use of this latter approach, however, depends greatly on the particular management style of the city manager. In Oakland's case, department managers were given complete freedom to propose those budget reductions they deemed most appropriate.

Notwithstanding the process undertaken, budget reductions did equal the amount requested by the city council. While the public described these reductions as "scare tactics" and as "not realistic" because other revenues, such as state-surplus revenues, were not taken into consideration, the reductions were based upon assumptions valid at that time. It would have been premature for Oakland's elected officials to have assumed that any portion of these revenues would be forthcoming, since it was impossible to predict what actions, if any, the state legislature would take to help local governments offset the effects of Proposition 13. The only other alternative would have been to wait until after the election to see what the state would do to assist financially troubled cities. Because this strategy prevailed in most California municipalities,[71] many citizens were never made aware of the anticipated impact on public services of the expected revenue loss. Therefore, the reduce-the-fat mentality prevailed in most cities for lack of information to the contrary. The political philosophy of an elected body also played an important part in the stand local government assumed on Proposition 13 prior to the June election. A more conservative political body might not have wanted to take an official stand against such a property-tax-relief measure. This was definitely not the case in Oakland.

Oakland's elected officials made several assumptions upon which to base the city's Jarvis-Gann budget. Service reductions were, therefore, accurately based on the criteria set forth by the city council. The proposed service reductions reflected actual expectations of the effect of Proposition 13. Throughout the entire process, however, one important impact of Proposition 13 was not apparent to the public. The effect of the initiative on the loss of the city's tax-increment funds, because it did not directly influence prevailing public services, was never highlighted to the public. The *Public Service Impact Statement* only indicated that the loss of these funds would permit "very limited redevelopment activities in the Central Business District."[72] The precise impact of this revenue loss was not adequately explained. Many specific projects of citywide interest were affected. These included the City Center Project, which involved the construction of a new parking garage and acquisition of land for commercial and retail development; the Chinatown Project, which funded acquisition of land for a major commercial redevelopment project; and Victorian Row, a major downtown redevelopment effort to rehabilitate a portion of the city's Victorian housing stock.[73] These projects are part of the city's efforts to revitalize what is referred to as its central business district. Citizens were ignorant of the impact of Proposition 13 on these important tax-increment projects.

Soon after the city council approved the final Proposition 13 budget, notices were mailed to about 1,050 employees who were scheduled to be terminated in the event of the passage of Proposition 13.[74] The difference between this number and the 1,330 layoffs initially predicted was created by vacant positions, many of which were not filled because of the uncertainties surrounding the possible implementation of the Jarvis-Gann Initiative. This action proved embarrassing, since only a small fraction of the anticipated employee terminations ever materialized. The city is only required, according to union agreements, to give employees two weeks advance notice prior to termination. The preoccupation of city staff with Proposition 13 created this embarrassing situation, which is still talked about at city hall today. In this respect, the term *scare tactics* proved to be a justifiable allegation. City officials could have waited until the middle of June before sending out these notices. While the city's receipt of state surplus revenues was not yet known at the time the notices were mailed, the city council adopted additional revenues which clearly reduced the magnitude of the projected budget deficit. This would have been a more realistic approach to informing the city's work force of required employee terminations.

On the more positive side, though much criticism was generated toward the city because of anticipated employee layoffs, the composition of those employees to be terminated proved to be equitable. The city's work force, at the time, included 13 percent management, 24 percent sworn, and 63 percent other employees. The first category includes management, supervisory, and professional employees. Sworn employees include uniformed police and fire personnel. The "other" category encompasses clerical, technical, craft, and field employees. Although not planned, the composition of projected layoffs proved to be proportional to the makeup of the city's work force. Therefore, the city could not be criticized for not reducing management employees in the same proportion as other city employees.[75] This coincidental occurrence served to limit criticism against the city in this area of its Jarvis-Gann Emergency Budget.

In addition to the effect of Proposition 13 on those public services already noted, the prospect that this measure might be implemented had a direct impact on other aspects of Oakland's city government. For example, in February the city manager imposed a citywide hiring freeze on all vacant positions to decrease the number of employees who might be terminated as a result of the passage of Proposition 13. Also the city council in April defeated a measure to increase the city's sewer-service charge. This fee increase was designed to acquire money for the maintenance and replacement of city sewers. The council based its decision on the prevailing political climate.[76] Additionally, the city manager had proposed the purchase of a new building to house several city departments that occupied rented office space. The city council rejected this proposal, responding that "this is not the time to talk about . . . buying a building in light of the hundreds of employees which may have to be laid off under Proposition 13."[77]

This mode of thinking, however, did not prevail all the time. The city council in February voted to increase its members' own automobile allowances from $170 to $185 per month and the mayor's automobile allowance from $250 to $275 per month. The annual cost of this expenditure was increased from $19,320 to $21,060, for a total increase of $1,740.[78] In theory, this increase in city expenditures meant that other public services had to be reduced accordingly to balance the city's budget under the anticipated Proposition 13 revenue loss.

The difficult process undertaken in Oakland to arrive at an acceptable Proposition 13 budget did contain areas for possible improvement. Oakland, however, was one of the few cities in California to prepare and adopt an official Jarvis-Gann budget. It was also one of the few cities in California to post signs on public facilities warning citizens of the possible effect of the passage of Proposition 13.[79] This exercise, though substantially mitigated by subsequent actions, served to relate anticipated revenue losses to "real" reductions in public services. It enhanced public awareness of what effects such a drastic cut in revenues would have on prevailing public services. Oakland residents gained insights not available to the great majority of citizens in other California municipalities. This increased level of awareness, however, did not necessarily lend insight into future events. The actual impact of Proposition 13 on city finances and public services is examined in the next chapter.

Notes

1. "Jarvis-Gann Budget Reductions," Oakland Director of Budget and Management Services, to Oakland Department Managers, 15 March 1978, files of Office of Budget and Management Services, Oakland, Calif.

2. Director of Budget and Management Services, *Jarvis-Gann*

Emergency Budget: Fiscal Year 1978–1979 (Oakland, Calif.: Office of Budget and Management Services, April 1978), p. i.

3. Ibid., p. ii.

4. Ibid., p. i.

5. Public-safety services include the city's police and fire departments. Cultural and recreational services include the city's office of parks and recreation, museum department, and library department.

6. Director of Budget and Management Services, *Jarvis-Gann Emergency Budget,* pp. v–vi. The number of program reductions was ascertained from pages 1 through 280. General government includes mayor/council, city manager, city clerk, city attorney, personnel, city planning, city auditor, city physician, retirement administration, finance, budget and management services, and housing conservation. Nondepartmental includes the following budgets: miscellaneous, community promotion, insurance and liability claims, employee benefits, central service overhead and capital expenditures.

7. *Jarvis-Gann Emergency Budget.*

8. Director of Budget and Management Services, *Contingency Budgets B and C—Jarvis-Gann Emergency Budget: Fiscal Year 1978–1979* (Oakland, Calif.: Office of Budget and Management Services, April 1978), pp. 3–4. The number of program reductions was ascertained from pages 7 through 47.

9. Director of Budget and Management Services, *Jarvis-Gann Emergency Budget.*

10. *Jarvis-Gann Emergency Budget,* 15 March 1978, p. 1.

11. Ibid.

12. Ibid., p. 3.

13. Ibid., p. 2.

14. Ibid.

15. Sue Soennichsen, "Jarvis-Gannized Budget Refined by City Council," *The Montclarion,* 26 April 1978, p. 1.

16. Ibid.

17. City Clerk, *City Council Meeting Minutes* (Oakland, Calif.: Office of City Clerk, 18 April 1978), p. 1.

18. Soennichsen, "Jarvis-Gannized Budget, p. 1.

19. Ibid.

20. Ibid.

21. City Clerk, *City Council Meeting Minutes,* 18 April 1978, p. 1.

22. Ibid.

23. Ibid.

24. Director of Budget and Management Services, *Issue Paper, Jarvis-Gann Alternative Budgets, Fiscal Year 1978–79* (Oakland, Calif.: Office of Budget and Management Services, 25 April 1978), p. 1.

25. Director of Budget and Management Services, *Contingency Budgets B and C,* pp. 3–4. The number of program reductions was ascertained from pages 7 through 47.

26. Director of Budget and Management Services, *Issue Paper,* p. 4.

27. Ibid.

28. Ibid.

29. City Clerk, *City Council Meeting Minutes,* 27 April 1978, p. 1.

30. Ibid.

31. Ibid., p. 2.

32. Ibid.

33. Sue Soennichsen, "Proposition 13 Budget Cut 35%, Closing Signs to be Posted," *The Montclarion,* 3 May 1978, p. 1.

34. City Clerk, *City Council Meeting Minutes,* 27 April 1978, p. 2.

35. *Jarvis-Gann Emergency Budget,* 4 May 1978, p. 2.

36. The city council's adopted Jarvis-Gann Emergency Budget indicated operating and capital expenditures of $81.1 million. This figure, however, erroneously included $1 million in bond funds, which are financed out of restricted funds.

37. Director of Budget and Management Services, *Contingency Budgets B and C,* pp. 3–4. The number of program reductions was ascertained from pages 7 through 47. The modifications to this budget were determined from *Jarvis-Gann Emergency Budget—Fiscal Year 1978-79,* 4 May 1978, p. 2.

38. Ernie Cox, "Wilson Attacks Trib on Jarvis Coverage," *Oakland Tribune,* 10 May 1978, sec. A, p. 5. Reprinted with permission.

39. Ibid.

40. City Clerk, *City Council Meeting Minutes,* 9 May 1978, p. 1.

41. Ibid.; Cox, "Wilson Attacks Trib."

42. Cox, "Wilson Attacks Trib."

43. City Clerk, *City Council Meeting Minutes,* 9 May 1978, pp. 1–2.

44. City Council, *Resolution 57201 C.M.S.,* Oakland City Council, Oakland, Calif., 9 May 1978. This resolution also contains many routine phrases required of all budget resolutions.

45. Cox, "Wilson Attacks Trib."

46. Director of Budget and Management Services, *Public Service Impact Statement—Jarvis-Gann Emergency Budget: FY 1978-79* (Oakland Calif.: Office of Budget and Management Services, May 1978), pp. 1–10.

47. Director of Budget and Management Services, *Contingency Budgets B and C,* pp. 1–4; and *Jarvis-Gann Emergency Budget,* 4 May 1978, p. 2.

48. Director of Budget and Management Services, *Public Service Impact Statement,* pp. 1–10.

49. Director of Budget and Management Services, *Contingency Budgets B and C,* pp. 5–6.

50. Gene Ayres, "Ax Is Set to Fall on City Facilities," *Oakland Tribune,* 10 May 1978, sec. A, p. 4. Reprinted with permission.

51. Ibid.

52. Ibid.

53. Ibid.

54. Ibid.

55. Ibid.

56. Ibid.

57. City Manager, "Proposition 13—Posters Announcing Possible Closures and/or Service Reductions," *Administrative Bulletin,* Office of the City Manager, Oakland, Calif., 2 May 1978, p. 1.

58. Ibid.

59. Ibid.

60. City Manager, "Proposition 13," 1 June 1978, p. 1.

61. Ernie Cox, "City Jarvis Notices Irk Cop," *Oakland Tribune,* 5 May 1978, sec. D, p. 27. Reprinted with permission.

62. Ibid.

63. Will Jones, "Mayor Wilson's Warning: Jarvis Means City Chaos," *Oakland Tribune,* 2 April 1978, sec. A, p. 1.

64. Ibid.

65. Ibid.

66. Gene Ayres, "Barbs Fly as Speakers Debate Property-Tax Cut Pros and Cons," *Oakland Tribune,* 2 April 1978, sec. A, p. 1. Reprinted with permission.

67. Ibid.

68. Ibid.

69. Ibid.

70. Suzanne Foucault, special projects director, League of California Cities, Berkeley, Calif., interview held 11 January 1979.

71. Ibid.

72. Director of Budget and Management Services, *Public Service Impact Statement,* p. 10.

73. City Manager, *Recommended Budget for Fiscal Year 1978–79* (Oakland, Calif.: Office of City Manager, May 1978), pp. G-1, G-2, and G-3. This was the city's regular budget for fiscal year 1978–1979, which was never utilized because of the passage of Proposition 13.

74. Thirteen hundred and thirty city positions were proposed for reductions. Of this amount, about 280 were vacant. Notices were only mailed out to employees—not vacant positions. Notices were sent to about 1,050 city employees.

75. Of the 1,330 positions to be reduced, 178 (13 percent) were manage-

ment, 318 (24 percent) were sworn police and fire personnel, and 834 (63 percent) were classified as "other" employees. The actual composition of the city's work force was obtained from data-processing manager, *Meet and Confer Monthly Salary Report,* Computer Report No. MC84LBYP, Data-processing department, Oakland, Calif., 31 March 1978. These data reflect the composition of the city's work force during the preparation of the adopted Jarvis-Gann Emergency Budget.

76. Ernie Cox, "City Tightens Purse Strings," *Oakland Tribune,* 16 May 1978, sec. D, p. 27.

77. Sue Soennichsen, "Proposition 13 Shadow on Lease," *The Mont-clarion,* 10 May 1978, p. 5. Reprinted with permission.

78. Cox, "City Tightens Purse Strings."

79. Suzanne Foucault, interview.

5 Actual Impact

Introduction

On 6 June 1978, Proposition 13 overwhelmingly passed by nearly a two-to-one margin on a statewide basis. Oakland, however, was one of the few cities in California that voted against the initiative. The statewide vote was 4.3 million in favor, 2.3 million against. The Oakland vote, on the other hand, was 42,060 in favor and 46,118 against.[1] The results of this voting pattern, by district, clearly reflected the socioeconomic composition of Oakland's population. The city's more affluent hill area, with 81-percent voter turnout, reflected the statewide vote. This area endorsed Proposition 13 by nearly a two-to-one margin. The city's so-called flatlands, with only 60-percent voter turnout, defeated the measure by a two-to-one margin.[2]

The Oakland vote was typical of what political observers had noted of the election on a statewide basis. As with other large cities, Oakland's poor and minority citizens, many of whom are renters and reside in the flatlands, consistently voted against the initiative. The city's more affluent hill-area residents, many of whom are homeowners, enthusiastically voted for the initiative. Soon after the election, many citizens believed that the city council would reduce a greater level of public services in the hill area because of that area's pro-Proposition 13 vote.[3] This prediction did not hold true.

Prior to the election, city officials predicted that Oakland would lose $32.9 million in revenues and be forced to eliminate 1,330 positions from its work force. Termination notices had already been mailed to these employees. Morale among city workers was at an all-time low. The city's Jarvis-Gann Emergency Budget had already been adopted and was scheduled to be implemented on 1 July 1978—the effective date of the initiative. Local newspapers, immediately after the election, reported "City Hall appears to be in a [state] of shock," "there was a feeling of suspended animation" among city employees, and "rumors abounded" concerning the fate of hundreds of city workers.[4] One department manager was quoted as saying "he [was] appalled that no one [was] trying to stop . . . cutbacks before checking out alternative revenue sources."[5] This feeling did not prevail for very long.

Oakland's anti-Proposition 13 vote was immediately seized upon by the city's elected officials as a mandate to soften the anticipated impact of the initiative on city finances and public services. The city council held five special emergency sessions during the last two weeks of June. The pace during this period was frantic. There was little time for the council to act because of the mandated 1 July 1978 deadline for the imposition of new taxes. This short time-frame was further aggravated by the fact that a majority of the council had taken an out-of-state trip for one week during this crucial period. A quorum could not be obtained during this time so a city-council meeting had to be canceled.[6]

What the council did during this two-week period was hard to fathom. Against substantial citizen turnout and quite vocal opposition, the city's elected officials mandated increases in the city's revenues by several million dollars. This was accomplished through increases in the city's transient-occupancy tax, business license tax, and real estate transfer tax. The city council also adopted a new admissions tax, a 5-percent levy on all admissions to entertainment establishments. This tax was repealed a few months later. During the last week of June, the state legislature adopted Senate Bill 154 which distributed over $4 billion in state-surplus revenues to local governments in an effort to counteract the effect of the Jarvis-Gann Initiative. Oakland's share of these revenues amounted to over $9 million. These additional funds, together with other revenue adjustments, substantially reduced the impact of Proposition 13 on the city of Oakland. These actions expanded the city coffers by nearly $19 million, reducing the expected Proposition 13 budget deficit by more than one-half.

During these special-council hearings, many citizens thought the city's controversial employee license fee, previously approved by the city council and contested in the courts, would be implemented on 1 July 1978. This revenue source had recently been declared legal by the California Supreme Court.[7] This fee, which amounted to a 1-percent levy on all income earned in Oakland over $6,500, would have generated an additional $12 million in city revenues.[8] Because of great opposition from the business community, the implementation of this tax was postponed until 1 January 1979. A few months later, when the heat of Proposition 13 had subsided, the city's elected officials, again because of vehement opposition to this tax from the business community, voted for its repeal. The requirements of the Jarvis-Gann Initiative now make necessary a two-thirds vote of the qualified electorate before this or any other tax can legally be implemented. Since such a vote is difficult to obtain on any issue, let alone one involving taxes, it is unlikely that this potential revenue source will ever become a reality.

The city council, during July and August, held five public workshops to further review departmental budgets. These meetings were designed to explore additional areas of the city's budget for economies and possible future budget reductions. City officials, during this period, methodically reviewed every departmental budget in the city. This only served to educate the city's elected officials, since no official action was taken by the council to further decrease any departmental budget. This was ironic since the press had labeled these hearings as a prelude to "a sweeping reorganization of city government"[9] which would "slash millions from the next fiscal year's budget."[10] The city council's actions during these hearings did not live up to these expectations. No additional economies were achieved and no reorganization resulted from this nearly two-month effort of reviewing the city's operations.

A couple of months later, in mid-October, the city council, with little fanfare and no public discussion, routinely adopted the city's revised Proposition 13 budget. This budget was nearly 90 percent of the city's projected normal budget for fiscal year 1978–1979. When all the dust had settled, the city's final Proposition 13 budget reduction amounted to $14.3 million, which eliminated 227 positions, all but 70 of which were vacant by the start of the new fiscal year. The final budget cut was slightly over 40 percent of the anticipated reduction. Staffing was reduced by only 17 percent of what had been originally predicted. These final figures lend credence to the allegations of scare tactics aimed at city officials during the city's campaign against the Jarvis-Gann Initiative. It is difficult to place blame, however, since the original budget reduction was based on the incorrect assumption of no replacement revenues.

Although the preoccupation with Proposition 13 has greatly subsided at city hall, it continues to have a direct impact on city finances and public services. The city council maintained the citywide hiring freeze throughout fiscal year 1978–1979. City officials also increased various user fees and charges in order to make public services more self-sustaining. Even with these efforts, the city faced a budget deficit for fiscal year 1979–1980. The city, in an effort to help offset this deficit, is dependent upon the continued receipt of state-surplus revenues. Even with the continuation of state aid, the council again had to undergo the arduous process of reducing programs to balance the city's budget.

This chapter examines the above events in detail. The topics discussed include the distribution of state-surplus revenues, the adoption of replacement revenues by the city council, the additional Proposition 13 budget hearings held to make further economies, the adoption of the final version of Oakland's Proposition 13 budget, and the actual financial and operational impact of this budget on prevailing public services. The continuing impact of Proposition 13 is also discussed.

State-Surplus Revenues

On 8 June 1978—two days after Proposition 13 had been approved—the governor addressed a special joint session of the state legislature. This session was held to assess the effects of this measure on local governments. Prior to the election, the governor had been a strong opponent of the initiative. Now that the people had spoken, however, the tone of the governor's rhetoric changed. The governor's speech, while not containing many specifics, did encourage cooperation among the legislators in implementing Proposition 13. The key points by the governor in this address were as follows.[11]

There will be no new taxes. "Voters have told us they want a tax cut; they don't want a shell game." The state must share the burden of Proposition 13. The governor indicated that he would propose budget cuts of at least $3 billion in the existing state budget and suggested that this money be combined with state-surplus revenues to provide resources to assist local governments.

The governor said he would work with the legislature to distribute the 1-percent property-tax revenues which would be collected under Proposition 13. He stated that the entire amount of state-surplus revenues would be committed to meet the needs of "our public schools and local governments." He recommended for the first year only "$4 billion in direct aid [to local governments] and $1 billion [to] be set aside in an emergency loan fund."

The governor stated that after 1 July 1978, he would make additional proposals concerning the long-term implications of Proposition 13. He also stated that the federal government will enjoy a $2 billion windfall under the Jarvis-Gann Initiative and suggested that federal policies be reexamined to direct these revenues back to California. Finally, the governor reminded the business community that it will reap a substantial savings, about $3 billion annually, and that business has a moral obligation to invest this money in California to create more jobs and to improve the economy.

The spirit in Sacramento was one of cooperation. There was little time to act. The legislature immediately went to work on the state's response to Proposition 13. Senate Bill 154, adopted on 24 June 1978, was the legislative vehicle used for this purpose. This bill allocated state-surplus revenues and post-Proposition 13 property taxes to California's local governments. Senate Bill 2212, passed by the legislature one week later, was a "trailer" amendment designed to slightly modify and refine some of the provisions of Senate Bill 154. These two pieces of legislation formed the state's response to ease the impact of the Jarvis-Gann Initiative on local governments. The leadership for these bills was provided by the state legislature. Neither the governor's staff nor the office of planning and research initiated anything of substance in these Proposition 13 legislative efforts.[12] The governor and his staff had not undertaken any contingency planning before the election to identify possible options to mitigate the full effect of the Jarvis-Gann Initiative.[13] The governor's staff did, however, fully cooperate with the legislature to adopt and implement this legislation in a timely manner.

Senate Bill 154 contained several provisions to provide fiscal relief to local governments. The bill gave direct financial aid to counties, cities, school districts, and special districts. Additionally, it established a local agency emergency loan fund and a local agency indebtedness fund. It also set the property-tax rate at $4 per $100 of assessed valuation, the maximum rate permissible under Proposition 13. To further aid counties, the state assumed responsibility for certain health and welfare functions previously financed by counties. The legislative counsel's digest, outlining the provisions of Senate Bill 154, is set forth in figure 5-1.[14] The portions of this legislation pertaining to municipalities are examined in greater detail below.

Property-Tax Revenues. The 1-percent post-Jarvis-Gann Initiative property-tax revenues were distributed to all taxing jurisdictions. The allocation for cities was based upon their average share of countywide property-tax revenues during the three fiscal years prior to the passage of Proposition 13 (fiscal years 1975-1976, 1976-1977, and 1977-1978).[15]

Allocation of Surplus Revenues. Two hundred and fifty million dollars in state-surplus revenues were distributed to cities. Individual cities received a portion of these funds based upon their share of the statewide property-tax loss. From this amount, the state subtracted one-third of each city's unallocated General Fund reserves in excess of 5 percent of total revenues for fiscal year 1977-1978.[16]

Conditions of Receiving Surplus. Two conditions were imposed upon cities in accepting state-surplus revenues. First, the funds had to be used to maintain existing levels of police and fire services, except where efficiencies could be achieved without lowering these service levels. This provision, for all practical purposes, mandated police and fire budgets at their fiscal year 1977-1978 funding levels. Second, cities were prohibited from granting salary increases to their employees greater than the increases allowed for state workers. The governor, in vetoing the pay raise for state employees, froze the salaries of municipal employees during fiscal year 1978-1979. Promotions, fringe-benefit increases, merit increases, longevity increments, and educational increments were excluded from this requirement.[17]

Local Agency Emergency Loan Fund. The sum of $870 million was set aside in this fund. The purpose of this fund, administered by the Pooled Money Investment Board, was to establish a "lender of last resort" where local governments' tax-anticipation notes, if not accepted at normal interest

Revises the California Education Code, California Government Code, Health and Safety Code, Revenue and Taxation Code, and the Welfare and Institutions Code

Provision 1

This bill has as its purpose the partial relief of local government from the temporary difficulties brought about by the approval of Proposition 13 at the June 6, 1978, election.

Provision 2

This bill would appropriate funds from the General Fund to Section A of the State School Fund, in lieu of statutorily prescribed appropriations, for the 1978–79 fiscal year and would prescribe a method of computing the state support for school districts and county superintendents of schools.

Provision 3

This bill would appropriate funds for various categorical aid programs operated by school districts and county superintendents of schools.

Provision 4

The bill would appropriate funds from the General Fund to Section B of the State School Fund and would provide for the apportionment of such funds to community college districts in the 1978–79 fiscal year.

Provision 5

It would provide for the distribution by the State Controller, in accordance with a specified procedure, of $250,000,000 to cities, and $436,000,000 to counties and cities and counties, for the 1978–79 fiscal year. Such amounts would be required to be given first for police and fire programs.

Provision 6

It would provide for the distribution, in accordance with a specified procedure, of $125,000,000 to special districts for the 1978–79 fiscal year.

Provision 7

It would limit the use of state funds for cost-of-living salary increases in the 1978–79 fiscal year and would require each city, county, and city and county, the Department of Finance, and the Legislative Analyst to report with respect to expenditures and revenues of such local agencies.

Provision 8

It would appropriate $870,000,000 to the Local Agency Emergency Loan Fund, which would be created in the State Treasury, to be available for short-term loans to be made by the Pooled Money Investment Board to local agencies, in accordance with a specified procedure.

Figure 5–1. Senate Bill No. 154, Post-Proposition 13 Legislation

Provision 9

It would appropriate $30,000,000 to the Local Agency Indebtedness Fund, which would be created in the State Treasury, to be available for loans to be made by the Pooled Money Investment Board to local agencies for the purpose of making payments due on certain nonvoter approved bonds during the 1978–79 fiscal year.

Provision 10

This bill would (a) reduce moneys made available under this bill to counties determined by the State Director of Health Services to have made a disproportionate reduction in net county costs for health services, as prescribed, which the director determines will be detrimental to the health needs of the public or indigents; (b) waive the requirement of county matching funds otherwise required in order to obtain funding of county alcoholism programs during the 1978–79 fiscal year; (c) waive the requirement for county financial participation in funding county programs under the Short-Doyle Act during the 1978–79 fiscal year.

Provision 11

The bill would provide for the imposition of a property tax by counties at the rate of $4 per $100 of assessed valuation and for the distribution of the revenues derived from such tax to each such county and to the local agencies, school districts, and community college districts within such county, and to the county superintendent of schools.

Provision 12

The bill would require the state to pay the following for the 1978–79 fiscal year only: (a) all county costs for Medi-Cal and the State Supplementary Program; (b) all county costs for the Aid to Families with Dependent Children Program, except the state would pay 95 percent of the nonfederal share of grant costs for providing children with foster care, subject to a specified condition; (c) each county's share of the administrative costs for the federal Food Stamp Program.

Provision 13

The bill would limit the annual cost-of-living increases for the State Supplementary Program and the Aid to Families with Dependent Children Program grant amounts for the 1978–79 fiscal year to any cost-of-living increase granted state employees by the Budget Act of 1978, but not to exceed that otherwise provided by existing law.

Provision 14

The bill would also appropriate specified amounts from the General Fund to the State Department of Social Services and the State Department of Health Services for each county's share of the welfare programs specified in the bill.

Provision 15

The bill would state that there are no state-mandated local costs that require reinbursement for a specified reason.

Provision 16

The bill would take effect immediately as an urgency statute.

Figure 5-1 continued

rates at banks, could be purchased by the state. The intent was to provide loans at prevailing interest rates to those cities that experienced cash-flow problems at a time when private lenders were unwilling to purchase tax-anticipation notes.[18]

Local Agency Indebtedness Fund. Thirty million dollars was allocated to this fund. The purpose of this fund, also administered by the Pooled Money Investment Board, was to ensure that local governments could make payments on nonvoter-approved bond indebtedness. The state determined that it was in the public interest to protect the credit of local governments by insuring local governments against bond default. Loans would be made for a maximum period of three years at prevailing interest rates.[19]

As previously indicated, the supreme court declared the salary freeze imposed by Senate Bill 154 unconstitutional. Therefore, local governments were free to honor contractual obligations with employee unions governing annual salary increases. Prior to this court ruling, local governments that authorized pay raises for their employees were precluded from receiving their share of state-surplus revenues. Statewide, two counties, seventy-five cities, and twenty-nine special districts had granted pay increases to their workers. These local governments subsequently received their expected share of these funds, amounting to about $27 million.[20]

The $4.2 billion allocated to local governments under Senate Bill 154 restored 60 percent of the property-tax loss suffered under Proposition 13. The disbursement of these funds among counties, cities, school districts, and special districts is set forth in table 5-1.[21] The net property-tax loss to local governments, originally estimated to be $7 billion, was actually $2.8 billion after the allocation of state-surplus revenues. The additional revenues enabled local governments to greatly reduce the potential impact of the Jarvis-Gann Initiative. These funds also provided local governments with an orderly transition to a post-Proposition 13 revenue base.

The distribution of state-surplus revenues served to postpone the real impact of Proposition 13 for one year. The governor said these funds would be provided for one year only. He has, however, included $4.4 billion in the state's fiscal year 1979–1980 budget to continue this program. This funding level incorporates a 7-percent increase over and above the amount allocated during fiscal year 1978–1979.[22] The final legislation adopted to divvy up these funds to local governments is discussed in chapter 6.

Senate Bill 154 was drafted and adopted within a two-week period—6 June 1978 to 24 June 1978. Six days later, on 30 June 1978, the state legislature passed clean-up legislation to slightly modify and refine the provisions and requirements of Senate Bill 154 relating to the allocation of state-surplus revenues, school financing, and the disbursement of property-tax revenues. This legislation, Senate Bill 2212, made various definitional and tech-

Table 5-1
Distribution of California State-Surplus Revenues by Type of Government,
Fiscal Year 1978–1979

Government	Revenue Reduction [a]	State Surplus [a]	Net Loss [a]
Counties [b]	$2.2	$1.5	$ .7
Cities [c]	.8	.3	.5
School districts	3.6	2.3	1.3
Special districts	.4	.1	.3
Totals	$7.0	$4.2	$2.8

[a] Billions of dollars.
[b] Includes city and county of San Francisco.
[c] Excludes city and county of San Francisco.

nical changes and revisions in the original bailout legislation.[23] The original legislation was not substantially altered, only refined.

The requirements of Senate Bill 154 have far-reaching implications for local governments. These ramifications include state interference in the operations of local governments, the state assumption of various health and welfare programs, and the use of state aid to finance traditional local government services. This infringement on home rule and local discretion removed decision making for many local government functions from city hall to Sacramento. These implications are discussed in chapter 6.

Council Approves Replacement Revenues

City officials spent several months planning for the possible implementation of Proposition 13. Staff had spent many hundreds of hours preparing alternative financial plans to enable the city to cope successfully with this mandate. The original criterion was simple. The city council would provide no replacement revenues if Proposition 13 was adopted. After all, the people would have expressed their desires on governmental taxation at the polls. The Oakland vote, however, provided the city's elected officials with a rationale for softening the impact of this measure on the city. No one could have predicted at the time that the council, in less than a two-week period, would mandate sufficient revenues to make the previously adopted Jarvis-Gann Emergency Budget a meaningless financial plan. The process the council underwent in approving these replacement revenues is examined below.

The first post-Proposition 13 meeting was held by city officials on 13 June 1978. At this meeting the city manager summarized the impact of the initiative on Oakland's revenues and suggested possible alternative revenues the city council might wish to consider to offset this revenue loss. These revenues included increases in the city's transient-occupancy tax, real estate transfer tax, and business license tax, and a possible Port of Oakland reimbursement for services rendered by the city.[24] The Port of Oakland is a quasi-autonomous agency operated by a Board of Port Commissioners appointed by the city council upon nomination from the mayor. The port had been receiving numerous city services free of charge for a number of years.

The mayor then called upon the city's Sacramento representative, previously requested to attend this meeting, to discuss the possible allocation of property taxes under Proposition 13 and the availability of state-surplus revenues. She stated "that the situation in Sacramento changes daily, and that it appears probable that the state will not allocate property tax revenue to cities on a proportional basis."[25] She reported that the state's surplus revenues were estimated to be $5.8 billion, but that the figure was also changing daily. She stated further that "it appears some of the surplus-state money will be allocated to government agencies; however, the allocation formula [is] not known at this time."[26] The city manager then announced that a resolution had been prepared recommending a method of allocating property taxes and distributing the state-surplus revenues. This document, approved unanimously by the city council, encouraged the state legislature to allocate property taxes based on the amount of such revenues lost by a public agency and to distribute state-surplus revenues to cities in order to replace needed and essential services.[27] This resolution also requested the mayor to inform state legislators of the city's position on these matters. The full contents of this resolution are set forth in figure 5–2.

During this meeting, eleven individuals asked to speak regarding the city's Jarvis-Gann Emergency Budget. They included union representatives, business leaders, city employees, and property owners. The demands presented were as varied as the interests represented. Union representatives and city employees opposed the layoff of civil-service employees and urged the council to find replacement revenues. They reminded city officials that Oakland citizens voted against Proposition 13 and did not want public services reduced. Representatives of the business community and property owners discouraged any new taxes, saying that the people of the state had voiced their opposition to increasing governmental taxation and spending. A few citizens mentioned that service reductions would hit the city's poor and minority population the hardest. In short, the public discussion was vociferous and reflected Oakland's split vote on this measure.

The mayor responded by stating that it was impossible to determine precisely how many city employees would have to be terminated because of

---

Oakland City Council Resolution No. 57298 C.M.S.[a]

Resolution Recommending Method of Allocating Real Property Taxes and Distribution of State Surplus Funds.

Whereas, as a result of the passage of Proposition 13 at the June 6, 1978, election, the City of Oakland is faced with a financial crisis if needed basic services, including police and fire protection, to its citizens are to continue at a responsible level; and

Whereas, the state legislature is now considering how to allocate property taxes within each county; and

Whereas, the state legislature is also considering the basis to distribute surplus funds retained by the state to alleviate the financial crisis of local public agencies; and

Whereas, it is the sense of the City Council that any reasonable method of allocating such taxes and distributing such surplus must take into consideration the prior revenues received from property taxes in the prior fiscal year, and proportionate loss in such taxes of each public agency in the 1978–79 fiscal year; now therefore, be it

Resolved: That the City Council strongly supports state legislation that allocates property taxes on the basis of prior revenues received from such taxes and the proportionate loss in 1977–78 fiscal year of such revenues; and, be it

Further Resolved: That the City Council strongly recommends that the surplus funds retained by the state be distributed to the cities to replace needed and essential public services; and, be it

Further Resolved: That the Mayor is requested to write to the local legislators of the city to inform them of the City of Oakland's position.

---

[a]Adopted by the city council on 13 June 1978.

Figure 5–2. Resolution Recommending Allocation of Real Property Taxes and State-Surplus Revenues

the uncertain situation in the state capital. The city manager stated that by raising certain taxes and if the city received a portion of the state's surplus revenues, the number of employees laid off could be reduced to 641.[28] One council member, distraught by the apparent windfall of profits under Proposition 13 to the business community, "tried to launch a movement to make the business community pay the same taxes as they did before [the measure] passed."[29] This official made the motion that the city council suggest that the state legislature place the matter before the voters in the upcoming November general election. The mayor ruled the motion out of order after it failed to spark any support from other council members. Another city official suggested that the matter be placed "on the back burner."[30] This issue was subsequently dropped for lack of interest among city officials.

Upon completion of the staff presentation and public discussion, the mayor closed the meeting by stating that it appeared the situation in Sacramento was in a state of flux and, because of this, the city council should wait a few days before taking any action. By delaying action, they might be able to determine what the state legislature would do regarding the allocation of property-tax revenues and the distribution of state-surplus revenues.[31] City officials did not know at this time that it would not be until the last week in June that the state legislature would take action on these vital issues. In the interim, the council proceeded to adopt its own replacement revenues.

The next special meeting on Proposition 13 was held by city officials only two days later on 15 June 1978. The city manager opened the meeting by providing the city council with a list of policy decisions for their immediate consideration. These contained possible additional revenue sources and alternatives for allocating the additional funds back to city departments. The same revenues discussed at the previous meeting—increases in the city's transient-occupancy tax, real estate transfer tax, and business license tax— were again introduced for the council's consideration.[32] The city manager also discussed recent changes in the city's financial condition.

He stated that the city's real estate transfer tax, previously thought to be invalidated by Proposition 13, would be continued, even though there was some question as to its legality. This decision was made because this tax had been in effect prior to the effective date of the initiative.[33] This revenue source amounted to $4.2 million. This good news was nullified by the fact that staff felt that Congress would not continue the Public Works Employment Act (antirecessionary payments), from which the city was expected to receive about $4.2 million during fiscal year 1978–1979.[34] This assumption proved to be true because Congress, a few months later, failed to extend this fiscal assistance program. The city manager also informed council members that the Oakland-Piedmont Municipal Court had recently approved increases in city bails and fines for moving-vehicle violations and parking-code violations. These increases, which were scheduled to go into effect on 1 July 1978, would bring an additional $1.2 million into the city's treasury.[35] After hearing this report, the city council began the difficult task of discussing alternative replacement revenues.

The city manager suggested that the council consider increasing the city's transient-occupancy tax from 6 to 8 percent and that it determine whether the additional funds, amounting to $0.3 million, should be used to finance the chamber of commerce's convention and visitors bureau.[36] A representative of the chamber of commerce addressed the council, stressing the importance of the convention and visitors bureau and its efforts to attract tourists to Oakland. No one spoke in opposition to this tax increase. With little discussion, the council unanimously agreed to increase this tax and to use the additional funds to finance the program.[37] The Convention Center Fund, normally used to subsidize the chamber, had been eliminated in the city's previously approved Jarvis-Gann Emergency Budget. By increasing this revenue source, city funding for the program had been restored in an amount equivalent to what had been eliminated a few months earlier.

Possible increases in the city's business license tax were then considered. This tax is based on the annual gross receipts of a business. Various categories of businesses are taxed at different rates, ranging from $0.60 to $13.95 per $1,000 of gross receipts.[38] The city manager stated that staff recommendations for increasing various rates of this tax would amount to an additional $1.7 million in revenues. One council member made the motion that this revenue source should be increased by $5 million, "particularly from residential and commercial rental-property owners, who are benefiting most from the passage of Proposition 13."[39] Another council member thought that such action was premature and that the city should wait until the status of the state's surplus revenues had been determined before increasing this tax. This official stated that Oakland had been losing businesses and that such a tax increase would hurt the city's efforts to retain businesses and attract new ones.[40] A compromise motion was then introduced. It recommended approving the increase in this tax recommended by the city manager and directed him to provide the city council with possible additional increases from this source at its next meeting. These increases were to "target businesses that gained most from Proposition 13."[41] Six individuals spoke to the council opposing the tax, but to no avail. After the public discussion, the council voted unanimously to approve the recommendation.[42]

In the midst of increasing city revenues, one council member suggested that the city council postpone the implementation of the city's controversial employee license fee, which had previously been approved and scheduled to go into effect on 1 July 1978.[43] The city attorney advised that because of the restrictions imposed by Proposition 13 relative to new taxes, the council should postpone this tax for six months—until 1 January 1979.[44] The mayor responded that "if it were not for the legal implications [of Proposition 13] he would support the indefinite postponement of this tax, but that he felt it would be irresponsible to preclude the possibility of ever enacting [this tax] due to the city's financial situation."[45]

A motion was made favoring the mayor's position. The council's stand on this tax was a pleasant surprise to the several representatives of the business community who were present at this meeting. Only one citizen addressed the council in opposition to this action. He stated that the revenue generated from this tax should be used to maintain public services reduced by Proposition 13. After hearing this appeal, the council unanimously voted to implement the mayor's proposal.[46] Several months later, on 12 December 1978, the council again considered the enactment of the employee license fee.[47] Citizen turnout at this meeting was unusually great. Of the thirty-seven individuals who addressed the council, thirty-four spoke against this tax. Among them was Oakland's former mayor, John Reading, who had originally introduced this new form of taxation. Only three citizens spoke in favor of the tax, stressing the much-needed revenue it would generate for the city. A motion was then introduced to repeal this tax. Against the wishes of the mayor, who favored a further postponement of the tax, city officials, by a five-to-four vote, narrowly approved the repeal of this highly publicized and much-debated revenue source.[48]

After the city council had approved additional revenues and postponed the implementation of the employee license fee, the city manager again presented options for restoring public services. The first gave priority to restoring police and fire services. The second restored fewer funds in the police and fire departments and allocated them to several cultural and recreational programs.[49] One council member spoke in favor of the second alternative, stating that "it gives more of our city back."[50] Other council members agreed, but pointed out the need for police and fire services to the community.[51] A motion was made to restore as many city programs as possible by approving the second budget-restoration alternative. The city council approved this recommendation unanimously.[52] A subsequent motion was made to restore additional funds, should they become available, to police and fire services. This motion, with little discussion, was also approved unanimously.[53]

Prior to the close of the meeting, one council member congratulated the city council for "dealing calmly and rationally with a potentially explosive situation."[54] The mayor praised the council, noting "the contrast between the city's actions and the hysterical tone of some nearby . . . governments he would not mention by name."[55]

The next special meeting was not held until eight days later. The reason for this hiatus during such a critical period just prior to the implementation of Proposition 13 proved embarrassing. The mayor and four council members attended a week-long meeting of elected officials in Atlanta, Georgia. In addition to the conspicuous absence of city officials during this period, the press had noted that the cost of this trip, which was about $3,000, was paid for by the taxpayers.[56] Just prior to the trip, the press referred to the council as "undaunted by the voters' 'reduce spending' message [Proposition 13]."[57] The lost time, however, was quickly recaptured upon their return. Several million dollars in additional revenues were authorized during the last week in June.

The third public hearing dealing with the impact of Proposition 13 was held by city officials on 23 June 1978. Prior to it, the city manager had distributed a staff report to council members outlining possible new revenue sources. This report analyzed three existing revenue sources—increases in the city's business license tax, utility consumption tax, and real estate transfer tax—and a new revenue source: a city admissions tax.[58] These revenues, in total, would raise nearly $10 million in additional local funds. This report also analyzed increases in selected categories of the business license tax applicable to owners of residential-rental property. This information had been requested by the city council at its previous meeting. Armed with these financial options, council members were ready to consider possible additional taxes to further counteract the revenue loss suffered by Proposition 13. It should be noted that these additional revenues were not staff recommendations but merely a "shopping list" of potential revenues submitted for the council's consideration.

A report on the status of state legislation to help local governments was the first order of business. The mayor requested the city's Sacramento representative to advise the city council of the latest information on the allocation of property taxes and the distribution of state-surplus revenues. She indicated that the state legislature had recently adopted Senate Bill 154. This legislation authorized cities to receive a prorated share of the 1-percent property-tax revenue and allocated approximately $250 million in state-surplus funds to cities on a one-time basis. Oakland's share of these funds was estimated to be about $7.5 million.[59] The final figure had not yet been determined because the distribution of these revenues was still being calculated by the state controller. She also indicated that this legislation required cities to maintain pre-Proposition 13 service levels in their police and fire departments.[60] Council members were elated about this good news since these additional funds would help the city mitigate the impact of Proposition 13 on public services. City officials would not find out until several months later, when the final distribution of these funds had been determined, that Oakland would actually receive $9.3 million.

After this report, the city manager informed the city council that he had worked out an agreement with the Port of Oakland whereby the port agreed to reimburse the city approximately $1 million annually for the cost of city services rendered to the port.[61] The port's executive director then addressed the council, outlining the services that the port had agreed to pay for, stating "the Port of Oakland will cooperate with the city during [its] financial crisis."[62] The services for which the city would receive compensation included those provided to the port by the police department, fire department, personnel department, office of general services, office of public works, and office of finance. These services included airport security, operation of a fireboat, personnel services, street lighting, street sweeping, engineering, and financial services.[63] Heretofore, the port had been receiving these services free of charge, or at a fraction of their actual cost. This action, in addition to giving the city an additional $1 million annually in revenues, served to make those city services rendered to the port cost-covering. The city council, with little discussion, unanimously agreed to approve a motion to accept the port's proposal to pay for these services.[64]

The city council then directed its attention toward creating additional revenues. The city manager recommended that the council consider possible increases in the city's business license tax. Council members had approved selected increases in this tax at their previous meeting. They were now considering additional increases for those property owners who "benefited tremendously from the windfalls created by Proposition 13."[65] The city manager recommended several "equity and cost recovery adjustments"[66] in an effort to update various categories of this tax and to make the administration of this tax cost-covering relative to other categories. The council, with almost no discussion, approved this recommendation unanimously.[67] One council member then made the motion that this tax be increased for owners of residential-rental properties who gained most from the passage of Proposition 13. The recommended increase in this category of the tax was over 1,500 percent.[68] After additional discussion concerning the benefits received by such individuals under the Jarvis-Gann Initiative, the council voted unanimously to approve this increase.[69] The city manager then indicated that if all categories of the business license tax were doubled, excluding residential-rental properties, an additional $2 million in revenues could be raised. The motion was introduced and, with little discussion, approved unanimously.[70] One council member suggested that the tax rate applicable to owners of commercial properties be increased by the same amount approved for owners of residential-rental properties—1,550 percent. Another city official pointed out that Oakland already had many vacant commercial properties in its downtown area and that such a tax increase would be counterproductive to the city's efforts to revitalize its center-city area. After additional discussion, the motion was defeated by a two-to-one margin.[71]

During the council's deliberations on increasing the city's business license tax, twenty-three citizens addressed the council, setting forth their concerns about this revenue source. As at previous city hearings on Proposition 13, the speakers represented divergent interests. Once again, the city council heard arguments on both sides of the issue. A clear majority of those present were members of the business community and property owners. These speakers protested that "new taxes would discourage business growth in Oakland at a time when the city is trying to revitalize the business community and attract new industries and businesses into the city."[72] Representatives of employee unions and certain community groups argued that the additional revenues were needed to retain public services and minimize employee terminations. Both sides argued with great vehemence, each representing different, yet equally defensible, points of view. After this tumultuous public discussion it was obvious that the pleas of the business community and property owners fell on deaf ears.

Prior to the close of this meeting, one council member suggested that the city council consider increasing the city's real estate transfer tax. Another council member recommended that city officials implement an admissions tax on all entertainment events.[73] These possible taxes, if approved, would generate about $5 million annually in additional city revenues. The mayor stated that consideration of these revenues should be postponed and that another meeting should be held to consider these possible taxes. Other members agreed with the mayor's recommendation.[74] These agenda items were, therefore, delayed until the council's next Proposition 13 session.

On 27 June 1978, the city council held its fourth special meeting on the implementation of Proposition 13. It was to consider possible increases in the real estate transfer tax and the enactment of a new admissions tax, a discussion which had been tabled from the previous meeting. The city manager began by presenting a report summarizing the revenues previously approved by the council and outlining the possible new revenues that could be generated by increasing the taxes discussed above.[75] If the real estate transfer tax levied against the sales price of all real property sold within the city was increased from 0.5 to 0.75 percent, an additional $3 million in revenues would accrue to the city annually. The new admissions tax, a 5-percent surcharge on admission prices paid at entertainment establishments, would bring in about $1.5 million annually in additional city revenues. The city manager also suggested additional budget restorations for virtually every department in the city, giving priority to police and fire services.[76] After this report, the mayor opened the hearing for public discussion.

Citizen attendance at this meeting was greater than at any of the previous Proposition 13 sessions. Forty-five individuals addressed the city council on the proposed tax increases.[77] The majority of these persons were affiliated with the local Board of Realtors and the Apartment House Association. Members of the Board of Realtors protested against increasing the real estate transfer tax, stating that the tax would have an adverse impact on Oakland's real estate industry. They also emphasized to city officials that California voters had overwhelmingly approved Proposition 13 and were against new taxes. The president of the Apartment House Association stated, "You can't balance your budget by killing business."[78] This individual made the most dramatic appeal against new taxes, angrily stating, "I'm going to ask the news media to record your votes by name so we'll know who to vote against in the next election."[79] Various speakers addressed the council for nearly two hours protesting against increasing this tax. The opposition was highly organized, yet their appeals had little impact on council members.

A handful of citizens spoke against the implementation of the new admissions tax. Several small theater owners appeared and said that "lower-income people might be priced out of entertainment by this new tax."[80] Representatives of the Golden State Warriors, a franchised basketball team, and the Oakland Raiders, the city's famous football team, testified "they would have to pay the tax themselves if it began immediately because most season tickets had already been printed and sold."[81] The arguments posed by these individuals did influence the city council. The final vote on this tax is examined below.

A few speakers were in favor of these tax increases. They reminded the city council that Oakland's citizens had voted against Proposition 13 and did not want any reductions in city services. They also said that service reductions and employee layoffs would hit the city's poor and minority citizens the hardest. One speaker maintained that the real estate industry stood to gain most from the passage of Proposition 13 and could afford the increase in real estate taxes. After the public discussion on these taxes, council members commenced their deliberations.

The mayor began by stating that "it is a vast responsibility to represent all of the people and that any increases in taxes imposed by council can be set aside later if it becomes advisable to do so."[82] He reminded those attending the meeting that "council members are also business people who [would also] be affected by the new taxes."[83] The mayor concluded his remarks by stating that Oakland voters were against Proposition 13 and did not want any reductions in public services.

After the mayor finished his brief talk, one council member, saying that "the real estate market will be able to pay for it,"[84] made a motion to double the real estate transfer tax from 0.5 to 1 percent. Another member of the council immediately introduced an amendment to this motion, limiting the increase to only 50 percent. This official stated that such a drastic tax increase was unfair to the real estate industry. After additional discussion, the city council adopted this amended motion with only one dissenting vote.[85]

The admissions tax was the next order of business. One council member recommended that city officials establish an admissions tax of 5 percent on all entertainment events within the city. Another council member argued that this tax would unduly burden Oakland's highly successful sports franchises since season tickets had already been printed and sold.[86] This council member won a partial victory when a motion to postpone the implementation of this tax for six months (until 1 January 1979) was approved with little discussion by a three-to-one margin.[87] A couple of months later, on 19

September 1978, city officials reconsidered the implementation of this tax.[88] The city council had received letters protesting this tax from the Oakland Coliseum, the Ringling Brothers/Barnum and Bailey Circus, the Ice Capades, the Ice Follies, and the Harlem Globetrotters.[89] This organized opposition served its purpose. The mayor stated that he had reconsidered his support of this tax and considered that it was "regressive and would hurt the working person."[90] He also stated that this tax might hinder the city's efforts to retain its highly popular sports franchises. With little discussion, the city council unanimously voted to approve a motion to repeal the admissions tax.[91]

After city officials approved these tax increases, one council member suggested that the city's business license tax be increased for commercial-rental-property owners to the same level mandated for residential-rental-property owners.[92] This additional revenue source had been discussed at previous council meetings but no official action had been taken. This council member stated that "commercial properties had received just as much tax relief from Proposition 13 as had residential properties."[93] One individual, a local attorney and property owner, spoke against this tax increase. He protested that this tax was unfair, that it would hinder the city's effort to retain businesses, and that it would be against the intent of Proposition 13.[94] After additional discussion, the mayor recommended that the matter be continued until the next special session. Consideration of this additional revenue source was deferred to what would be the council's final meeting on Proposition 13.

Just before the end of this meeting, the mayor recommended that the budget restorations proposed by the city manager be approved with the stipulation that the council could modify them at a later date. These restorations added back funds to every city department in an amount equal to what the city council had mandated in additional revenues and the amount the city expected to receive from state-surplus revenues.[95] Council members, with almost no discussion, approved the mayor's recommendation unanimously.[96] The council left the door open to make changes in the city manager's recommendations because a series of additional Proposition 13 budget sessions had been scheduled during July and August. These hearings, which did not alter the city manager's budget restorations, are discussed in the following section of this chapter.

The city council held its final meeting on 29 June 1978, two days before the effective date of Proposition 13. Compared with the previous revenue-generating sessions, this meeting proved to be somewhat anticlimatic. The city manager began the meeting by presenting a report outlining the city's normal budget, now a moot issue, the Jarvis-Gann Emergency Budget, departmental-budget restorations, and the final cut remaining in each department.[97] After the previous meeting, one council member had requested two alternative financial plans that would hold back $4 million in funds which the council could allocate back to individual departments after the scheduled budget hearings. This plan would give the council flexibility in making additions to departmental budgets based on its perceptions of the relative needs of individual departments. The city manager had prepared these financial options in advance of this meeting. The first alternative decreased all departmental budgets by a total of $4 million. The second reduced all departmental budgets, excluding the police and fire departments. The first option required the termination of an additional 350 city employees. The second plan necessitated the termination of an additional 410 employees.[98] After this report was presented, the mayor opened the meeting for public discussion on the matter.

The mayor said he was opposed to this recommendation because of the increased employee layoffs involved. A representative of Oakland's largest public-employee union addressed the council, voicing his opposition to this plan. He also objected to the additional number of city employees that would have to be terminated. He then requested the postponement of all employee layoffs. One council member asked the city manager if such an action was possible. The city manager responded by indicating that "the present budget is based on every advantage available to the city and some projected sources of revenue might not materialize."[99] He also stated, "it would cost approximately $100,000 to postpone all layoffs until the end of July and, if any money is held back, it will result in additional layoffs."[100] After additional discussion, the mayor obtained the consent of the council to direct that no action be taken on the recommendation to hold back funds for later disbursement by the council.[101]

The city council then directed its attention to an item deferred from its previous meeting: increasing the business license tax as it applied to commercial-rental property. Six individuals spoke against this tax increase. These persons, most of whom were local property owners, protested implementation of this tax increase, citing the same reasons raised at the previous meeting. After this discussion, a motion was made to increase this tax.[102] One council member stated that he would oppose the motion because "there is more market for rental-residential properties than for commercial properties [in Oakland]."[103] Other members generally agreed with this position. After additional discussion, the council member who introduced the motion stated it was obvious there was not enough support to pass the measure.[104] The motion was withdrawn. The protests had proved to be successful. This is one of the few taxes that was not increased by the council during its many meetings on Proposition 13.

There was one final item of business. The city manager informed city officials that they had inadvertently increased the portion of the business license tax applicable to hotels and motels by 1,550 percent during their meeting of 23 June 1978. This was the meeting at which the city council approved increases in this tax applicable to residential-rental properties. The mayor agreed that it was not the intent of the council to approve an increase for this category of the tax. With little discussion, council members unanimously approved a motion to amend the previous legislation, exempting hotels and motels from this tax increase.[105] This action served to reduce annual revenues from this source by about $0.2 million. This vote was the final action the council took on acquiring replacement revenues for those lost by the passage of Proposition 13. Two days later, the requirements of Proposition 13 became effective.

During the five special Proposition 13 sessions held by the city council, an additional $7.1 million was approved in replacement revenues, all designed to counteract the anticipated impact of the Jarvis-Gann Initiative. The council had mandated increases in the city's transient-occupancy tax, business license tax, and real estate transfer tax. Of this amount, $0.3 million went to subsidize the chamber of commerce's convention and visitors bureau. The remaining funds—$6.8 million—were added back to departmental budgets. Another $2.2 million was raised through the actions of other local agencies. This included traffic bail and fine increases approved by the municipal court and Port of Oakland reimbursements for city services. These funds, together with the city's allotment of state-surplus revenues, provided a total of $18.6 million in replacement revenues. The additional city revenues are listed in table 5-2.[106] In addition to these revenues, the city reduced its miscellaneous budget by some $2.4 million. These funds were budgeted under the original Jarvis-Gann Emergency Budget in the form of a contingency fund for employee layoffs.[107] Funds were previously allocated for terminal vacation and sick-leave pay based on the massive employee layoffs predicted under Proposition 13. Most of these funds

Table 5-2
Additional Oakland City Revenues, Final Jarvis-Gann Budget, Fiscal Year 1978-1979

Revenue Source	Amount (millions of $)
Increase in transient occupancy tax	0.3
Increase in business license tax	3.8
Increase in real estate transfer tax	3.0
Port of Oakland reimbursement for city services	1.0
Traffic bail and fine increases	1.2
Distribution of state-surplus revenues	9.3
Total additional revenues	18.6

were no longer needed and were subsequently added back to departmental budgets.

The total amount restored to the city's Proposition 13 budget was $21 million, which was used to restore 118 programs throughout every department in the city, resulting in a restoration of over 1,100 city positions. A tabulation of departmental restorations, programs, and positions is presented in table 5-3.[108] The final financial and operational impact of the city's revised Proposition 13 budget is discussed in subsequent sections of this chapter.

Additional Proposition 13 Budget Hearings

The mayor, during the last week of June, informed the city council that he had requested the city manager to schedule a series of post-Proposition 13 departmental-budget hearings.[109] The official purpose of these hearings was to review the impact of Proposition 13 on departmental operations.[110] The mayor said that these hearings "may result in the reallocation of available [city] funds."[111] The hearings were highly publicized by the local press. Newspaper articles appeared informing the public of the date and time of these meetings.[112] The local press stated that these meetings were designed "to consider possible modifications in the proposed new city budget, drawn up since the passage of Proposition 13,"[113] and "to give the City Council its first detailed look at the impact of Proposition 13 and to plan what some say will be a sweeping reorganization of city government."[114] Another article said the purpose of the meeting was "to slash millions from the next fiscal year's budget, a year when the city expects to be hit harder by the effects of Proposition 13 than it was this year."[115] Because of this publicity buildup, the city's department managers, who had been requested to attend these meetings to explain their departments' budgets and operations, felt that additional budget reductions would be made. The climate at city hall was one of apprehension. What actually happened at these budget hearings is examined below.

The first budget hearing was held by the city council on 6 July 1978. The city manager made some opening comments concerning the city's Proposition 13 budget. He stated that this budget was based on utilizing available one-time savings, additional replacement revenues, state-surplus revenues, and normal estimated city revenues. He also noted that failure to receive any of these funds would leave the budget out of balance.[116] The city manager then asked several department managers to explain the impact of Proposition 13 on their respective budgets and to describe their departmental operations.

City officials proceeded to review nine departmental budgets. These

Table 5–3

Oakland City Budget Restorations, Final Jarvis-Gann Budget, Fiscal Year 1978–1979

Departments	Amount (millions of $)	Percent	Programs [a]	Positions
Police	3.7	54	25	236
Fire	3.7	77	12	149
Public works	3.2	70	4	156
General services	3.9	89	9	94
Parks and recreation	2.4	71	38	197
Library	1.2	71	1	111
Museum	0.9	75	20	46
General government	2.0	69	6	114
Nondepartmental	(2.4)	(77)	3	—
Total restorations	18.6	57	118	1,103

Note: Discretionary funds, excluding tax-increment and bond funds.

[a] Includes programs reduced or eliminated.

were the office of the mayor/council, office of the city manager, office of the city clerk, office of the city attorney, personnel department, office of the city physician, city planning department, office of the city auditor, and retirement administration department. No citizens asked to address the city council concerning the impact of Proposition 13 on these city-staff departments. All these departmental budgets were approved by the council.[117]

During the course of reviewing these budgets, council members raised questions concerning some departments' operations. The city council asked the city manager to analyze the staffing of the retirement administration department in light of the number of employees who had been transferred from the city's own retirement system to the Public Employees Retirement System, which is administered by the state. They noted that staffing in this department over the years had remained constant, while the number of employees enrolled in the city's retirement system had been significantly reduced.[118] The city manager came to the defense of this department, saying, "Don't forget there were charges not long ago that this department was not being run very well. There are $100 million in retirement funds administered by this department."[119] No further action was taken on reducing personnel in this department.[120] The council also considered increasing personnel in the office of the city physician but took no action to implement this proposal.[121]

This meeting did have one positive outcome. The city council, after hearing a report from the city manager, unanimously approved a motion to continue the city's hiring freeze throughout fiscal year 1978–1979.[122] This action came after the city manager had informed city officials that a freeze on hiring could possibly save the city as much as $4 million annually. This was based on the estimate that, through attrition alone, about 200 city positions would be eliminated during the year. The council qualified its action by informing the city manager that he could fill vacancies where an exceptional need existed.[123] This term *exceptional need,* however, was never defined. The administration of this hiring policy, properly, was left to the city manager.

Council members held their next budget meeting on 13 July 1978. After the initial budget hearing, the city manager had briefed all department managers on the desired method of presentation. They were instructed to describe the impact of Proposition 13 on their respective budgets and to explain briefly their departmental operations. During this meeting, the city council reviewed three departmental budgets: the office of parks and recreation, the library department, and the museum department. About a dozen citizens addressed the council, expressing their concerns over the adverse effect of Proposition 13 on the public services provided by these departments. All departmental budgets were approved by the council.[124]

Council members, during this meeting, only questioned reductions in one department. The mayor stated that it appeared that administrative reductions in the office of parks and recreation were relatively low compared with program reductions. The department manager was requested to furnish a report to the council outlining the reasons for these reductions.[125] A report was subsequently provided. After reviewing this report, the council decided not to alter the budget reductions in this department. In addition to this scrutiny, the council indicated that if additional funds became available, priority would be given to restoring junior and senior high school recreational programs which had been sorely cut.[126] Additional funds, however, never became available and no program restorations were made.

One department manager told the council that "because of layoff procedures, sometimes the most competent personnel are laid off due to their lower seniority status."[127] One council member said he was concerned about this problem and others agreed. After some discussion, a motion was unanimously adopted to direct the city's Civil Service Commission to review the city's "last-hired, first-fired" layoff procedures in an effort to correct this problem. The city's personnel director was subsequently instructed to meet with representatives of public-employee unions on this matter since the city has contractual obligations with these unions requiring this procedure. Union representatives opposed changes, asserting that this was a meet-and-confer matter subject to negotiation. The policy was not changed.[128]

On 20 July 1978, the city council reviewed nine city budgets. These included the office of general services, office of community development, office of economic development and employment, and the city's nondepartmental budgets which include employee benefits, insurance and liability claims, debt service, miscellaneous budget, coliseum support, and community promotion. No citizens requested to speak on the impact of Proposition 13 on these budgets. The city council approved all budgets as presented.[129] The council did, however, raise several questions concerning departmental operations.

In examining the office of general services, one council member requested information on the number of city vehicles driven outside Oakland.[130] The city manager stated that he would provide this information to the city council within one week.[131] This report revealed that a total of twenty-nine vehicles were assigned to employees and that nine of these were driven outside the city. All but one of these automobiles were driven by police officers. The city manager said that the "Supreme Court ruled that the use of these vehicles was 'custom and practice for police captains' and could not be taken away."[132] He also noted that most employees assigned automobiles were on call and that mileage reimbursement would cost the city approximately the same as the vehicles.[133] After hearing this report, the council took no action to reduce the number of vehicles driven by employees.

During this meeting, the city council approved additional funding for the city's community-promotion budget. This budget is used to allocate funds to community groups which are deemed to promote Oakland. One council member requested that the Oakland Ballet Company be funded at the same level as the previous year, $3,150.[134] A motion was introduced and unanimously approved to restore funding for this organization. These funds had previously been eliminated from the city's Proposition 13 budget.

The fourth budget hearing was held by the city council on 27 July 1978. During this meeting, city officials reviewed the police and fire department budgets. After discussing these budgets, one council member reminded the police chief and fire chief that the council had taken a position to use additional funds, should they become available, to maintain the city's public-safety services. Both budgets were approved as submitted.[135] After council discussion on these budgets, which consume nearly two-thirds of the city's total budget, only two citizens asked to address city officials.

One individual, representing the Consumer Affairs Council of Alameda County, questioned excessive overtime costs in the police department.[136] The police chief immediately responded, stating that state law required a constant level of staffing for police operations. The mayor stated that this issue had been studied before and that no correctional solution had been developed.[137] The police chief subsequently submitted a report to the city council on these overtime costs. After reviewing this document, city officials took no action to reduce these costs.

A member of the board of the Oakland Municipal Employees Retirement System expressed his concern to the council about the alleged inequities in the city's pension systems for sworn and civilian personnel. He emphasized the additional costs the city had to pay in retirement benefits for sworn personnel and requested that the mayor form a commission to review this matter. The mayor said he would consider this request.[138] No action, however, was ever taken on this proposal.[139] It should be noted that the city's retirement systems are mandated by the city charter and changes require a majority vote of the city's electorate.[140]

This speaker also requested information on the city manager's salary. The mayor indicated that the top salary set for Oakland's city manager was $55,000 and that the current city manager agreed to accept the position at $53,000, the same amount paid to the city's previous city manager. The mayor also noted that the city manager, at no additional cost, had agreed to continue the duties of acting city attorney,[141] the position held by him prior to his present appointment.

The final post-Proposition 13 budget hearing was held on 10 August 1978. During this meeting, the city council reviewed the budgets of the office of finance, the office of budget and management services, the office of public works, and the city's capital improvement plan. No citizens asked to address the council on these city budgets. All budgets were subsequently approved as submitted.[142]

During this hearing, the finance director told the council he questioned the usefulness of the city's present computer system. He stated, "there is a need for the city to purchase updated computer equipment and to streamline its procedures."[143] One council member requested that the city manager provide the council "with a report detailing the cost to purchase updated computer equipment and the amount of money it would ultimately save the city."[144] Other members agreed with this request. The city manager responded by stating that a management consulting firm had agreed to donate its services to the city "to analyze the city's budget process, accounting methods, and computer operations."[145] He also stated that he would submit recommendations on this matter to the council in approximately two months.[146] The consulting firm to which the city manager referred reviewed only the city's budgetary process. No commitment was ever made by this company to review the city's accounting system or computer operations.[147] The city council never received the follow-up report promised by the city manager.

During these five meetings, council members examined every departmental budget in the city, including the capital improvement plan. A summary of those budgets reviewed is set forth in table 5-4. In slightly more than a month, the city council spent nearly ten hours somewhat cursorily scrutinizing budgets totaling almost $100 million which authorized funding

Table 5–4
Oakland Department Budget Hearings, Final Jarvis-Gann Budget, Fiscal Year 1978–1979

6 July 1978

Office of the mayor/council
Office of the city manager
Office of the city clerk
Office of the city attorney
Personnel department
Office of the city physician
City planning department
Office of the city auditor
Retirement administration department

13 July 1978

Office of parks and recreation
Library department
Museum department

20 July 1978

Office of general services
Office of community development
Office of economic development and employment
Nondepartmental budgets

27 July 1978

Police department
Fire department

10 August 1978

Office of finance
Office of budget and management services
Office of public works
Capital improvement plan

Note: Discretionary funds for these departments amount to $98.7 million.

for over 3,600 city positions. The changes made in the city's Proposition 13 budget were minor. The council restored funds for the Oakland Ballet Company in the amount of $3,150. The most worthwhile result of this process was the hiring freeze mandated by the council, which was estimated to save the city nearly $4 million during fiscal year 1978–1979.

Halfway through these hearings, the mayor expressed reservations concerning the merits of these meetings. He stated that "[he] wondered whether [the meetings] were accomplishing anything."[148] The city manager responded by stating that the "meetings were worthwhile even if they set the tone for what is promised to be a major overhaul of the system by next year's budget."[149] In retrospect, the hearings did little more than to educate the council on departmental operations. This proved to be worthwhile since council members had to approve subsequent budget reductions in order to balance Oakland's budget for fiscal year 1979–1980. Their newly found familiarity with departmental operations served to expedite this difficult process.

City Council Adopts Revised Proposition 13 Budget

After restoration of the $18.6 million in replacement revenues, Oakland's revised Proposition 13 budget, including both operating and capital expenditures, amounted to $98.7 million. The city's normal budget, which would have become operational if Proposition 13 had been defeated, was expected to be $113 million. The city's modified financial plan required a reduction of public services amounting to $14.3 million, encompassing 102 programs in nineteen city departments. The final reduction necessitated the elimination of 227 city positions. A departmental listing of these final reductions is set forth in table 5–5.[150]

On 17 October 1978, after the turmoil surrounding the Jarvis-Gann Initiative had subsided, the city council considered the adoption of a resolution authorizing modifications in the city's original Jarvis-Gann Emergency Budget.[151] The city manager presented a short report to city officials outlining Oakland's normal budget, the revised Proposition 13 budget, and the final budget reductions, which represented the difference between these two financial plans.[152] The revised Proposition 13 budget incorporated the

Table 5–5
Oakland City Budget Reduction, Final Jarvis-Gann Budget, Fiscal Year 1978–1979

Departments	Amount (millions of $)	Percent	Programs[a]	Positions
Police	3.1	8	12	31
Fire	1.1	4	2	2
Public works	1.4	12	20	78
General services	0.5	7	13	39
Parks and recreation	1.0	12	19	34
Library	0.5	14	11	10
Museum	0.3	12	6	6
General government	0.9	12	15	27
Nondepartmental	5.5	62	4	—
Total reduction	14.3	13	102	227

Note: Discretionary funds, excluding tax-increment and bond funds.

[a] Includes programs reduced or eliminated.

additional replacement revenues mandated by the city council, the city's estimated receipt of state-surplus revenues, and all council-approved program restorations.[153]

The citizen interest generated by the adoption of this financial plan was the antithesis of what had prevailed during earlier public meetings on the city's Proposition 13 budget. Not one citizen asked to address city officials on this agenda item. The city council, with little discussion, unanimously approved a motion adopting the modified budget as presented.[154] The complete text of this resolution is presented in figure 5-3.[155] The adoption of this final Proposition 13 budget, which represented the culmination of a process lasting several months, was not even publicized in the local press.[156] It was apparent that citizen interest had waned.

Oakland City Council Resolution No. 57602 C.M.S. [a]

Resolution Amending Resolution Number 57201 C.M.S. Adopting a Budget as the Financial Plan for Conducting the Affairs of the City for Fiscal Year 1978–79 and Appropriating Additional Moneys to Provide for the Expenditures Proposed by Said Amended Budget

Whereas, the City Council has adopted resolution number 57201 C.M.S. which adopted a budget as the financial plan for conducting the affairs of the City for Fiscal Year 1978–79 and appropriated moneys to provide for the expenditures proposed by said budget; and

Whereas, the City Council has increased certain local taxes which were not contemplated at the time the original budget was adopted, and certain other revenue items have been reestimated based on the latest available information; and

Whereas, the City Council has reviewed departmental and nondepartmental budgets in public hearings in view of the reestimated amount of nonrestricted resources available for Fiscal Year 1978–79; now, therefore, be it

Resolved: That the nonrestricted fund budget of the City is increased by $18,822,833, from $80,052,400[b] to $98,875,233, and an additional $18,822,833 is hereby appropriated; and be it

Further Resolved: That the City Manager is hereby authorized to expend in accordance with the laws of the State of California and the City of Oakland on behalf of the City Council, $98,875,233 in nonrestricted funds in accordance with the amended budget as shown below:

---

[a] Adopted by the city council on 17 October 1978.

[b] This figure differs from the budget figure in Resolution 57201 C.M.S. by $1,020,000. The amount originally allocated for debt service was reallocated to departmental budgets, since Proposition 13 did not affect voter-approved bond indebtedness.

Figure 5-3. Oakland Budget Resolution, Final Jarvis-Gann Budget, Fiscal Year 1978–1979

Operating Expenditures	*Amount*
0100 Mayor/Council	$328,791
0200 City Manager	484,361
0300 City Clerk	276,864
0400 City Attorney	544,618
0500 Personnel	420,320
0600 City Planning	514,793
0700 City Auditor	166,290
0800 City Physician	77,235
0900 Retirement Administration	125,537
1000 Finance	1,688,099
2100 Police	34,563,309
2200 Fire	26,204,492
3000 Public Works	10,063,289
4000 General Services	3,343,656
5000 Parks and Recreation	3,561,294
6100 Library	3,230,270
6200 Museum	2,273,586
6300 Paramount Theatre	160,400
7300 Community Development	544,768
8100 Employee Benefits	1,446,900
8200 Insurance and Liability Claims	875,404
8400 Miscellaneous	1,136,807
8600 Coliseum Support	750,000
8800 Community Promotion	342,150
9000 Budget and Management Services	1,053,000
9300 Central Service Overhead	(940,000)
Subtotal, Operating Expenditures	$98,236,233

Capital Improvements

3000 Public Works	$639,000
Subtotal, Capital Improvements	$639,000
Grand Total	$98,875,233

and be it

Further Resolved: That the funds appropriated under this resolution, and resolution number 57201 C.M.S., shall be appropriated from the following funds as hereby amended:

101 General Purpose Fund	$87,986,233
211 Revenue Sharing Fund	5,900,000
291 City Street Fund	2,032,000
293 Select System Fund	1,856,000
295 Traffic Safety Fund	1,101,000
Total	$98,875,233

and be it

Further Resolved: That the City Manager is hereby authorized to transfer appropriations from the General Fund to the Public Works Employment Act Fund when and if Congress shall act to amend the Public Works Employment Act, and when revenues from this source shall be determined.

Figure 5–3 continued

The actual impact of Oakland's revised Proposition 13 budget was dramatically less than what had been predicted. A comparison of the city's anticipated budget reduction, the council-approved restorations, and the final reduction is examined in table 5–6.[157] The changes made in the city's original Jarvis-Gann Emergency Budget greatly exceeded the fine-tune adjustments predicted by the city manager prior to the passage of Proposition 13. The actual financial and operational impact of Oakland's revised Proposition 13 budget is examined below.

The Proposition 13 budget adopted by city officials allocated the city's estimated discretionary funds to city departments for fiscal year 1978–1979. The city council had previously approved the restricted-fund portion of the city budget.[158] Restricted funds are earmarked for specific purposes and are nondiscretionary in nature. These funds, which constitute about one-third of Oakland's total budget,[159] are mainly received under various federal grant programs. They include the Comprehensive Employment and Training Act (CETA; Department of Labor), Community Development Block Grant (Department of Housing and Urban Development), Community Action Program (Office of Economic Opportunity), Head Start Program (Department of Health, Education, and Welfare), and Federal Aid Urban Grant (Department of Housing and Urban Development). The city expected to receive nearly $36 million during fiscal year 1978–1979 from these federal programs,[160] which were not impacted by the passage of Proposition 13.

Table 5–6
Comparison of Oakland City Budget Reductions, Original Reduction versus Final Reduction, Fiscal Year 1978–1979

	Original Cut		Restorations		Final Cut	
Departments	Amount (millions of $)	Positions	Amount (millions of $)	Positions	Amount (millions of $)	Positions
Police	6.8	267	3.7	236	3.1	31
Fire	4.8	151	3.7	149	1.1	2
Public works	4.6	234	3.2	156	1.4	78
General services	4.4	133	3.9	94	0.5	39
Parks and recreation	3.4	231	2.4	197	1.0	34
Library	1.7	121	1.2	111	0.5	10
Museum	1.2	52	0.9	46	0.3	6
General government	2.9	141	2.0	114	0.9	27
Nondepartmental	3.1	—	(2.4)	—	5.5	—
Totals	32.9	1,330	18.6	1,103	14.3	227

Note: Discretionary funds, excluding tax-increment and bond funds.

When they are included, the city's total budget, including both discretionary and nondiscretionary funds, amounts to about $138 million.[161]

Actual Financial Impact

The city's normal discretionary fund budget for fiscal year 1978–1979, $113
million, authorized funding for over 3,800 positions, including CETA-
funded personnel. The modified Proposition 13 budget, amounting to $98.7
million, provided funding for nearly 3,600 city employees, 710 of whom are
CETA-funded personnel. The revised Jarvis-Gann budget reduced Oakland's operating and capital budget by slightly over one-tenth and, in so
doing, eliminated about 6 percent of the city's authorized positions. While
the magnitude of this budget reduction was certainly not as great as predicted, it did have a measurable impact on many city departments. The
financial effect of the modified Proposition 13 budget on specific city
departments is discussed below. This analysis is based on a comparison
between Oakland's expected normal budget for fiscal year 1978–1979 and
its revised Proposition 13 budget.

Police Department. This department's normal budget was $37.4 million,
which authorized 684 sworn and 359 civilian personnel. The revised Proposition 13 budget allocated $34.3 million, authorizing 658 sworn and 355
civilian personnel. This involved a reduction of $3.1 million and thirty-one
positions, twenty-six of which were sworn. The police department was operated at about 92 percent of its normal funding level with 97 percent of its
regular staffing complement. Funding was reduced by 8 percent, staffing by
3 percent.

Fire Department. This department's regular budget included $26.4 million,
which financed 597 positions: 579 sworn and 18 civilian. The final Jarvis-
Gann budget authorized $25.3 million, 577 sworn and 18 civilian positions.
This reduction amounted to $1.1 million and the elimination of two sworn
positions. The fire department was run at about 96 percent of its normal
funding level with 99 percent of its regular authorized staff. The final
reduction was funding by 4 percent, staffing 1 percent.

Office of Public Works. This department's normal funding and staffing
level involved $11.5 million and 537 city positions. The modified Proposi-
tion 13 budget allocated $10.1 million and authorized 459 city positions.
This involved a reduction of $1.4 million and seventy-eight city positions.
Public works was operated at nearly 88 percent of its regular funding level
with slightly over 85 percent of its normal authorized staffing. This represented a final cut of 12 percent in funding and 15 percent in staffing.

Office of General Services. This department's regular budget allocated $6.8 million and 404 personnel. The revised Jarvis-Gann budget authorized $6.3 million and 365 positions. The final reduction amounted to $0.5 million and thirty-nine positions. General services was authorized 93 percent of its regular funding level and 90 percent of its normal staffing. The final reduction in funding and staffing amounted to 7 percent and 10 percent, respectively.

Office of Parks and Recreation. This department's normal budget and staffing totaled $8.6 million and 505 personnel. The final Proposition 13 budget allocated $7.6 million and 471 positions. This required a reduction of $1 million and thirty-four positions. Parks and recreation received 88 percent of its normal funding and 93 percent of its regular staff complement. The actual reduction amounted to 12 percent in funding and 7 percent in staffing.

Library Department. This department's normal budget would have included $3.7 million and 207 personnel. The revised Jarvis-Gann budget, on the other hand, authorized expenditures of $3.2 million and a staff of 197 positions. This involved a reduction of $0.5 million and ten positions. The library was operated at 86 percent of its regular funding level with 95 percent of its normal staffing. The final cut in funds and staff amounted to 14 percent and 5 percent, respectively.

Museum Department. This department's regular budget would have allocated $2.5 million and authorized 132 personnel. The modified Proposition 13 budget included $2.2 million which financed 126 positions. This required a reduction of $0.3 million and six positions. The museum was financed at 88 percent of its regular funding level with 95 percent of its normal positions. The actual reduction in staff and funds amounted to 5 percent and 12 percent, respectively.

General Government. This area of the city budget, as mentioned earlier, encompasses city-staff departments. The general government departments include the mayor, council, city manager, city clerk, city attorney, personnel, city planning, city auditor, city physician, retirement administration, finance, and budget and management services. In contrast to the original Jarvis-Gann Emergency Budget, funding and staffing for the mayor, city auditor, and city physician were not reduced. These departmental budgets were restored to their normal funding and staffing levels. The normal budget for general government operations totaled $7.2 million, which authorized 394 positions. The revised Jarvis-Gann budget approved $6.3 million and 367 positions. The final reduction totaled $0.9 million and twenty-seven positions. These general government departments, on the average, were operated at 88 percent of their normal funding with 93 percent of their regular authorized staffing. The actual cut in funding was 12 percent; in staffing, 7 percent.

Nondepartmental. This portion of the city's budget, as noted in chapter 4, covers functions outside regular departmental operations. These include the miscellaneous budget, community promotion, insurance and liability claims, employee benefits, central service overhead, and capital improvements. These budgets, because of their unique nature, contain no staffing. They are basically accounting categories to capture costs not associated with specific city departments. Insurance and liability claims, employee benefits, and central service overhead were restored to their normal funding levels. The normal budget for the city's nondepartmental activities amounted to $8.9 million. The final Proposition 13 budget allocated $3.4 million, requiring a reduction of $5.5 million. These nondepartmental budgets, on the average, were authorized funding at about 38 percent of their regular level. The final reduction in these budgets amounted to 62 percent.

Tax-Increment Projects. The city council had no choice but to maintain the reduction contained in the original Jarvis-Gann Emergency Budget. The normal tax-increment-project budget, prior to the passage of Proposition 13, was $6.4 million. The city expected to receive $2.7 million under the requirements imposed by the Jarvis-Gann Initiative. This funding source was reduced by $3.7 million, nearly 60 percent of the normal funding level. The final reduction amounted to 40 percent.

A departmental comparison of Oakland's normal budget for fiscal year 1978–1979 and its revised Proposition 13 budget for fiscal year 1978–1979 is presented in table 5–7.[162] This diagram sets forth the actual extent of funding and personnel reductions in each area of Oakland's city government. The impact of these reductions on public services is explained below.

Actual Public-Service Impact

The anticipated budget reduction under Proposition 13 was $32.9 million and 1,330 city positions. This reduction amounted to one-third of the city's discretionary funds and one-third of its total work force. The actual reduction, $14.3 million and 227 positions, decreased funding and staffing by 14 percent and 6 percent, respectively. Replacement revenues substantially mitigated the potential impact of Proposition 13. While the operational effect of the Jarvis-Gann Initiative was not as drastic as anticipated, it did leave measurable impact on Oakland's public services. This is described below.[163] These reductions were implemented with the beginning of the

Table 5-7

Comparison of Oakland City Budgets, Normal Budget versus Final Jarvis-Gann Budget, Fiscal Year 1978-1979

Departments	Normal		Jarvis-Gann		Reduction	
	Budget (millions of $)	Staffing	Budget (millions of $)	Staffing	Budget (millions of $)	Staffing
Police	37.4	1,043	34.3	1,012	3.1	31
Fire	26.4	597	25.3	595	1.1	2
Public works	11.5	537	10.1	459	1.4	78
General services	6.8	404	6.3	365	0.5	39
Parks and recreation	8.6	505	7.6	471	1.0	34
Library	3.7	207	3.2	197	0.5	10
Museum	2.5	132	2.2	126	0.3	6
General government	7.2	394	6.3	367	0.9	27
Nondepartmental	8.9	—	3.4	—	5.5	—
Totals	113.0	3,819	98.7	3,592	14.3	227

Note: Discretionary funds, excluding tax-increment and bond funds.

city's 1978-1979 fiscal year, which commenced on 1 July 1978. The public immediately felt the impact of these service reductions.

Police Department. A reorganization in the bureau of services resulted in the assignment of additional law-enforcement duties to the remaining police officers within this division. In other parts of the department, the responsibilities of those positions eliminated were assigned to other police officers.

Fire Department. An administrative reorganization, which consolidated operations, resulted in the elimination of two high-level sworn positions. The duties of these positions were assumed by other sworn personnel. An operational reorganization in the department resulted in the implementation of variable staffing within fire companies. This enabled the department to achieve a sizable savings without reducing positions.

Office of Public Works. Hand sweeping in west and north Oakland has been eliminated. An increase in street litter is expected to result. Machine street sweeping is now done less frequently in residential areas. Streets are cleaned once every four to five weeks, instead of once every three to four weeks. Street maintenance is done less frequently. Deferred maintenance of the city's streets will ultimately result. This impact will be felt in future years.

Personnel reductions in the traffic engineering department have resulted in longer response times in handling citizen requests for traffic-control studies.

A reduction in the Weed Abatement Program has increased response times in handling citizen complaints. An accumulation of weeds and debris may result on the city's vacant lots, increasing fire hazards in such areas.

Office of General Services. Fire-alarm boxes have been removed on a city-wide basis. The personnel responsible for their maintenance and repair have been eliminated. Security guards at the city hall building have been eliminated. Smoke detectors and an after-hours electronic entry system are being installed. The city hall switchboard has been eliminated. All incoming telephone calls must now be made directly to city departments. Telephone information assistance and after-hours telephone service, previously available to citizens, have been eliminated.

A street-lighting energy-conservation program has been implemented, replacing existing street lamps with energy-saving lamps.

About one-third of the city's Walk/Don't Walk signs on traffic signals have been removed without significantly increasing pedestrian or vehicular hazards.

Office of Parks and Recreation. Studio II, a cultural arts center located at the Arroyo Recreation Center, has been permanently closed. The park ranger force has been reduced by one-half. Park security and fire-prevention activities have been reduced accordingly.

Twenty part-time positions at the city's recreation centers have been eliminated. Fewer supervised and organized recreational activities are available at these locations. Eight gardener positions have been eliminated, resulting in a decrease in the maintenance level and litter control at city parks and recreation centers.

Library Department. Hours at the city's main library have been reduced by nearly 20 percent during the summer months. The main library is now open fifty hours per week instead of sixty-two hours per week during the summer. Library hours have been reduced by 20 percent at branch libraries throughout the city.

Two bookmobiles have been eliminated in the Spanish-speaking and Asian communities. The citywide library film-loan service has been abolished.

Museum Department. Hours at the city's museum have been reduced by 13 percent, eliminating the only evening hours this facility is open to the public (that is, Friday nights). The museum aquarium has been closed; all aquatic exhibits have been postponed indefinitely.

The Oakes Observatory, site of presentations on California art, architecture, and history, has been closed. Periodic exhibits at the Oakes Gallery have been eliminated. This attraction is located at the main museum facility.

Office of the City Manager. The position of public information officer was eliminated.[164] The duties of this position were transferred to the deputy city manager. The position of employee relations officer was abolished. The responsibilities of this position were transferred to the city's personnel director. Due to reductions in the clerical staff, the remaining personnel have assumed additional duties.

Office of the City Clerk. Citizen requests for information and records now take longer to process.[165] Planned projects, such as records management, have been delayed. A backlog of typing, filing, and processing contracts and records has resulted. Due to reductions in the secretarial staff, the remaining personnel have assumed additional duties.

Office of City Attorney. To respond in a timely manner to departmental requests for legal advice and legal opinions, as well as to prepare contracts and agreements with vendors, long-term projects and assignments of a lower priority have not been accomplished.[166] Additional legal responsibilities have been assigned to the remaining professional staff.

Personnel Department. Departmental requests to fill personnel vacancies and requests for promotional examinations now take longer to process.[167] Special projects, such as departmental personnel-needs assessments and revisions to the city's Personnel Manual, have been postponed indefinitely. The remaining clerical staff have been assigned additional duties. A backlog of departmental filing and delays in the maintenance of personnel records have resulted.

City-Planning Department. There are no follow-up field inspections on zoning permits to determine if conditions of approval have been satisfied.[168] Enforcement is strictly on a complaint basis. More time is spent on current problems, less time on long-range planning activities. Planning studies undertaken are not as thorough or comprehensive. Response times to citizen requests (such as rezoning) are subject to longer delays. Action time on certain zoning and subdivision cases is slower.

Requests for certain information by the public cannot be complied with. Requests for studies by the Planning Commission and the Landmarks Preservation Advisory Board must be deferred or rejected.

Retirement Administration Department. The microfilming of retirement records has been postponed.[169] The remaining accounting staff has been assigned additional duties.

Office of Finance. The permits and licensing section now spends ten to fourteen days answering citizen inquiries that formerly took only a few days.[170] The parking violations bureau has a greater backlog of citizen complaints. Response to public inquiries has been delayed. Less time is available for auditing payments made under the city's business license tax. Unrealized revenues may result because of businesses understating their taxes.

Accounting controls are weaker because of slower reconciliations, less-frequent monitoring, and less-timely financial reporting. The consequence is an increased risk of error and fraud. A payroll computerization project, which would have ultimately lowered the costs of preparing the city's payroll, has been indefinitely postponed.

Data-Processing Department. This department now has no reserve capacity to meet emergency conditions.[171] No new systems of any kind are being developed. Departments are now forced to seek the assistance of outside contracts for the development of new applications. Only the most urgent requests for service are considered for action, such as those mandated by city ordinance, state law, or other external requirements.

New financial applications have been indefinitely postponed. These include the sales-tax-auditing system, parking-meter-collection auditing system, cabaret licensing, and transient-occupancy tax collections. The implementation of the city's planned payroll/personnel system has been postponed indefinitely.

Nondepartmental. The Convention Center Fund has been abolished. All transient-occupancy-tax revenues are now transferred into the city's General Fund to finance regular city operations.[172] This means that Oakland will not be able to build its Convention Center with local revenues. Other funding will have to be sought for this project.

The city council's policy of utilizing 100 percent of available tax-increment funds remained in effect.[173] Several tax-increment projects, including the Chinatown Project, Victorian Row, and City Center Project, will have to be delayed. Construction of these projects will take twice as long as anticipated, unless other funding sources are obtained.

The funding of community organizations under the Community Promotion Program has been substantially reduced. The city received requests for funding from over thirty community organizations which promote Oakland in various ways. Funding was provided for only three of these organizations. Requests for funds from the remaining organizations could not be honored.[174]

General-Fund support for capital-improvement projects has been reduced by about one-fourth. A minimal level of funding was maintained to enable the city to qualify for federal matching funds. Both the number and the magnitude of the city's capital-improvement projects have been reduced accordingly.

The anticipated impact of Proposition 13 on public services required the closure of some forty-four city facilities, including several fire stations, many branch libraries, and over a dozen park and recreational facilities. The impact of the actual service reductions on city facilities was not nearly as severe. The office of parks and recreation closed one crafts center, the library department eliminated two bookmobile vans, and the museum department permanently closed one exhibit and one gallery. A listing of those city facilities actually closed under the city's revised Proposition 13 budget is presented in table 5-8.[175]

A description of the actual impact of Proposition 13 on city services was prepared by the staff of the OBMS. This document was based on narrative descriptions prepared by department managers on the actual impact of the Jarvis-Gann Initiative on their respective operations. These reports were reviewed, edited, and assembled into a short publication entitled *Public Service Impact Statement—Jarvis-Gann Budget: Fiscal Year 1978-79.* This report was primarily used to inform city officials, both elected and appointed, of the actual impact of Proposition 13 on public services. This

Table 5-8
Closed Oakland City Facilities, Final Jarvis-Gann Budget, Fiscal Year 1978-1979

Facility	Address
Parks and recreation	
Studio II, Arroyo Viejo Recreation Center	7701 Krause Avenue
Library	
Main library	
two bookmobile vans	125 14th Street
Museum	
Aquarium Exhibit	Oakland Museum
Oakes Observatory Gallery	1000 Oak Street

document was not used extensively as a public-informational vehicle, but mainly as a staff report. Requests from citizens and community organizations concerning the actual impact of Proposition 13 on city services were minimal. Most requests for such information were received from public agencies, which were basically concerned with the impact of the Jarvis-Gann Initiative on other governmental organizations.

Local press coverage of the actual impact of Proposition 13 on Oakland's public services was minimal. Subsequent newspaper articles appeared describing the removal of Walk/Don't Walk pedestrian lights located on traffic signals, estimated to save nearly $90,000 annually;[176] the elimination of fire-alarm boxes throughout the city, projected to save $80,000 per year;[177] and the implementation of the city's street-lighting energy-conservation program, designed to save about $1.5 million annually.[178] Coincidentally, these last two economies would have resulted notwithstanding the passage of Proposition 13. The removal of the fire-alarm boxes and the conversion of street lights had already been planned prior to the enactment of the Jarvis-Gann Initiative.[179]

Continued Impact

Proposition 13 continues to affect Oakland in a number of different ways. Soon after the city's budget reductions had been implemented, the city manager announced a major review of the city's operations. This effort was designed to achieve additional economies to offset the city's projected financial deficit for fiscal year 1979–1980. Department managers had already been asked to submit proposed budget reductions to balance this budget. The city council also increased various user fees in order to create additional revenues. These events were a direct outgrowth of the passage of the Jarvis-Gann Initiative.

The requirements of Senate Bill 154, which allocated state-surplus revenues, have also created problems for city officials. Under the threat of possible litigation by the city's fire fighters' union, budget reductions were negotiated downward in the fire department. Shortly thereafter, the police officers' union brought suit against the city in an attempt to restore budget reductions implemented in the police department. The provisions of Senate Bill 154 which froze the salaries of local government employees were subsequently declared unconstitutional. Proposition 13 continues to have a direct impact on city operations. This impact is described in greater detail below.

Soon after the city council completed its post-Proposition 13 budget hearings, the city manager announced a major review of the city organization.[180] The purpose of this effort was to make further recommendations to the council on ways to achieve departmental efficiencies, since the city faced another budget deficit in fiscal year 1979–1980. This scrutiny of city operations involved three phases. First, the city auditor was instructed to review all city departments "with the objective of making the most economies [possible]."[181] Second, the services of a management consulting firm would be used to "look at the method by which the [city's] budget is prepared . . . and offer suggestions for ways to do [the budget] in a more efficient and businesslike manner."[182] The third phase involved extensive talks between the city manager and the budget director regarding the possible updating of the city's data-processing system.[183] The mayor also indicated that the city "may very well want to hire outside efficiency experts to come in and examine the city's structure and suggest methods for cost-cutting."[184]

While this rhetoric sounded impressive, the results of these plans were less than dramatic. The city auditor reviewed departmental operations on a time-available basis. No additional economies were realized from this exercise. The management consulting company did review and made recommendations on ways to improve the city's budgetary process. This firm even tested the use of zero-base budgeting in selected city departments. No savings, however, resulted from these efforts. While the discussions on the city's data-processing operations did take place, no alterations were made in this system. The financial impact of Proposition 13 postponed the purchase of new data-processing equipment.[185] The services of the efficiency experts, discussed by the mayor, were never utilized. In short, the review of the city organization did not live up to the predictions made by the mayor and city manager.

The purpose of this examination of city operations was to create additional savings to help offset Oakland's anticipated financial deficit in fiscal year 1979–1980. Estimated revenues for this fiscal year amounted to $98.2 million.[186] Carry-over fund balances, primarily due to the council-approved hiring freeze, were projected to be nearly $5.2 million,[187] $1 million more than originally predicted. The city's total resources, which include both revenues and fund balances, were $103.4 million.[188] City expenditures for fiscal year 1979–1980 were estimated to be $111.3 million.[189] Oakland, therefore, faced a potential financial deficit in the following fiscal year of nearly $8 million. This revenue shortage can be directly attributed to Proposition 13. Prior to the passage of the Jarvis-Gann Initiative, the city would have received additional property-tax revenues from increasing assessed valuations. The city council also had the option of increasing the city's property-tax rate to raise additional revenues. Both these revenue avenues have been severely limited by the requirements of Proposition 13. The property tax has become a nondiscretionary source of revenue. Pre-Proposition 13 property taxes provided 34 percent of Oakland's nonrestricted funds. Post-Proposition 13 property taxes accounted for only 14 percent of local revenues.[190]

The budget-reduction process necessary to balance Oakland's budget for fiscal year 1979–1980 was completed in June 1979. Department managers had been requested to prepare budget reductions in an amount necessary to offset the projected deficit.[191] One of the key revenue assumptions for this budget was the continued receipt of state-surplus revenues with no strings attached. The state legislation distributing these revenues during fiscal year 1978–1979, as previously mentioned, required local governments to maintain police and fire services at pre-Proposition 13 service levels, except where economies could be achieved without impacting these service levels. Luckily, this revenue source was continued at its former level, without this requirement. City departments, on the average, had to reduce their expenditures by about 7 percent. If police and fire services had been excluded from this reduction, the remaining city departments would have had to reduce their budgets by nearly 40 percent. The latter approach to balancing the city's budget would have virtually paralyzed all public services except police and fire. Figure 5–4 illustrates the magnitude of police and fire services in relation to other city services.[192]

Various legislative proposals were considered in Sacramento to continue state aid to local governments. These proposals are examined in chapter 6. The state legislature should approve such legislation in a timely manner to enable local governments, like Oakland, to incorporate these funds into their annual budgetary-planning process. The 1978 state legislation allocating surplus revenues was signed into law by the governor on 24 June 1978, only one week before the beginning of the new fiscal year.

Proposition 13 did not impose restrictions on increasing existing fees charged to citizens by local governments. Such fees are designed to capture the costs of providing public services. Oakland took advantage of this avenue to enhance the city's post-Proposition 13 revenue posture. The office of finance reviewed the fees charged by each city department with the goal of making such fees cover the costs of the services rendered. During fiscal year 1978–1979, the city council approved fee increases charged by the office of the city clerk,[193] city-planning department,[194] office of public works,[195] fire department,[196] office of parks and recreation,[197] office of general services,[198] police department,[199] and office of finance.[200] Hundreds of user fees charged by these departments were increased, some by as much as 400 percent.[201] While the office of finance reviewed departmental fees and suggested increases, department managers were given the final approval to increase such fees. All staff recommendations made to the city council relative to increasing user fees received prior approval of the department managers involved.[202] This effort, in addition to providing more revenues, made the public services provided by city departments more cost-covering. It also helped reduce the magnitude of the city's budget deficit for fiscal year 1979–1980.

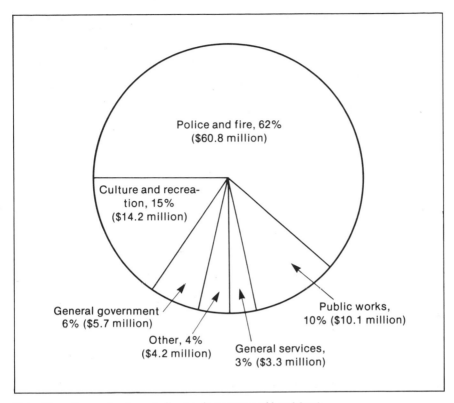

Note: Discretionary funds, excluding tax-increment and bond funds.

Figure 5-4. Allocation of Oakland City Expenditures, Final Jarvis-Gann
Budget, Fiscal Year 1978–1979

In addition to worrying about balancing the budget, city officials had
to cope with maintaining those Proposition 13 budget reductions mandated
in the city's fire and police departments. The city council was aware that
Senate Bill 154 placed limitations on reductions in municipal fire and police
services. City officials circumvented this requirement, however, by indicating that the reductions made in Oakland's public-safety services were
"economies," and did not affect prevailing service levels. Budget reductions in the fire and police departments were quickly contested by the
employee unions representing these uniformed employees.

Under the threat of possible litigation, city officials negotiated with
Local 55 of the International Fire Fighters Association on the fire-depart-
ment reductions mandated by the city's Proposition 13 budget. After
lengthy negotiations, a settlement was finally reached. The city agreed not
to reduce seventeen chief operators' positions. The fire fighters' union, in

turn, agreed to voluntarily cut two administrative positions: one assistant chief and one battalion chief. The fire department's budget, however, was reduced by the amount previously approved by the city council. This was accomplished through the implementation of what was referred to as "variable manning," whereby the fire department agreed not to fill vacant positions during fiscal year 1978–1979. This settlement enabled city officials to reduce the fire department's budget as planned without having to lay off any fire-fighting personnel. Both of the administrative positions eliminated were vacant. City officials agreed to the terms of this compromise because they did not want to become involved in the lengthy process of litigation on this issue. This compromise proved to be mutually advantageous.[203]

In retrospect, city officials could have sustained these reductions because the superior court subsequently ruled that this provision of Senate Bill 154 was unconstitutional. This decision resulted from a suit against the city initiated by the Oakland Police Officers Association. The circumstances surrounding this litigation are discussed below.

Following the city's compromise with the fire-fighters' union, the Oakland Police Officers Association commenced legal action against the city, contesting the budget reductions mandated in the police department under the requirements of Senate Bill 154.[204] The union argued that the city's actions in reducing police services violated this state legislation. The city attorney held that this provision of state law violated article 11 of the California Constitution, which governs the rights and powers granted by the state to charter cities. After considerable testimony, the superior court ruled in favor of the city, stating

> the rights and powers granted by the [state constitution] to chartered cities are of such a fundamental and important nature that the legislature may not by statute require as a condition that any of those rights and powers be given up or suspended or otherwise diluted as a condition of gaining any benefit from the state.[205]

The portion of Senate Bill 154 pertaining to the maintenance of police and fire services was declared unconstitutional.[206] The city was permitted to maintain the reductions mandated by the city council in police services. The Oakland Police Officers Association immediately appealed this decision. The determination of the Proposition 13-related reductions in the police department is now pending in the court of appeals.[207]

The requirements of Senate Bill 154 posed additional problems for city officials. After the city council approved the revised Proposition 13 budget, additional revenues, over and above what had been anticipated, were received. These funds, resulting primarily from an increase in the city's post-Proposition 13 property-tax revenues ($4.1 million) and a greater-than-expected fund balance on 30 June 1978 ($0.8 million), amounted to slightly over $5 million.[208] These additional revenues, because of the salary freeze mandated by Senate Bill 154, were not appropriated to city departments. Instead, these funds were set aside in a "litigation contingency," pending a determination of the constitutionality of this provision of Senate Bill 154. This salary freeze had been contested by several local governments. On 15 February 1979, the California Supreme Court declared this portion of Senate Bill 154 unconstitutional.[209] The court ruled "that wage restrictions in the [state] bailout legislation violated the contract clause of the constitution and the home rule powers of charter cities and counties."[210] These funds were subsequently allocated to city employees according to existing contractual agreements between the city and public-employee unions.

Commentary

While Proposition 13 overwhelmingly passed on a statewide basis, the measure was defeated in Oakland by a margin of about 4,000 votes. The Oakland vote primarily reflected the socioeconomic composition of the community. The timely analysis by city officials of the potential impact of this legislation on Oakland, combined with the great amount of publicity this analysis received prior to the election, may have contributed to this voting pattern. This is difficult if not impossible to determine, however, since Oakland has many minority and poor citizens, many of whom are renters. Political observers, after analyzing the election results, pointed out that such individuals consistently voted against the Jarvis-Gann Initiative.[211] The subsequent actions taken by Oakland's city officials resulted primarily from the city's anti-Proposition 13 vote.

While it took several months of political and administrative turmoil to arrive at a satisfactory Jarvis-Gann Emergency Budget, it took only a few weeks to restore millions of dollars to city departments. When the final Proposition 13 budget was completed, the anticipated budget reduction and the impact of this reduction on public services bore no resemblance to reality. The final financial deficit was less than one-half of what had been predicted. Replacement revenues were used to restore over three-fourths of those city positions scheduled to be eliminated. The actual number of employees terminated was only a fraction of what had been anticipated. About half of the estimated program reductions were restored and only a few city facilities were actually closed. Table 5-9 examines the anticipated budget reduction, the council-approved budget restorations, and the actual cuts made to the city's budget as a result of the passage of Proposition 13.

All departmental budgets, with the exception of three, were reduced as a result of the revenue loss created by the Jarvis-Gann Initiative. Two of these departments—the office of the city auditor and the office of the city

Table 5–9
Oakland, Comparison of Reductions, Original versus Final Jarvis-Gann Budget, Fiscal Year 1978–1979

Category	Original Cut	Restorations	Final Cut
Budget reduction (millions of $)	32.9	18.6	14.3
Positions eliminated	1,330	1,103	227
Incumbents eliminated	1,050	980	70
Program reductions [a]	220	118	102
City facilities closed	41	37	4

Note: Discretionary funds, excluding tax-increment and bond funds.
[a] Includes programs reduced or eliminated.

physician—were basically maintained at their pre-Proposition 13 funding and staffing levels. The funds of a third department—the office of the mayor—were increased by slightly over $63,000, or 52 percent.[212] These additional funds resulted from a requested increase in the mayor's travel budget. It would have been more prudent, and possibly would have enhanced the mayor's image, if his department had reflected a good-faith budget reduction of at least a few thousand dollars. The office of the mayor was the only city department whose budget showed such a dramatic increase.

Initially, over 1,000 notices of termination were mailed to city employees. As the city council approved replacement revenues, subsequent letters rescinding these notices were distributed. The pace of this effort was frantic. It was difficult to "get a handle on" the actual number of employees scheduled to be terminated because of Proposition 13. Newspaper articles closely monitored the council's actions during June, continually informing the public of the revised number of employees due to lose their jobs. The number of employees to be laid off was revised downward during this period from 1,050 to 70. One local newspaper even provided citizens with a "city-budget tally," comparing the city's anticipated budget reductions with the council-approved replacement revenues.[213]

In total, 227 city positions were actually eliminated from Oakland's work force. Of this number, 19 percent were management, 12 percent were sworn, and 69 percent were "other" employees.[214] This first category includes management, supervisory, and professional employees. Sworn personnel includes uniformed police and fire employees. The "other" category represents clerical, technical, craft, and field employees. The actual composition of the city's work force at this time was 14 percent management, 23 percent sworn, and 63 percent "other."[215] This analysis reveals that city officials eliminated a greater proportion of management positions and relatively few sworn positions.

Upon closer examination, however, a different picture emerges. Most of the positions eliminated were vacant. Of the seventy employees actually terminated, only one was management and none were sworn employees.[216] The remaining layoffs included clerical, technical, craft, and field employees. This means that virtually all of those employees who lost their jobs were blue-collar-type city workers in lower-level positions. About three-fourths of the employees terminated were semiskilled laborers and street sweepers.[217] The vacant positions eliminated, however, still impacted the delivery of public services. By eliminating vacant positions, the duties assigned to these positions were either eliminated or partly transferred to other city employees. The final impact of Proposition 13 on Oakland's public services reflects the effect of all positions eliminated, both filled and vacant.

The post-Proposition 13 budget hearings held by the city council proved to be anticlimactic. The Jarvis-Gann Initiative had already passed, the council had adopted considerable replacement revenues, and the actual impact of the initiative, while not as great as predicted, was already being felt by Oakland's citizens. These budget hearings, while not living up to their expectations, did serve two important purposes. Council members did receive a review, though somewhat cursory, of the city's departmental operations. Also, the city council continued the citywide hiring freeze throughout fiscal year 1978–1979. This action was estimated to have saved the city about $4 million. This saving was incorporated into the financial projections for the following fiscal year.

Not long after these hearings, the mayor announced that he would discontinue the long-time practice of allowing the city to pay for the dinners of council members before their Tuesday night meetings. Eliminating this fringe benefit would save the city around $5,000 annually.[218] This matter was subsequently referred to the Council Ways and Means Committee for study and recommendation. Abolishing this fringe benefit, while not saving a great deal of money, would have shown that city officials were serious about cutting unnecessary city expenses. A "lid" was ultimately placed on the cost of these meals at $8.50 per person.[219] A few months later, in November, the amount of this meal allowance was increased to $10.[220] This benefit was also expanded to include designated staff members of departments and the mayor who attended evening council meetings.[221] The city council did, however, impose restrictions on its own out-of-state travel, limiting such travel to one trip per person each year.[222] This latter sacrifice appeared to be too little too late.

The continuing impact of Proposition 13 on Oakland is very real. Prior to the passage of this measure, many of the city's user fees did not cover the costs of the services provided. City officials are now aware of the need to make certain city services cost-covering. The city's fiscal climate has changed. This has been exhibited in the council's actions since the passage of the Jarvis-Gann Initiative. The city's hiring freeze will also have a direct impact on public services. Presently, the duties of vacant positions are being transferred to other city personnel. Ultimately, the reallocation of these duties will reach a point of diminishing return as staff resources are stretched to maintain existing public services.

The city's projected budget deficit for fiscal year 1979–1980 has been balanced. A future deficit could result because of an unfavorable court decision on the budget reductions mandated in the police department. If the ruling of the superior court is reversed and funds are restored, the city's resources could be reduced accordingly, creating a deficit in future years. Even with the planned-budget reductions, state-surplus revenues are needed to make the city's budget balance. Without the receipt of these revenues, Oakland's Proposition 13-related budget deficit would have been $23.6 million. State-surplus revenues, however, reduced the magnitude of this revenue shortfall by $9.3 million, permitting the city to spread the revenue loss created by Proposition 13 over a longer period.

The city's resources were cut by over $14 million by Proposition 13, reducing public services in most departments. New programs are being scrutinized as never before. One new program, the city's affirmative action program governing city contracts for the purchase of supplies and commodities and the construction of public-works projects, warrants special attention. During fiscal year 1977–1978, city contracts for these purposes exceeded $11 million.[223] About 6 percent of this amount went to local minority businesses.[224] The city council, greatly concerned over the lack of minority participation in these contracts, approved a new affirmative action plan to boost minority involvement in this area of city government. This plan gives a 3-percent bidding preference to Oakland firms and a 5-percent bidding preference to minority-owned Oakland businesses.[225]

City officials, in adopting this plan, authorized the use of local tax dollars to subsidize Oakland-based firms. While affirmative action is a desirable goal, efforts should have been directed toward enhancing the competitiveness of such firms, rather than toward awarding city contracts to other than the lowest bidder. The costs of these goods and services will now be greater. Assuming the city's resources remain constant, other areas of the city budget—those providing direct public services—will have to be further reduced in the future. The logic of this plan seems faulty. If other cities adopt similar policies, Oakland firms will lose their competitive position in these cities. Only time will tell what actual dollar impact this program will have on city expenditures.

In retrospect, the allegations of scare tactics against city officials prior to the passage of Proposition 13 were justified. The anticipated effect of the Jarvis-Gann Initiative bore little resemblance to the actual impact of this measure. The initial direction given to the city manager by the city council for preparing Oakland's Jarvis-Gann Emergency Budget—to assume no replacement revenues—proved to be false. At this time, however, the council was not aware that Oakland's citizens would vote against this initiative. Furthermore, they were not aware that the city would receive state-surplus revenues. While the Oakland mandate was not substantial, it did provide council members with a political rationale for adopting replacement revenues. These additional revenues greatly mitigated the potential impact of the Jarvis-Gann Initiative in Oakland.

One editorial appearing a couple of weeks after the city council had mandated replacement revenues describes the feelings of many citizens in Oakland relative to the intent of Proposition 13. This writer stated

> ... our city officials warned that there would be well over 1,000 city employees laid off, with drastic reductions in fire and police services. The fact is that a relatively insignificant [number] of city employees have been laid off. The layoffs included such nonvital employees as street sweepers, a stage hand, a welder, etc. Actually no layoffs would have been required if some of the excessive salaries of top administrators had been reduced.[226]

This sentiment still prevails among a great many Oakland citizens.

Notes

1. March Fong Eu, *Statement of Vote: Primary Election, June 6, 1978* (Sacramento, Calif.: Office of Secretary of State, July 1978), p. 190.

2. Sue Soennichsen, "Business Taxes are Increased," *The Montclarion,* 28 June 1978, p. 1.

3. Sue Soennichsen, "Oakland's Vote on Jarvis: A Plus in Sacramento?" *The Montclarion*, 21 June 1978, p. 1.

4. Sue Soennichsen, "Gloom and Rumors in Oakland's City Hall," *The Montclarion*, 14 June 1978, p. 1.

5. Ibid., p. 2.

6. Sue Soennichsen, "To Junket or Not to Junket," *The Montclarion,* 14 June 1978, p. 1.

7. Richard Spencer, "Oakland Employee Fee Upheld," *Oakland Tribune,* 30 May 1978, sec. A, p. 1.

8. Sue Soennichsen, "Employee License Fee Puts Council in Quandary," *The Montclarion,* 7 July 1978, p. 1. The actual figure cited by the city manager was $12.25 million annually.

9. Ernie Cox, "City Council Looks at Future Budgets—Reorganized City Government Seen," *Oakland Tribune,* 5 July 1978, sec. E, p. 47.

10. Ernie Cox, "Hiring Freeze to Cut 200, Save $4 Million Annually," *Oakland Tribune,* 7 July 1978, sec. D, p. 25.

11. *Legislative Bulletin* (League of California Cities), 9 June 1978, p. 3.

12. Samuel E. Wood, "The 'Sleeper' in Proposition 13: Statewide Planning's Chance to Work," *Cry California,* 3(Fall 1978):8.

13. Ibid.

14. California, Senate, *Senate Bill 154* (Sacramento, 24 June 1978), pp. 1–2.

15. Ibid., sec. 24, subparagraph (1)(B), p. 27.

16. Ibid., sec. 15, subsection 16250, paragraphs (c) through (e), p. 12.

17. Ibid., sec. 15, subsection 16250, paragraph (g) and subsection 16280, pp. 12, 13, and 18.

18. Ibid., sec. 16, pp. 19–21.

19. Ibid., sec. 18, pp. 21–23.

20. "State OK's '13' Bailout Funds," *Oakland Tribune,* 8 March 1979, sec. B, p. 5.

21. California, Assembly, Revenue and Taxation Committee, Willie L. Brown, Jr., chairman, *Summary of Legislation Implementing Proposition 13 for Fiscal Year 1978-79,* (Sacramento, 2 October 1978), p. 87.

22. Lynn M. Suter, *Legislative Committee Report* (Sacramento, Calif.: Office of Lynn Suter, legislative consultant, 13 February 1979), p. 2.

23. California, Senate, *Senate Bill 2212* (Sacramento, 30 June 1978).

24. City Manager, *Effects of Proposition 13 on Property Tax Related Revenue* (Oakland, Calif.: Office of City Manager, 13 June 1978), p. 1; idem, *Policy Matters for Specific Council Attention* (Oakland, Calif.: Office of City Manager, 13 June 1978), p. 1.

25. City Clerk, *City Council Meeting Minutes* (Oakland, Calif.: Office of City Clerk, 13 June 1978), p. 1.

26. Ibid.

27. City Council, *Resolution 57298 C.M.S.,* Oakland City Council, Oakland, Calif., 13 June 1978.

28. Ernie Cox, "Council Stalled on Budget Cuts," *Oakland Tribune,* 14 June 1978, sec. C, p. 31.

29. Ibid.

30. Ibid.

31. City Clerk, *City Council Meeting Minutes,* 13 June 1978, p. 2.

32. City Manager, *Priority Decisions for Consideration* (Oakland, Calif.: Office of City Manager, 15 June 1978), pp. 1–3.

33. City Clerk, *City Council Meeting Minutes,* 15 June 1978, p. 2.

34. City Manager, *Recommended Budget for Fiscal Year 1978-79* (Oakland, Calif.: Office of City Manager, May 1978), p. A-6.

35. City Manager, *Additional Revenue Projected* (Oakland, Calif.: Office of City Manager, 15 June 1978), p. 1.

36. City Clerk, *City Council Meeting Minutes,* 15 June 1978, p. 2.

37. Ibid.

38. Director of Budget and Management Services, *Public Service Impact Statement—Jarvis-Gann Emergency Budget: Fiscal Year 1978-79* (Oakland, Calif.: Office of Budget and Management Services, September 1978), p. 7.

39. Sue Soennichsen, "Reductions in Proposition 13 Cutbacks," *The Montclarion,* 21 June 1978, p. 1.

40. City Clerk, *City Council Meeting Minutes,* 15 June 1978, p. 3.

41. Ibid.

42. Ibid.

43. Ibid., p. 2.

44. Ibid.

45. Ibid., p. 3.

46. Ibid.

47. City Clerk, *City Council Meeting Minutes,* 12 December 1978, p. 3.

48. Ibid., p. 4.

49. City Manager, *Priority Decisions for Consideration* (Oakland, Calif.: Office of City Manager, 15 June 1978), p. 2.

50. Ernie Cox, "'Error' Gives City Extra $5.6 Million," *Oakland Tribune,* 15 June 1978, sec. A, p. 1.

51. City Clerk, *City Council Meeting Minutes,* 15 June 1978, p. 2.

52. Ibid.

53. Ibid.

54. Soennichsen, "Reductions in Proposition 13 Cutbacks," p. 8.

55. Ibid.

56. Soennichsen, "To Junket or Not to Junket," p. 1.

57. Ibid.

58. "Revenue Alternatives," Oakland Assistant to Director of Finance, to Oakland City Manager, 22 June 1978, files of Office of Budget and Management Services, Oakland, Calif.

59. City Clerk, *City Council Meeting Minutes,* 23 June 1978, p. 1.

60. Ernie Cox, "City Cuts Could Start Tomorrow," *Oakland Tribune,* 26 June 1978, sec. C, p. 21.

61. City Clerk, *City Council Meeting Minutes,* 23 June 1978, p. 1.

62. Ibid.

63. Walter A. Abernathy, executive director, Port of Oakland, letter to Board of Port Commissioners, Port of Oakland, Oakland, Calif., 23 June 1978, pp. 1–2.

64. City Clerk, *City Council Meeting Minutes,* 23 June 1978, p. 1.

65. Ibid., p. 2.

66. Ibid.

67. Ibid.

68. Ibid.

69. Ibid.

70. Ibid.

71. Ibid.

72. Ernie Cox, "Council Pushes Through New Business Taxes," *Oakland Tribune,* 24 June 1978, sec. A, p. 1. Reprinted with permission.

73. City Clerk, *City Council Meeting Minutes,* 23 June 1978, p. 3.

74. Ibid.

75. City Manager, *Budget Restoration Projection* (Oakland, Calif.: Office of City Manager, 27 June 1978), p. 1.

76. Ibid., p. 2.

77. City Clerk, *City Council Meeting Minutes,* 27 June 1978, p. 1.

78. Barbara Wood, "Two More Taxes Okayed by Council," *The Montclarion,* 5 July 1978, p. 1.

79. Ibid., pp. 1, 8.

80. Ibid., p. 8.

81. Ibid.

82. City Clerk, *City Council Meeting Minutes,* 27 June 1978, p. 1.

83. Wood, "Two More Taxes," p. 8.

84. Soennichsen, "Business Taxes Are Increased," p. 8.

85. City Clerk, *City Council Meeting Minutes,* 27 June 1978, p. 1.

86. Ibid., p. 2.

87. Ibid.

88. City Clerk, *City Council Meeting Minutes,* 19 September 1978, p. 1.

89. Ibid.

90. Sue Soennichsen, "Entertainment Tax Repealed by Council," *The Montclarion,* 27 September 1978, p. 1.

91. City Clerk, *City Council Meeting Minutes,* 19 September 1978, p. 2.

92. City Clerk, *City Council Meeting Minutes,* 27 June 1978, p. 2.

93. Soennichsen, "Business Taxes Are Increased, p. 8.

94. City Clerk, *City Council Meeting Minutes,* 27 June 1978, p. 2.

95. City Manager, *Budget Restoration Projection,* p. 1.

96. City Clerk, *City Council Meeting Minutes,* 27 June 1978, p. 2.

97. City Manager, *Jarvis-Gann Budget* (Oakland, Calif.: Office of City Manager, 29 June 1978), p. 1.

98. City Manager, *Four-Million Dollar Hold Back in Ratio to Original Cut* (Oakland, Calif.: Office of the City Manager, 29 June 1978), p. 1.

99. City Clerk, *City Council Meeting Minutes,* 29 June 1978, p. 1.

100. Ibid.

101. Ibid.

102. Ibid.

103. Ibid.

104. Ibid., p. 2.

105. Ibid.

106. These revenue sources and the amount the city was to receive under each were taken from *City Council Meeting Minutes* of 15 June, 23 June, 27 June, and 29 June 1978, previously cited.

107. Director of Budget and Management Services, *Jarvis-Gann Emergency Budget: Fiscal Year 1978–79* (Oakland, Calif.: Office of Budget and Management Services, April 1978), p. 273.

108. These figures were obtained by comparing the city's adopted Jarvis-Gann Emergency Budget (Director of Budget and Management Services, *Contingency Budgets B and C—Jarvis-Gann Emergency Budget: Fiscal Year 1978–79,* April 1978) and the modifications made by the City Council ("Jarvis-Gann Emergency Budget—Fiscal Year 1978-79," Director of Budget and Management Services, to Oakland City Manager, 4 May 1978) with the final Jarvis-Gann Budget (director of Budget and Management Services, *Jarvis-Gann Budget: Fiscal Year 1978–79,* 5 July 1978).

109. Lionel J. Wilson, mayor, to Oakland City Council, 27 June 1978, files of Office of Budget and Management Services, Oakland, Calif.: p. 1.

110. Ibid.

111. Ibid.

112. Sue Soennichsen, "Budget Session Scheduled," *The Montclarion,* 12 July 1978, p. 1; and Cox, "City Council Looks at Future Budgets," sec. E, p. 47.

113. Soennichsen, "Budget Sessions Scheduled," p. 1.

114. Cox, "City Council Looks at Future Budgets," sec. E, p. 47.

115. Cox, "Hiring Freeze to Cut 200," sec. D, p. 25.

116. City Clerk, *City Council Meeting Minutes,* 6 July 1978, p. 1.

117. Ibid., pp. 1–3.

118. Ibid., p. 3.

119. Cox, "Hiring Freeze to Cut 200," sec. D, p. 25. Reprinted with permission.

120. City Clerk, *City Council Meeting Minutes,* 6 July 1978, p. 3.

121. Ibid., p. 2.

122. Ibid., p. 3.

123. Ibid.

124. City Clerk, *City Council Meeting Minutes,* 13 July 1978, pp. 1–2.

125. Ibid., p. 1.

126. Ibid.

127. Ibid.

128. Jayne Williams, acting personnel director, City of Oakland, interview held 28 February 1979.

129. City Clerk, *City Council Meeting Minutes,* 20 July 1978, pp. 1–2.

130. Ibid., p. 1.

131. Ibid.

132. Sue Soennichsen, "City Car Allowance Scrutinized," *The Montclarion*, 16 August 1978, p. 1.

133. Ibid.

134. City Clerk, *City Council Meeting Minutes,* 20 July 1978, p. 2.

135. City Clerk, *City Council Meeting Minutes,* 27 July 1978, pp. 1–2.

136. Ibid., p. 1.

137. Ibid., p. 2.

138. Ibid.

139. Walter Johnson, retirement administration manager, Retirement Administration Department, Oakland, Calif., interview held 28 February 1979.

140. Oakland City Charter, arts. 14 and 20, 5 November 1968.

141. City Clerk, *City Council Meeting Minutes,* 27 July 1978, p. 2.

142. City Clerk, *City Council Meeting Minutes,* 10 August 1978, pp. 1–2.

143. Ibid., p. 1.

144. Ibid.

145. Ibid.

146. Ibid.

147. David Curtis, senior consultant, Arthur Andersen and Co., San Francisco, interview held in Oakland, Calif., 28 February 1979.

148. Sue Soennichsen, "Budget Review," *The Montclarion*, 19 July 1978, p. 4. Reprinted with permission.

149. Ibid.

150. Director of Budget and Management Services, *Public Service Impact Statement—Jarvis-Gann Emergency Budget: Fiscal Year 1978-79,* p. 2. The number of positions reduced in the fire department was modified due to negotiations between the city and the International Association of Fire Fighters. This agreement was contained in city manager and vice president, IAFF, Local 55, *Letter of Understanding,* Oakland, 15 August 1978,

p. 1. The number of program reductions was obtained by comparing the city's adopted Jarvis-Gann Emergency Budget (Director of Budget and Management Services, *Contingency Budgets B and C—Jarvis-Gann Emergency Budget: Fiscal Year 1978–79,* April 1978) with the final Jarvis-Gann Budget (Director of Budget and Management Services, *Jarvis-Gann Budget: Fiscal Year 1978–79,* 5 July 1978).

151. City Clerk, *City Council Meeting Minutes,* 17 October 1978, p. 2.

152. "Recommendation to Pass a Resolution Adopting a Final Budget Plan and Appropriating Additional Nonrestricted Funds to Carry Out Said Final Budget Plan for Fiscal Year 1978–79," Oakland Budget Director to Oakland City Manager, 10 October 1978, files of Office of Budget and Management Services, Oakland, Calif., p. 2.

153. Ibid., p. 1.

154. City Clerk, *City Council Meeting Minutes,* 17 October 1978, p. 2.

155. City Council, *Resolution No. 57602 C.M.S.,* Oakland City Council, Oakland, Calif., 17 October 1978. This resolution also contains many routine phrases required of all budget resolutions.

156. A search through Oakland's two local newspapers, the *Oakland Tribune* and *The Montclarion,* failed to reveal any information on the city council's adoption of Oakland's final Proposition 13 budget.

157. The information contained in this figure was obtained from sources previously cited. Refer to note 37, chapter 4, for the source of the original cut; note 95, chapter 5, for the source of the restorations; and note 137, chapter 5, for the source of the final cut.

158. City Council, *Resolution No. 57317 C.M.S.,* Oakland City Council, Oakland, Calif., 27 June 1978.

159. City Manager, *Adopted Budget for Fiscal Year 1978–79* (Oakland, Calif.: Office of City Manager, October 1978), p. A-7.

160. Ibid.

161. Ibid., p. A-6.

162. The information contained in this table was obtained from sources previously cited. Refer to note 47, chapter 4, for normal budget; note 142, chapter 5, for the Jarvis-Gann budget; and note 137, chapter 5, for the reduction.

163. Director of Budget and Management Services, *Public Service Impact Statement—Jarvis-Gann Budget: Fiscal Year 1978–79,* pp. 3–5. The actual public-service impact of Proposition 13 on city services was taken from this document, unless otherwise noted.

164. Director of Budget and Management Services, *Jarvis-Gann Budget: Fiscal Year 1978–79,* 5 July 1978, p. 6.

165. Arrece Jameson, city clerk, City of Oakland, interview held 6 March 1979.

166. Oakland Assistant City Attorney, to Oakland City Manager, 21

November 1978, files of Office of Budget and Management Services, Oakland, Calif., p. 1.

167. Jayne Williams, acting personnel director, city of Oakland, interview held 6 March 1979.

168. "Impact of Proposition 13 on General Government Departments—FY 1978-79," Oakland Planning Director, to Oakland City Manager, 16 November 1978, files of Office of City Manager, Oakland, Calif., p. 1.

169. "Impact of Proposition 13 Reductions on Retirement Administration," Oakland Retirement Administration Manager, to Oakland City Manager's Office, 21 November 1978, files of Office of City Manager, Oakland, Calif., p. 1.

170. "Impact of Proposition 13 on the Office of Finance," Oakland Acting Director of Finance, to Oakland City Manager's Office, 21 November 1978, files of Office of City Manager, Oakland, Calif., p. 1.

171. James R. Burgardt, data-processing manager, city of Oakland, interview held 6 March 1979.

172. City Council, *Resolution 57201 C.M.S.*, Oakland City Council, Oakland, Calif., 9 May 1978. The portion of this resolution dealing with the Convention Center Fund was not modified.

173. Ibid. The portion of this resolution dealing with tax-increment funds was not modified.

174. The city's normal budget for fiscal year 1978-1979 (City Manager, *Recommended Budget for Fiscal Year 1978-79,* May 1978, pp. B-93 and B-94) contained requests for funding from over thirty community organizations.

175. The listing of closed city facilities was obtained from Director of Budget and Management Services, *Public Service Impact Statement— Jarvis-Gann Budget: Fiscal Year 1978-79,* pp. 3-5.

176. Ernie Cox, "'Walk' Lights to be Discontinued," *Oakland Tribune,* 14 July 1978, sec. E, p. 27.

177. Ernie Cox, "Fire Boxes Get Ax from '13,'" *Oakland Tribune,* 7 July 1978, sec. A, p. 1.

178. Sue Soennichsen, "City's New Lights Nearly Done," *The Montclarion,* 27 September 1978, p. 5.

179. These reductions were contained in City Manager, *Recommended Budget for Fiscal Year 1978-79,* May 1978, p. v. This budget was never considered by the city council due to the passage of Proposition 13 on 6 June 1978.

180. Sue Soennichsen, "City Setup to Receive Hard Review, Overhaul," *The Montclarion,* 16 August 1978, p. 1. Reprinted with permission.

181. Ibid.

182. Ibid.

183. Ibid.

184. Ibid.

185. Donald L. Bierman, budget director, city of Oakland, interview held 13 March 1979.

186. "Budget Reduction Alternatives for FY 1979–80 (nonrestricted funds)," Oakland City Manager, to Oakland City Council, 4 June 1979, files of Office of City Manager, Oakland, Calif., p. 4.

187. Ibid., p. 5 (table 1).

188. Ibid.

189. Ibid.

190. City Manager, *Adopted Budget for Fiscal Year 1978–79,* October 1978, p. A-5.

191. City Manager, "Financial Planning for FY 1978–79," *Administrative Bulletin,* Office of the City Manager, Oakland, Calif., 27 October 1978, p. 1.

192. The financial information for this figure was taken from City Manager, *Adopted Budget for Fiscal Year 1978–79,* p. A-8.

193. "Recommendation to Approve an Ordinance Amending Ordinance Number 9336 C.M.S. (Master Fee Schedule) to Amend Fees Assessed by the City Clerk," Oakland Director of Budget and Management Services, to Oakland City Manager, 17 August 1978, files of Office of City Manager, Oakland, Calif., p. 1.

194. "Recommendation to Approve an Ordinance Amending Ordinance Number 9336 C.M.S. (Master Fee Schedule) to Amend Fees Assessed by the City Planning Department," Oakland Director of Budget and Management Services, to Oakland City Manager, 31 August 1978, files of Office of City Manager, Oakland, Calif., p. 1.

195. "Recommendation to Pass an Amendment to Ordinance No. 9336, Master Fee Schedule, in Order to Increase Certain Parking Fees under the Jurisdiction of the Off-Street Parking Commission," Oakland Management Assistant, to Oakland City Manager, 10 October 1978, files of Office of City Manager, Oakland, Calif., p. 1.

196. "Recommendation to Approve an Ordinance Amending Ordinance Number 9336 C.M.S. (Master Fee Schedule) to Amend Fees Assessed by the Fire Prevention Bureau," Oakland Management Assistant, to Oakland City Manager, 19 October 1978, files of Office of City Manager, Oakland, Calif., p. 1.

197. "Recommendation to Approve an Ordinance Amending Ordinance Number 9336 C.M.S. (Master Fee Schedule) to Amend Fees Assessed by the Office of Parks and Recreation," Oakland Management Assistant, to Oakland City Manager, Oakland, Calif., p. 1.

198. "Recommendation to Pass an Ordinance Amending Ordinance No. 9336 C.M.S. (Master Fee Schedule) to Amend Fees Assessed by the

Office of General Services," Oakland Management Assistant, to Oakland City Manager, 6 December 1978, files of Office of City Manager, Oakland, Calif. p. 1.

199. "Recommendation to Approve an Ordinance Amending Ordinance Number 9336 C.M.S. (Master Fee Schedule) to Amend Fees Assessed by the Police Department," Oakland Management Assistant, to Oakland City Manager, 21 December 1978, files of Office of City Manager, Oakland, Calif., p. 1.

200. "Recommendation to Pass an Ordinance Amending Ordinance No. 9336 C.M.S. (Master Fee Schedule) to Add Fees Assessed by the Office of Finance," Oakland Director of Finance, to Oakland City Manager, 14 February 1979, files of Office of City Manager, Oakland, Calif., p. 1.

201. The planning department's subdivision fee was increased from $125 to $500. This was the most dramatic fee increase.

202. James L. English, management assistant, Oakland Office of Finance, interview held 13 February 1979.

203. The conditions of this agreement were contained in city manager and vice president, International Fire Fighters Association, Local 55, *Letter of Understanding,* Oakland, Calif., 15 August 1978, p. 1.

204. *Oakland Policy Officers Association et al.* v. *City of Oakland et al., Superior Court Case No. 512463-1,* Oakland, Calif., 29 December 1978.

205. Ibid., pp. 35-36.

206. Ibid., p. 36.

207. Ralph Kuchler, assistant to the city attorney, city of Oakland, interview held 13 March 1979.

208. "Recommendation to Pass a Resolution Adopting a Final Budget Plan and Appropriating Additional Nonrestricted Funds to Carry Out Said Final Budget Plan for Fiscal Year 1978-79," p. 3.

209. Marla Taylor, "Proposition 13 Pay Limitation Unconstitutional, Rules State Supreme Court," *California Public Employee Relations Special Reporting Series,* no. 8. (20 February 1979), p. 1.

210. Ibid.

211. Fred Garretson, "Bay's Core Cities Voted 'No' on Proposition 13," *Oakland Tribune,* 18 June 1978, sec. A, p. 9.

212. City Manager, *Adopted Budget for Fiscal Year 1978-79,* p. B-2.

213. Sue Soennichsen, "City Budget Tally," *The Montclarion,* 28 June 1978, p. 4.

214. Of the 227 positions actually eliminated, 42 (19 percent) were management, 28 (12 percent) were sworn police and fire personnel, and 157 (69 percent) were classified as "other" employees.

215. The actual composition of the city's work force was obtained from Data-processing Manager, *Meet and Confer Monthly Salary Report,* Computer Report No. MC84LBYP, Data Processing Department, Oakland

Calif., 23 June 1978. These data reflect the composition of the city's work force prior to 1 July 1978, the effective date of employee layoffs.

216. City Manager, *Layoffs 6/28/78* (Oakland, Calif.: Office of City Manager, 28 June 1978), pp. 1–4. This was the final employee layoff list compiled by the city manager.

217. Ibid.

218. Ernie Cox, "City Council Trims Own Sails," *Oakland Tribune*, 3 August 1978, sec. B, p. 17.

219. Ibid.

220. City Council *Resolution 57691 C.M.S.,* Oakland City Council, Oakland, Calif., 21 November 1978.

221. Ibid.

222. Cox, "City Council Trims Own Sails," sec. B, p. 17.

223. The contracts awarded for supplies and commodities amounted to $5.3 million. Contracts for public-works projects during this same period were $5.8 million. This information was obtained from George S. Schneider, purchasing manager, office of general services, city of Oakland, interview held 15 february 1978; and Carl Kennedy, contract compliance officer, office of public works, city of Oakland, interview held 15 February 1978.

224. Ibid.

225. Ibid.

226. Lino D. Piccardo, "Lies about Proposition 13," editorial, *Oakland Tribune,* 19 July 1978, sec. B, p. 23. Reprinted with permission.

6 Statewide Reaction

Introduction

The requirements of the Jarvis-Gann Initiative became a reality on 1 July 1978. The impact of this measure on local governments, while not as severe as predicted, was still dramatic. The most immediate effect of the initiative was to reduce local government revenues by $7 billion. Statewide, property-tax revenues to local government were decreased from $12.4 billion to $5.4 billion. The distribution of this revenue loss among counties, cities, school districts, and special districts is illustrated in table 6-1.[1] Cities alone lost $800 million. The fiscal void created by this revenue loss was felt by local governments immediately.

Statewide, municipalities eliminated over 3,000 positions.[2] This figure does not include the number of positions not filled in anticipation of the passage of Proposition 13. Many of the public services performed by these positions were eliminated. The magnitude of this reduction was dependent upon a particular government's reliance on property-tax revenues. As indicated in chapter 2, property taxes generally constitute 50 percent of total school revenues, with a reliance range of 20 to 90 percent. Counties typically rely on property taxes for about 35 percent of their funds, with a range of 24 to 49 percent. Cities average 23 percent, but may use from 0 to 60 percent.

Table 6-1
California Property-Tax-Revenue Losses by Type of Government, Fiscal Year 1978-1979

Government	Before Proposition 13[a]	After Proposition 13[a]	Revenue Reduction[a]
Counties[b]	$ 3.8	1.6	2.2
Cities[c]	1.3	0.5	0.8
School districts	6.5	2.9	3.6
Special districts	0.8	0.4	0.4
Totals	$12.4	$5.4	$7.0

[a] Billions of dollars.
[b] Includes city and county of San Francisco.
[c] Excludes city and county of San Francisco.

The reliance of special districts on property-tax revenues varies between 0 and 100 percent.[3] While the Proposition 13 property-tax loss did not directly affect the twelve cities in California which do not levy a property tax, its influence was felt with varying force in other cities.

Local governments took quick action to counteract this revenue loss. While the Proposition 13 mandate imposed severe restrictions on new revenues, no limitations whatsoever were placed on increasing existing user fees and charges. Since the passage of the Jarvis-Gann Initiative, local governments have optimized the use of this revenue-generating tool. Over $100 million in new and additional revenues from a number of different sources have been approved by local elected municipal officials. These revenues resulted from increasing local user fees; licenses and permits; fines, forfeits, and penalties; service charges; and enterprise funds. A breakdown of these revenues is presented in table 6-2.[4]

Subsequent research revealed that nearly half of all cities increased existing taxes and fees.[5] This action stemmed primarily from a change in attitude on the part of local government officials. Two new policies have emerged as a result of Proposition 13. First is the expansion of the pay-as-you-go concept for financing public services. Second is the attitude that, with rapidly escalating costs throughout the marketplace, governments should not let their own charges for services lag in price, forcing all taxpayers to increasingly subsidize what had been largely paid for by users.[6]

In addition to the nontax revenues generated by local governments, the state legislature, as previously noted, adopted legislation distributing the state's surplus revenues. Over $4 billion was allocated to local governments. Cities received $250 million of these funds.[7] The exact status of these funds was not known by local government officials until one week before the new fiscal year. Prior to the passage of Proposition 13, state officials would make no commitment as to the distribution of these funds.

It was subsequently revealed that as early as May 1978, the chairman of the Senate Finance Committee, the chairman of the Assembly Ways and Means Committee, the State Department of Finance, and the leaders of both houses and their respective staffs were involved in conferences, reviewing memoranda and various proposals on distributing state-surplus revenues in anticipation of Proposition 13's passage.[8] There was a consensus of those involved that to inform the public of these efforts would be, in effect, to aid the proponents of the measure by underrating its drastic consequences.[9]

By election day (6 June 1978) both executive and legislative leaders had reached general agreement on the amount of state funds to be allocated to local governments, the controls on disbursement, and the process for allocating these funds to the thousands of local governments in California.[10] Between 6 June 1978 and 24 June 1978, a special legislative-conference

Table 6–2
California, Additional City Revenues from New or Increased Taxes, Fees, and Service Charges, Fiscal Year 1978–1979

Revenue Source	Amount (millions of $)
Taxes and franchises	32.5
Licenses and permits	7.6
Fines, forfeits, and penalties	1.4
Service charges	33.3
Enterprise funds	21.2
Other revenues	6.8
Total additional revenues	102.8

committee, which included the leadership of both houses and their fiscal committees, drafted the final legislation to allocate the state funds. This joint committee was guided by conclusions previously agreed upon prior to the passage of Proposition 13.[11]

Soon after this fiscal relief was provided to local governments, the governor signed Executive Order No. B–45–78, establishing the Commission on Government Reform.[12] By appointing this commission, the governor acknowledged that "there [was] an immediate need to develop fundamental reforms of government tax laws and spending programs at both the state and local levels [of government]."[13] The commission, headed by A. Alan Post, former state legislative analyst, consisted of fourteen members, representing local government, private enterprise, organized labor, academia, the legal profession, and citizen interests. The commission created four working committees to implement its mandate. The final recommendations of the commission, consisting of 117 pages, were issued on 5 February 1979, eight months after the passage of Proposition 13.[14] These recommendations, which have far-reaching implications for both state and local governments, have been submitted to the governor for his consideration.

The state's 1979–1980 legislative session was also dominated by the many issues arising from the implementation of Proposition 13. Various legislative proposals were introduced relating to controls on government spending and taxation. These proposals included placing limitations on user fees and charges assessed by local governments, the allocation of additional state-surplus revenues, and the implementation of additional spending and taxing restraints on both state and local governments. Other Proposition 13-related legislation was introduced, including renters' relief, county assessment practices, the distribution of property taxes, and tax-increment financing. Only two of these measures, additional replacement revenues and the renters' credit, were adopted. These measures were an outgrowth of the fiscal impact created by Proposition 13.

Last but not least, Paul Gann and Howard Jarvis are busily advocating additional governmental taxing and spending limitation proposals. Both catapulted to fame by the famous Jarvis-Gann Initiative, have gone their separate but somewhat related ways. Paul Gann, stating that citizens wanted a tax cut instead of a tax shift, instituted the Spirit of 13 movement aimed at limiting state and local government spending. This initiative was placed on the state's November 1979 special election ballot. It was subsequently approved by the voters. Howard Jarvis, angered over the continued existence of state-surplus revenues, began an initiative drive to eliminate California's income tax and business inventory tax. This measure was defeated by an overwhelming majority of the state's voters.

The above topics are examined in detail in this chapter. The subjects discussed include the efforts of the governor's Commission on Government Reform, the State Legislature's response to Proposition 13, the approval of additional replacement revenues, and the continuing tax and spending reform campaigns of Paul Gann and Howard Jarvis.

Commission on Government Reform

Within three weeks after the passage of Proposition 13, the governor signed Executive Order No. B-45-78,[15] establishing the Commission on Government Reform. In creating this commission, he acknowledged that there was an immediate need to develop fundamental reform of government tax laws and spending programs at both the state and local levels. This group was asked to examine the effects of the Jarvis-Gann Initiative at all levels of government, to review spending and taxing policies throughout the state, and to assess the need for reorganization of state and local governments to eliminate unnecessary programs and overlapping functions. The governor reminded the commission that "there are more than 5,200 units of local government in California, many of them with duplicating or overlapping services and jurisdictions."[16] He urged the commission to "make some kind of sense out of them."[17]

The specific goals of the commission, contained in the governor's Executive Order,[18] were to (1) study the long-term economic impacts of Proposition 13 on state and local government finances; (2) review the tax structures and financing of cities, counties, schools, and other special districts; (3) examine the functions and services provided by cities, counties, schools, and other special districts, and their relationship to one another and the state government; and (4) make recommendations for permanent reforms in the tax, revenue, and spending systems of both state and local government, as well as any reforms the commission believed necessary in the structure of state or local governmental entities.

Twelve members, including a chairman, were initially appointed to this commission. The League of Women Voters subsequently complained that the commission was dominated by too many experts and had insufficient citizen participation. The governor then expanded the membership to include two additional citizen representatives.[19] One was a member of the League of Women Voters, the other was a county supervisor. In the philosophy of Proposition 13, the governor's Executive Order stated that all members of the commission would serve without compensation. They were, however, permitted reimbursement for certain limited expenses. The full text of the governor's mandate is contained in figure 6-1.[20]

The commission immediately organized itself into four working committees. Each had the responsibility to study and propose findings and recommendations in one of the commission's four areas of responsibility. As no funds were provided the commission to accomplish the necessary research and data collection, it solicited the help of any knowledgeable individuals and organizations to volunteer their time and expertise. These individuals and organizations served on fifty-seven separate task forces. The fourteen persons serving on these task forces were mainly drawn from the academic community, while the forty organizations represented a broad spectrum of special purposes, ranging from the American Justice Institute to the Parent Teachers Association to the United Way.[21] The materials provided by these task forces were a major source of information upon which the commission based many of its findings and recommendations.

The commission, in analyzing the impact of Proposition 13, stated, "It [Proposition 13] unquestionably constituted the most significant fiscal act of the people of California in modern times."[22] The commission experienced great difficulty in measuring the effect of the initiative on local governments. A lack of adequate and timely information at the local governmental levels inhibited measurement of the full impact of the proposition. Additionally, at the time of the commission's report, only seven months had elapsed since the implementation of the initiative. For the most part, the commission noted, local governments had not had to significantly adjust their programs to meet lower revenues. Instead, state relief was provided to local governments which, along with available reserves, enabled most local governments to avoid, at least temporarily, the need to reduce or eliminate public services.[23] In short, Senate Bill 154 postponed the full impact of Proposition 13 for one year.

The commission's final report provided one of the most comprehensive analyses of the statewide ramifications of Proposition 13. This analysis included assessing the effect of this measure on property taxes; the federal government; the state government; local governments; public programs and

The Commission on Government Reform

Whereas, the passage of Proposition 13 has drastically reduced tax revenues available to cities, counties, schools and other special districts; and

Whereas, substantial financial assistance from the State will be necessary to enable local governments and districts to provide essential public services; and

Whereas, there is an immediate need to develop fundamental reforms of government tax laws and spending programs at both the State and local levels;

Now, therefore, I, Edmund G. Brown, Jr., Governor of the State of California, by virtue of the power and authority vested in me by the Constitution and statutes of the State of California, do hereby issue this order to become effective immediately:

1. There is established the Commission on Government Reform. Said Commission shall be composed of not more than 20 members appointed by the Governor, with a Chairperson to be designated by the Governor. Members of the Commission shall serve without compensation but shall be reimbursed for actual expenses.

2. The Commission shall meet on a regular basis to:
   (a) study the long-term economic impacts of Proposition 13 on state and local government finances;
   (b) review the tax structures and financing of cities, counties, schools and other special districts; and
   (c) examine the functions and services provided by cities, counties, schools and other special districts, and their relationship to one another and state government.

3. No later than January 15, 1979, the Commission shall deliver to the Governor and the Legislature an interim report summarizing its findings. The Commission's report shall also include recommendations for permanent reforms in the tax, revenue and spending systems of both state and local government, as well as any reforms the Commission believes necessary in the structure of state and local governmental entities.

4. The Commission shall be provided with whatever facilities and personnel are necessary to complete its assignment from within existing structures of state government. The Governor's Executive Secretary shall insure that all necessary resources are made available to the Commission.

5. All state agencies, departments, boards and commissions are hereby directed to assist and cooperate with the Commission in carrying out its responsibilities.

Figure 6–1. Governor of California, Executive Order No. B–45–78, Executive Department, State of California

services; public employees; and planning, land use, and development. The impact of Proposition 13 in these areas is briefly described below.

Property Taxes. Statewide, the property-tax rate was reduced by more than one-half. After allowances for state-funded property-tax reimbursement to local governments, the average property-tax rate in fiscal year 1977–1978 was $10.68 per $100 of assessed valuation. Under the Proposition 13 mandate, the statewide average-property-tax rate is projected to be $4.80 per $100 of assessed valuation. The maximum 1-percent full-cash value is equivalent to $4 per $100 of assessed value. The remaining $0.80 reflects ad valorem tax to retire voter-approved bond indebtedness. This action reduced property-tax revenues from $12.45 billion to $5.40 billion annually, a reduction of over $7 billion.[24]

Federal Government. Proposition 13 has had both direct and indirect effects on federal revenues. As a direct effect, additional federal tax liability resulting from smaller property-tax deductions taken by homeowners and rental, commercial, industrial, and agricultural property owners is expected to increase federal revenues in fiscal year 1978–1979 by over $1 billion. The indirect impact of Proposition 13 will have a countering, but not equal, impact on federal revenues. These factors include reduced purchases and services by the state government and denying cost-of-living increases to state employees and welfare recipients. As a consequence of the dampening effect on the national economy, it is expected that the federal government will lose about $0.4 billion in fiscal year 1978–1979. The net increase in federal tax revenues resulting from Proposition 13 is slightly over $0.6 billion in fiscal year 1978–1979.[25]

State Government. The initiative has had a direct fiscal impact on the state government by increasing certain tax revenues. It has a potential effect of restricting the legislature's ability to increase state taxes or to change the method of computing taxes in a manner which results in an increase, as well as prohibiting the legislature from enacting new taxes based on the value or sale of real property. Additionally, the state appropriated funds to reduce the immediate fiscal impact of Proposition 13 on local governments and public services. As a result, state expenditures in selected programs are expected to be affected in both the current and future budget periods.

On the positive side, the state is estimated to save over $638 million in its property-tax-relief programs. These include the Personal Property Tax Relief Program ($230 million), the Homeowners' Property Tax Relief Program ($400 million), and the Senior Citizens Property Tax Assistance Program ($8.4 million). As a result of the decreased level of property-tax deductions created by the property-tax savings mandated by Proposition 13, the state is estimated to receive additional revenues from personal-income taxes of about $82 million during 1978. The state will also receive an additional $150 million in corporate/noncorporate business tax revenues for the same period. This additional income is offset by the allocation of $5 billion in state-surplus revenues set aside for local governments.[26]

Local Governments. Proposition 13 has had its most severe effect on local governments, reducing local property-tax revenues by $7 billion in fiscal year 1978–1979. This represents a 57 percent decrease in expected property-tax revenues. This revenue loss was partly offset by the distribution of $4.2 billion in state aid. It was also mitigated by an increase in local taxes, fees, and charges amounting to $0.2 billion. The net property-tax loss to local governments, after the receipt of state-surplus revenues and increases in local taxes, fees, and charges, amounted to $2.6 billion. Therefore, the first-year impact of Proposition 13, $7 billion, was reduced by over 60 percent, to $2.6 billion. This was a dramatic revenue loss to counties ($0.7 billion), cities ($0.5 billion), school districts ($1.2 billion), and special districts ($0.2 billion).[27]

Public Programs and Services. Proposition 13 has caused a reprioritization of local programs and services. Some of this impact was due to the restrictions imposed by Senate Bill 154. Local governments have also had to reassess their critical programs and redirect resources to meet these priority services. Public library services, parks and recreational services, and cultural activities were most severely impacted by the redirection of funds to other programs. Counties decreased library services by nearly 12 percent and recreation and cultural activities by almost 18 percent. Cities reduced library services by over 9 percent and parks and recreation programs by nearly 8 percent.

Proposition 13 also adversely affected municipal bonds and local capital formation. Voter-approved bond indebtedness prior to 1 July 1978 was not affected. The 1-percent ceiling imposed by the initiative, and the limited local control over other revenue sources, virtually eliminated the future possibility of general obligation bonding to finance local capital facilities. The 1-percent tax-rate limit also greatly diminished the anticipated tax-increment revenues to local redevelopment agencies. Since Proposition 13 made no provision for outstanding tax-allocation bonds, some of these issues are in danger of default. Until new methods are found for securing long-term municipal debt, local governments are expected either to defer major capital improvements or to increase their use of benefit assessment districts, revenue bonds, and lease-back arrangements.[28]

Public Employees. The expected layoff of public employees resulting from Proposition 13 did not occur on a statewide basis. Approximately one-third of the local government employees who lost their jobs following passage of the initiative have been rehired. Nearly 26,300 local government employees were laid off after Proposition 13. Of this number, nearly 8,500 have been rehired, leaving an estimated net layoff of nearly 17,800 local government employees. Approximately one-half of all employees laid off were in the educational field.

Proposition 13 also directly affected the hiring policies of state and local governments. Immediately after the initiative was approved, the governor imposed a freeze on hiring new state employees. This hiring policy is still in effect. Many local governments adopted similar hiring-freeze policies. As a result of these actions, the state government has not filled over 3,100 positions. At the local government level, nearly 82,000 positions remain vacant on a statewide basis. Also, there is evidence that the rate of attrition in public service has accelerated since Proposition 13 because employees fear additional program reductions and layoffs. On the positive side, the hiring freeze and attrition permit future budgetary reductions in the number of authorized positions without requiring a comparable number of employee layoffs.[29]

Planning, Land Use, and Development. Proposition 13 is also expected to have a significant impact upon local planning and land-use decisions affecting new development. Cities and counties historically have shared with the developer the costs of new or expanded services and improvements required by new development. Proposition 13 makes it difficult, if not impossible, for local governments to finance from general revenue sources any of the additional services and capital-improvement needs created by community growth.

In response to this, many local governments have initiated or increased development fees and charges. This permits new construction to proceed but further adds to the already high cost of housing. Some communities may simply act to limit new growth and development in order to avoid increased service and improvement costs. Since property-tax revenues will not cover the cost of providing governmental services to new developments, a significant lack of incentive exists for cities to encourage new annexations and development. Also in the face of new revenue constraints, many local governments will more thoroughly analyze the economic implications of proposed developments. Additionally, an increasing number of new developments may be denied because adequate public services are not available to meet the increased demand created by such developments.[30]

The commission, after examining the fiscal implications of Proposition 13 and the information provided by its various task forces, arrived at three broad findings relative to the potential for government reform in California. These broad findings encompassed existing inequities in the state's governmental tax system, the potential for economies and cost reductions in government, and the overlap and duplication of programs and services within and among the various levels of government.[31] They determined that a yet-unanswered question arising from Proposition 13 is whether the cost of government can be contained and remaining tax inequities corrected without a significant reduction in services and a mass layoff of public employees. While some argue that both are needed, there is little evidence that the majority of people want significantly less from their government. Most people seem to want to pay less for government and to get what they pay for. Other people, however, want less government, as well as less-costly government and less-intrusive government.

The commission also found that whatever the nature and level of government expenditures in the future, a major challenge of Proposition 13 is to reestablish fiscal balance within and among the state and local governments. In recommending a strategy for achieving fiscal balance, the commission based its proposal on five findings and recommendations. These included an awareness of decreased local government revenues, that property-tax revenues will not rise as fast as inflation, that some local revenues can be generated to help offset the impact of Proposition 13, that local governments can hold down annual increases in their budgets, and that the state is expected to have another budget surplus of about $3 billion.[32] With these factors in mind, the commission found that permanent fiscal balance could be achieved by any combination of four approaches:[33]

1. Direct state assumption of all or part of the cost of local programs and services previously funded from local government revenues.

2. Sharing with local government a defined portion of state-collected-revenue sources on a long-term continuing basis, similar to current state subvention programs.

3. State sharing of revenue with local governments without an assurance of multiyear funding or source of revenue, such as categorical grant programs or the relief provided by Senate Bill 154.

4. Strengthening state revenues to the extent necessary to fund the newly assumed state fiscal obligations.

The commission's specific findings and recommendations impact may facets of state and local governments. These recommendations alone consumed over one-half of the commission's final report. It would be too lengthy to discuss all of these findings and recommendations, many of which pertain to state government, counties, school districts, special districts, and inequities in the present tax system. Only the findings and recommendations affecting local governments are examined. These areas include public-personnel costs, state-mandated costs, improving management processes, potential economies in local government functions, financing public services, and the organization of local government.

Public-Personnel Costs

Merit Increases. Public employees in California almost uniformly receive annual increases of one step (5 percent) in their customary five-step salary ranges based on satisfactory performance. Merit increases have tended to become almost automatic and regarded as a right. There is good cause for not perfunctorily awarding merit increases to all government employees. The commission recommended that employees and employers should be given notice that merit increases are to be awarded only on the basis of merit, not merely by serving a year of employment.[34]

Retirement Systems. One of the critical problems in public employment is the fiscal implications of retirement systems. Costs, in many systems, are in a runaway status. One reason is the multiplicity of systems. The largest system in California is the Public Employees Retirement System. Participation in this system is voluntary and based on individualized contracts between jurisdictions and the state. Therefore, many governments have different retirement systems. Twenty counties are members of the 1937 act retirement system. Three counties and twelve cities have self-administered systems, and thirty-eight cities have private insurance or trust fund systems. Additionally, the state has two other retirement systems: one limited to legislators and judges and one for employees of the University of California. The commission recommended that one public-employee-retirement system be established through a constitutional amendment, and a single public-employee plan be instituted with uniform retirement benefits.[35]

State-Mandated Costs

The commission found that an oppressive number and variety of state mandates are enacted each year. Each further constrains the ability of local governments to establish local expenditure priorities and to allocate available local resources to meet these priorities. Although certain mandates are in the statewide interest and local implementation is preferred over the creation of new state agencies, the cost of implementing new mandates should be fully reimbursed to local governments by the state. Although procedures for reimbursement of mandated costs have been established by statute, the use of disclaimer language in new legislation and the occurrence of anticipated local costs represent a growing financial burden on local governments. The commission recommended that the primary goal of a state-mandated-costs system should be the requirement that the legislature fully fund the mandated costs of legislative and administrative decisions which result in new or increased program costs at the local-governmental level.[36]

Improving Management Processes

Budgeting. The commission was hampered in its investigation into the impact of Proposition 13 on local governments because of inadequate and untimely local government financial information. The commission recommended that local governments be included, on a priority basis, in the proposed new state-budgeting system. The fiscal evaluation of the state allocations to local governments would then reflect consistent, up-to-date, reliable budgetary data. The method of implementing this recommendation should be determined with representation and participation from local governments.[37]

Cash-Flow Management. The commission made three recommendations concerning cash-flow management. One, state and local government finance officers should use an elcctronic fund-transfer system for major routine disbursement functions when the ratio is favorable. Two, local governments should make greater use of the state treasurer's Pooled Investment Programs to maximize the interest return on idle-cash balances. Three, the state legislature should review and streamline constitutional or statutory restrictions inhibiting or prohibiting local governments from contracting with financial institutions for cost-effective cash-management services.[38]

Disposition of Surplus Property. The commission recommended that governmental agencies should review and evaluate their land and real property holdings. They should then dispose of property determined to be in excess of their present and planned needs. Also all "future need" property should be productively used during the interim period. This could be accomplished through the use of a lease, an agreement to rent or share property, or by using properties for such public purposes as parks and recreation.[39]

Potential Economies in Local Government Functions

Local Autonomy. The commission recognized that local governments will be forced by limited revenues to reduce the cost and improve the efficiency of programs and services traditionally provided and funded locally. The commission felt that it is imperative that such decisions be made at the local level and based upon local priorities, and that local officials be given full responsibility and maximum flexibility in making program and expenditure adjustments. The role of the state should be to facilitate such local decisions, not to proscribe or obstruct them.[40]

Local Program Economies. The commission recognized that local program economies can be achieved in a variety of ways and urged local governments to consider such options as private-sector and intergovernmental contracting; consolidation of services; joint purchasing and data processing; joint use of costly or specialized equipment; and the civilianization of administrative, technical, and clerical functions in police and fire agencies.[41]

Deferred Maintenance. Local governments may be unable in the future to finance the major reconstruction or replacement of equipment and facilities which have deteriorated as a result of inadequate maintenance. The unchecked deterioration of public facilities has historically fueled the decay of urban areas, generating an enormous social and economic cost which must be borne by the entire population. The commission specifically urged against the deferral of routine maintenance of public equipment and facilities as an economy measure.[42]

Financing Public Services

Tax Expenditures. A tax expenditure is a revenue loss attributable to provisions of the tax laws which allow a special exclusion, exemption, or deduction from gross income, which in turn provide a special credit, a preferential rate of tax, or a deferral of tax liability. The commission noted that the amount of tax expenditures by local governments has become so large that separate management of tax items could produce significant budgetary changes. The commission recommended that the state implement legislation to establish a requirement for a local government tax-expenditure budget to parallel the requirement for the state budget.[43]

Federal Funds. One of the problems in governmental finance is the limited legislative review of the proposed expenditure of federal appropriations at the local level once a grant has been made by Washington. The commission recommended that local governments develop and implement an improved system for monitoring the receipt and expenditure of federal funds for all purposes.[44]

Local Taxes, Fees, and Charges. The commission determined that user fees and charges can be an efficient and equitable way of financing certain

public services. The willingness of people to pay the cost of a service demonstrates the existence of effective demand, and government can produce the
service at a level which meets the demand. The commission also recognized
the possible disadvantages of new or increased service fees and charges.
These disadvantages include the lack of experience among governments in
pricing their services. High fees might artificially reduce the demand for a
needed service. As fees are increased, low-income people become less able
to pay, thereby diminishing their use of the service. And there are increased
administrative costs associated with the collection and accounting of fees.
The commission also noted the ripple effect of new fees (for example, an
entertainment tax can deprive senior citizens of much enjoyment, development fees are invariably passed on in higher-housing prices, and increased
hospital charges may increase the cost of health insurance).

The commission made several recommendations relative to user fees
and charges. One, local governments, after taking into account the disadvantages of new fees, should consider the adoption of user fees and service
charges where a group of beneficiaries from a specific service can be identified, where the cost of the service can be determined, and where the service
is not found to be of general communitywide benefit. Any fees and charges
should be applied exclusively to the purpose for which the fee or charge is
levied. Two, fees and charges should not deprive disadvantaged citizens of
any needed service, and funds from other sources should be used as necessary to ensure that this does not occur. Three, the enactment of user fees or
service charges to support public services should be considered as an alternative to elimination of that service for reasons of economy.[45]

Proposition 13 Limitations. The commission found that the authority to
impose local taxes is severely constrained by existing law and almost precluded by the two-thirds vote requirement in Proposition 13. The commission made three recommendations to ease this burden.

1. That local governments be given maximum authority and flexibility
in the adoption of local taxes, fees, and charges and that statutory restrictions on such flexibility be removed.

2. That legislation be adopted which would give general law cities
plenary power over municipal affairs, effectively giving such cities the same
powers enjoyed by charter cities to levy local taxes, fees, and service
charges. The intention of this proposal is neither to limit the legislature's
authority to enact comprehensive legislation in an area otherwise deemed a
"municipal affair" nor to restrict in any way the home-rule powers of
chartered cities.

3. That local governments enhance their capacity to set reasonable fees
and to analyze the fiscal effects of such fees by implementing modern cost-
analysis techniques and strengthening cost-accounting procedures.[46]

Sharing of State Revenues with Local Governments. The commission felt that the one-time sharing of state funds with local governments under Senate Bills 154 and 2212 was a necessary and appropriate response to the immediate loss of local revenue resulting from Proposition 13. The commission acknowledged, however, that these pieces of legislation have shifted power and control from local governments to the state and have significantly diminished local discretion and authority over revenues and expenditure priorities. The long-term effect of such legislation is likely to be bigger, more-complex state government and weaker, less-responsive local government with less home rule. California has long been known as a strong home-rule state and one of the most detrimental effects of Proposition 13 will be a diminution of local control. Such legislation, in effect, takes government away from the people. The commission strongly affirmed the view that local governments should have maximum control over local revenues, including shared state revenues, while the state should relieve local government of the burden of funding those functions which are essentially state-wide in nature.

To correct these situations, the commission urged the governor and the legislature to implement permanent reforms which will allow local governments maximum authority to generate local revenues and provide an assured level of state-collected revenue on a continuing basis. Minimum constraints should be imposed on legislation designed to close the gap between local revenues and local needs. Such reforms, implemented in a timely manner, are preferred over a second-year, one-time sharing of state funds similar to Senate Bills 154 and 2212.[47]

Additional State Revenue Sharing. The commission, in acknowledging the problems mentioned above, recommended that in any sharing of additional state revenues local governments be allowed full responsibility and flexibility in the use of such funds according to local expenditure priorities. Specifically, none of the constraints found in Senate Bills 154 and 2212, nor any similar provisions, should be attached to any future program for the sharing of state funds with local governments. These provisions included the "reserve deduction," the prohibition against wage and salary increases, and the prioritization of public services. The reserve deduction penalized local governments that prudently accumulated General-Fund reserves in anticipation of the passage of Proposition 13. The prohibition against wage and salary increases placed public employees at a distinct disadvantage compared to private-sector employees in a time of high inflation, abrogated existing memoranda of understanding, and seriously distorted the local collective-bargaining process. Prioritization in the use of state funds mandated statutory preferences for police, fire, and certain health and educational programs, regardless of local needs and priorities.[48]

Permanent Fiscal Relief. The commission recommended that a defined and guaranteed portion of the state's 4.75-percent sales-tax revenue be distributed among cities and counties to fill the remaining gap between local needs and local revenues after taking into consideration any state assumption of local program costs; adjusted and reallocated property-tax revenues; shared revenue sources which are not directly affected by Proposition 13; and increases in local taxes, fees, and service charges. This additional sales-tax revenue should be appropriated to counties and cities on a per capita basis or by some other means which more nearly represents allocation on the basis of need.[49]

Distribution of Sales and Use Tax. The commission recognized the inequities inherent in the current distribution of sales and use taxes to local governments. Current distribution of these tax funds is based on the point of sale. The recommendation was made to amend the current distribution formula with respect to the existing 1-percent state-collected local sales and use tax to provide for allocation on the basis of population rather than point of sale or by some other means which more nearly represents distribution of these taxes on the basis of local need.[50]

Debt Financing for Local Capital Improvements and Redevelopment. Proposition 13 virtually eliminated the future use of general obligation bonding to finance local capital facilities. It also greatly reduced the effectiveness of tax-increment financing as the major tool for the funding of redevelopment projects. To ameliorate these conditions, the commission urged the governor and legislature to immediately study and evaluate alternative means of financing local capital facilities and redevelopment projects and to develop and adopt implementing legislation on an urgency basis. The commission also recommended that the legislature enact a statute or, if necessary, propose a constitutional amendment which would authorize cities and counties that have utilized tax increments to secure existing obligations for redevelopment and to levy special assessments for the purpose of supplementing property-tax revenues available for repayment of such redevelopment indebtedness, whether bonded or not. As an alternative solution, the recommendation was made to increase the use of benefit assessment districts, revenue bonds, and lease-back arrangements to finance needed facilities and redevelopment activities.[51]

Revenue and Expenditure Limitation Measures. The commission acknowledged that there is considerable public and legislative interest concerning the enactment of constitutional revenue and expenditure limitation measures. Such measures can contain a wide range and variety of provisions which are likely to have far-reaching and unanticipated effects. There is little evidence regarding the impact of these measures from the experience of other states. The commission took no position on any particular revenue or expenditure limitation measure but recommended that a limitation be placed on combined state and local spending and revenues.

The commission favored a limit expressed in terms relating to a fixed percentage of the personal income of all citizens of the state. Such a limit should be established by statute and reinforced by well-defined and statutorily established processes. If this fails, the commission believed that it would probably be necessary to enforce the limit by placing it in the constitution. The commission urged that any such measure should be carefully drafted and that the total and long-range implications should be thoroughly assessed and made public prior to submitting it to a vote of the people.[52]

Private Provision of Public Services. The commission did not find clear evidence that any given public service categorically can be provided more efficiently and effectively by the proprietary or nonproprietary private sector than by government inself. One exception to this is in volunteer-service agencies where operating costs are very low because most services are provided by unpaid staff. The commission did determine, however, that private delivery of public services can offer several advantages. Services may cost less or be performed better as a result of market competition; specialized skills not available within the government agency may be obtained; and such action limits the growth in the number of government employees. Also by contracting out for services, government can avoid large outlay costs for specialized equipment and facilities, provide greater flexibility in program adjustments, and promote increased objectivity in evaluation of the services rendered.

It was noted, however, that these advantages may not be realized and they can be offset by significant disadvantages. These disadvantages were not elaborated. The commission recognized that the opportunities of a particular arrangement vary widely among governmental jurisdictions and the types of service in question.

The commission recommended that state and local officials periodically consider whether purchase-of-service contracts might prove the most efficient and effective means of providing public services. Such periodic review should allow state and local governments to evaluate the need, demand, and appropriate level and structure of the service under current circumstances; the increased (or decreased) availability of qualified contractors; and the experience of other governmental agencies with contracting for comparable services. It was also recommended that the governor and legislature act to remove constitutional and statutory barriers to private delivery of public services in order to give maximum flexibility to state and local officials in the design of services and the allocation of available resources.[53]

Organization of Local Government

The commission noted that both the laws and citizens of California have fostered, allowed, and encouraged an enormously large and complex system of local government full of diversity and disparities. Accordingly, there are many complex and diverse problems to be solved. The commission believed that simplistic and blanket solutions are not the answer. Instead, the commission focused on processes by which the governmental structure and the allocation of functions within each county can be examined in a "bottom-up" approach against such criteria as efficiency, effectiveness, public accessibility, and responsiveness.

To achieve these objectives, the commission made two recommendations: (1) that the governor and the legislature review existing legal and fiscal barriers to local government boundary reform and simplification, with the goal of rationalizing the distribution of local governmental functions and costs, promoting citizen accountability, and providing for the effective delivery of governmental services and programs; and (2) that state legislation be enacted to encourage the establishment of a Local Government Review and Evaluation Commission in each county, with the following authority and goals.

The authority of these commissions would include three areas of responsibility. One, they would make recommendations which would be implemented by all elements of local governments, including private providers of governmental services, joint powers agencies, counties, cities, community college districts, school districts, and special districts. Two, they would look into all matters which could improve the efficiency and effectiveness of the delivery of services by all elements of government at the local level. Such recommendations would be case-specific regarding the structure, process, management, and financing of the delivery of the service examined. Three, these commissions would demand and obtain access to the information needed to carry out their functions.

The goals of these commissions would be to reduce or eliminate unnecessary, unwanted, or lower-priority services; improve the efficiency or effectiveness of the delivery of services; and eliminate unnecessary overlap and duplication of services. They would also strive to improve the management of the public-work force; increase the sharing of equipment, facilities, personnel, and revenue among and within various agencies of government at the different levels; reallocate functions among or within government agencies; and improve intergovernmental coordination and cooperation.

The government review and evaluation commissions would be largely state-funded and given a limited time after the enactment of the enabling legislation to complete their purpose. The products would be a comprehensive public report which would be submitted to the appropriate legislative body of the affected jurisdiction within the county. The recommendations would be implemented with the use of available and appropriate resources.[54]

Proposition 13 primarily affected the revenue posture of California's many local governments. The responses of these governments, to date, have been both varied and diverse. Due to the autonomous nature of local governments, a coordinated response to Proposition 13 is impossible. Yet with fewer funds available to finance public services, a greater degree of planning and reorganization is essential. The leadership and direction for this challenge must come from the state. The commission's findings and recommendations provide the governor with the policy options and directions needed for a comprehensive and timely response to the challenge raised by the Jarvis-Gann Initiative.

The charter and leadership of the commission, its broad responsibilities, the diverse background and personal interests of its members, as well as the wide-ranging membership of its various task forces, all help to legitimize its conclusions. The commission's recommendations, if implemented, could provide an opportunity for the state to emerge from the impact of Proposition 13 with a more rational distribution of governmental functions within a more responsible, cost-effective, and efficient governmental structure. Such a response would also serve to enhance the image of government in the eyes of the public.

It should be kept in mind that the recommendations of the commission are advisory only. They only become operational if the governor or the state legislature take appropriate and timely action. Responsibility for the implementation of administrative and legislative decisions is now in the hands of the state's elected officials. Only time will tell if a rational, coordinated, and comprehensive response to Proposition 13 will be adopted. To date, the prognosis is not favorable. The commission's recommendations received adverse press coverage, and there has been relatively little follow-up by the governor or state legislature. The legislature did, however, approve second-year bailout funds, eliminating the requirement to maintain police and fire services as a condition to receiving aid.

The public's awareness and scrutiny of all levels of government has reached an all-time high. As governments continue to react to Proposition 13, citizen interest is bound to increase, possibly forcing some form of publicly acceptable response. If elected officials fail to respond, the initiative process remains open as a continued vehicle for change. The threat of yet another initiative limiting taxation and spending is a further impetus for governmental reform. The popularity of such an initiative is dependent upon the image projected by governments in their continued response to Proposition 13.

State Legislature's Response

The California Legislature, after the June 1978 election, became preoccupied with various legislative proposals relating to Proposition 13. The legislators moved quickly to provide direct fiscal relief to the state's many local governments. Senate Bills 154 and 2212 were the vehicles used to achieve this goal. Other revenue and taxation measures introduced during this session either fell by the wayside or became moot with the adoption of the Jarvis-Gann Initiative.[55] Senate Bill 1, for example, became null and void as a result of the enactment of the initiative.

These additional legislative proposals, also introduced as a result of the passage of Proposition 13, included restricting state and local government spending,[56] limiting the provisions of the Jarvis-Gann Initiative to residential properties only,[57] subjecting local governments to the scrutiny of the state's "Little Hoover Commission,"[58] and modifying the formula used to allocate the state's surplus revenues.[59] This latter proposal, introduced as a result of intensive lobbying by local governments, would have removed the General-Fund Reserve restrictions imposed by Senate Bills 154 and 2212.

The pace during the last few months of this legislative session was hectic. The many measures introduced relating to Proposition 13, combined with the heavy lobbying by all levels of local governments (cities, counties, school districts, and special districts) and public-employee unions, proved to be unprecedented. Assembly Speaker Leo McCarthy, in referring to this legislative session, said it was "the most chaotic he had seen in ten years as a legislator."[60] The 1977–1978 session adjourned on 1 September 1978. The passage of Proposition 13 made it one of the most unusual in California's history.

The state's 1979 legislative session, which convened on 4 December 1978, was also dominated by Proposition 13-related legislation. Much of the legislation introduced dealt primarily with the many ramifications surrounding the implementation of the Jarvis-Gann Initiative. Because of the plethora of new legislation, the leadership of the assembly established a standing policy committee to review the various proposals relating to Proposition 13. The Assembly Revenue and Taxation Committee acted as the basic clearinghouse committee for such legislation, using the policy committee recommendations as part of its decision-making process. The senate funneled the majority of its Proposition 13-related legislation through its Finance Committee.[61]

Many legislative proposals were introduced to correct inequities inherent in the Jarvis-Gann Initiative,[62] facilitate the repayment of redevelopment projects financed with tax-increment funds,[63] and provide continued fiscal relief to local governments.[64] At the same time that the state legislature was attempting to ease the fiscal constraints created by Proposition 13, legislation was introduced to limit government taxation and spending.[65] Proposals were also introduced to impose restrictions on increases in user fees and charges[66] and provide additional tax relief to renters.[67] Of the many measures considered, only two (increased renters' relief and additional replacement revenues) were adopted.

Many politicians began the session complaining that renters in their districts did not share in the tax benefits provided by Proposition 13.[68] Their response, after months of debate and compromise, was finally agreed upon a few minutes before midnight on the eve of their adjournment.[69] Known as the "renters' bill," Assembly Bill 1151, introduced by Assemblyman Michael Ross (Los Angeles), increased the current renters' income-tax credit of $37 per year to $60 per year for single persons and $137 per year for married couples or heads of households. This credit is applied as a deduction to a renter's annual taxable income. Opponents of this legislation complained bitterly that the bill discriminated against single renters.[70]

After the passage of Proposition 13, the state legislature and the governor had only three weeks in which to approve legislation to distribute the state's surplus revenues to local governments. Despite the time constraints, the bill was enacted in late June. Even with twelve-months lead time, the new long-term bailout plan was not adopted by the legislature until 20 July 1979, and signed by the governor on 24 July 1979, three weeks into the new fiscal year.[71] This fiscal-relief plan, implemented with the passage of Assembly Bill 8, was amended ten times before it was finally approved. It is very confusing, consisting of nearly 200 pages of complex provisions and special formulas.[72] As was the case with Senate Bill 154, subsequent cleanup legislation was adopted (Assembly Bill 1019 and Senate Bill 186) to refine and clarify portions of this bill.

This bill provided for a shift of about one-third of the schools' property-tax revenues to cities, counties, and special districts. More state aid will replace the property-tax loss to education. The shifted property-tax revenues are roughly equal to the fiscal year 1978–1979 state block-grant funds to local agencies.[73] Additionally, the state assumed fiscal responsibility for various health and welfare programs administered by counties. The Local Agency Emergency Loan Fund and the Local Agency Indebtedness Fund, previously established by Senate Bill 154, were maintained.[74] The legislative council's digest, outlining the provisions of Assembly Bill 8, is set forth in figure 6–2.[75] The portions of this legislation pertaining to municipalities are examined in greater detail below.

Revises the California Education Code, California Government Code, Health and Safety Code, Revenue and Taxation Code, and the Welfare and Institutions Code

Provision 1

This bill would provide for a revised method of computing revenue limits of and apportionments to school districts. The amount of the revenue limit would be adjusted pursuant to a specified inflation adjustment.

Provision 2

This bill would require the transfer of a specified amount for the 1979–80 fiscal year to the State School Fund, in lieu of those specific statutes of the Budget Act of 1979, and would make the receipt of such funds subject to certain conditions. It would also enact new statutes requiring the annual transfer of specific amounts from the General Fund to the State School Fund for the 1980–81 fiscal year and fiscal years thereafter.

Provision 3

This bill would provide beginning July 1, 1980, for the annual appropriation of $144,300,000 from the General Fund to the State Teachers' Retirement Fund, such amount to be adjusted for changes in the California Consumer Price Index. This bill would also provide for the annual transfer of additional amounts according to a specified schedule.

Provision 4

This bill would provide for the apportionment of funds to qualifying school districts for the purpose of deferred maintenance.

Provision 5

This bill would enact the Emergency School Classroom Law of 1979 which would authorize the State Allocation Board to acquire portable classrooms and require the board to lease such facilities to qualifying school districts. This bill would appropriate $13,000,000 from the General Fund for this purpose.

Provision 6

This bill would authorize a school district to enter into certain leases and agreements with a nonprofit corporation for the lease of school facilities with provision for the imposition of an owner's development lien by the school district, as specified, on all property in the territory to be benefited to pay the district's lease obligation.

Provision 7

Current law permits, until June 1, 1980, any school district to lease real property or buildings on a district-owned site to private persons, firms, or corporations and authorizes joint use of such buildings. This bill would delete the provision repealing such law as of June 1, 1980.

Figure 6–2. Assembly Bill No. 8, Post-Proposition 13 Legislation

Provision 8

This bill would, among other things, limit the number of years fees imposed for interim classroom and related facilities can be collected following approval of a residential development.

Provision 9

This bill would also affect various miscellaneous provisions such as those relating to the use of bond proceeds available for certain vocational education facilities, provisions relating to staffing ration, provisions defining "miscellaneous funds" for school apportionment purposes, provisions relating to testing of pupil participants in bilingual education programs, and provisions dealing with the use of instructional materials adopted by the State Board of Education.

Provision 10

This bill would specify that, unless the legislature enacts legislation providing otherwise, certain educational programs will become inoperative on specified dates between June 30, 1981, and June 30, 1984.

Provision 11

This bill would provide different methods by which the county auditor would allocate property tax revenues and would provide methods for adjusting such allocations when local agencies have changed jurisdictional areas and functions.

Provision 12

Existing law requires that in determining the amount of specified state funds to be distributed to a local agency, a deduction, as specified, be made if the local agency's general fund reserve balance, as defined, exceeded a specified amount. Existing law also requires funds distributed to a city to be used as specified for police and fire protection programs. This bill would eliminate these requirements as to any city formed during or after fiscal year 1977–78. This bill would revise the definitions of the reserve balances. This bill would require the State Controller to make any necessary reconciliations in state funds allocated to counties and cities no later than August 10, 1979.

Provision 13

Existing law requires that the amount allocated to a county or city and county be reduced by an amount equal to the county or city and county share of state funds received for the support of certain needy children in institutions, boarding homes, and foster homes. This bill would eliminate such reductions.

Provision 14

This bill would also appropriate $221,000 for allocation and distribution by the State Controller to certain cities, as specified.

Provision 15

Under existing law, there is in the State Treasury the Local Agency Indebtedness Fund which is available for loans made by the Pooled Money Investment Board to local agencies for the purposes of making payments due on certain nonvoter approved bonds during the 1978–79

Figure 6–2 continued

fiscal year. This bill would permit the Pooled Money Investment Board to also make such loans during the 1979–80 fiscal year.

Provision 16

The bill would provide for reductions, as specified, in monies for local assistance in fiscal year 1980–81 and thereafter, under specified conditions.

Provision 17

This bill would provide for an audit of financial transactions of local governments by the State Auditor General.

Provision 18

This bill would provide that the state pay the county 10 percent share for Short-Doyle plans and county alcoholism programs until July 1, 1982, except that the state would pay such county share with respect to state hospital services under both programs only until January 1, 1980.

Provision 19

Under existing law, counties pay a specified annual share of the cost of the California Medical Assistance Program and the State Supplementary Program for the aged, blind, and disabled. The share is adjusted annually and is based on the county's taxable assessed value of assessed property. This bill provides for the state assumption of various costs associated with the administration of these programs.

Provision 20

Under existing law, the administration of public social services in each county is a county function and responsibility, except that the State Department of Social Services is required to contract with the federal government for the administration of the State Supplementary Program. This bill would require the department to implement in all counties by July 1, 1984, a centralized delivery system as specified. It would require the department to submit to the legislature a detailed work plan for implementation of the system and annual reports.

Provision 21

This bill would require each county to submit annually to the State Director of Health Services a plan and budget for county health services as defined. The net county costs of health services specified in the budget would be annually appropriated to the County Health Service Fund for allocation to counties, as specified.

Provision 22

This bill provides that no appropriation is made by this act, nor is any obligation created thereby, and provides that the other remedies and procedures for providing reimbursement shall have no application to the bill.

Provision 23

This bill would take effect immediately as an urgency statute.

Figure 6–2 continued

Allocation of Additional Revenues. Cities will receive $207 million in additional property-tax revenues. Cities are scheduled to receive about 83 percent of the amount they obtained under Senate Bill 154. State aid was cut primarily because cities are considered able to utilize other revenue sources, such as user fees and charges, as replacement revenues. This curtailment also enabled the state legislature to reduce state subventions for homeowners' and business inventory exemptions during fiscal year 1979–1980.[76]

Conditions of Receiving Aid. Unlike Senate Bill 154, which contained several restrictions upon those cities accepting state aid, Assembly Bill 8 has few strings attached. The only prohibitions are against detrimental health-care cuts and maintenance of certain adult and summer school programs. These conditions primarily affect counties and school districts. The provision for maintaining police and fire services was not included in this legislation, due to the heavy lobbying from municipalities and the recommendations of the Commission on Government Reform.[77]

Allocation of Property Taxes. Under Senate Bill 154, the increased revenue from the growth of assessed valuation (new construction, changes of ownership, and the 2-percent annual-valuation growth) was distributed proportionately countywide among all jurisdictions, even if only one jurisdiction provided all the necessary new services. Under the provisions of Assembly Bill 8, the revenue from the growth of assessed valuation is allocated among the jurisdictions on the basis of location.[78] This allocation formula is more equitable, since the government providing the services will benefit from the increased revenue.

Jurisdictional Changes. Senate Bill 154 contained no provisions for dividing up property taxes for annexations and incorporations. The 1979 legislation stated that in cases of annexations, incorporations, functional consolidations, or boundary changes, the affected government agencies must mutually agree upon the amount of property taxes to be exchanged. No jurisdictional change can occur until agreement is reached. During such negotiations, the revenues from the annual-tax-growth increment will be impounded. In the case of new incorporations, the Local Agency Formation Commission (LAFCO) will determine the amount of property taxes to be exchanged.[79]

Future Deflator Factor. One of the key provisions of Assembly Bill 8 is a safety valve known as the "deflator" clause. Starting in fiscal year 1980–1981, bailout revenues to local governments could be reduced if state revenues are significantly lower than anticipated. Fifty percent of the shortfall would be reflected in across-the-board reductions in school revenue limits.

The remaining 50 percent would be affected through cuts in state reimbursements to local governments.[80]

The Commission on State Finance was established to monitor the deflator provision. This commission is composed of seven members: four members of the legislature, the director of finance, the state controller, and the state treasurer. The commission is integral to the flow of revenues under this legislation. Its purpose is to forecast state revenues and expenditures and to project the anticipated surplus or deficit on a quarterly basis. The commission has been designed as the state agency charged with determining whether the deflator clause will be triggered.

Local Property-Tax Reductions. Any local agencies receiving property-tax revenues may elect to refund all or part of their annual allocation to property taxpayers within their jurisdiction. Such refunds are to be proportional to the amount of assessed value on each taxpayer's bill. Prior to this provision, no mechanism existed by which to return excess property-tax revenues to property owners.[81] Now if the additional property-tax revenues are not needed, they may appropriately be returned to the taxpayers.

Senate Audits of Local Government Programs. Assembly Bill 8 authorized the state auditor general to conduct financial and performance audits and evaluations of local government programs funded with state bailout funds. The legislature determined that since a significant portion of local budgets are funded by the state, the state should have the capability to determine funding priorities and evaluate the efficiency and necessity of state-supported local programs. The state auditor general will perform these audits at the direction of the legislature and its various committees.[82]

While Senate Bill 154 allocated $4.2 billion to local governments, Assembly Bill 8 authorized $4.9 billion—over a 10-percent increase. A comparison of the disbursement of revenues to local governments under both measures is presented in table 6-3.[83] As this table reveals, counties, school districts, and special districts received additional funds under the second-year bailout plan. Municipalities were the only level of government which received less, by about $100 million. The approval of replacement revenues served again to postpone the true fiscal impact of Proposition 13.

Despite a full year to work on a long-term measure, the legislature spent most of its time and energy on finances and little time on programs. Questions of efficiency, consolidation, and duplication were only briefly raised. Other issues regarding the size and scope of government were given only token consideration. Because the state coffers were still bulging, the pressure to do anything different was not there. The second-year bailout plan provides enough money to keep the structure and organization of local governments much as they were prior to Proposition 13.[84]

Table 6–3
California Comparison of Replacement Revenues SB 154 and AB 8 by Type of Government, Fiscal Year 1979–1980

Government	SB 154 [a]	AB 8 [a]	Difference [a]
Counties [b]	$1.5	$1.6	$0.1
Cities [c]	0.3	0.2	(0.1)
School districts	2.3	2.9	0.6
Special districts	0.1	0.2	0.1
Totals	$4.2	$4.9	$0.7

[a] Billions of dollars.
[b] Includes city and county of San Francisco.
[c] Excludes city and county of San Francisco.

The new replacement revenue package will cost the taxpayers $4.9 billion. The 1981 cost is projected to be $5.3 billion, over a 9-percent increase. Even though the new plan has a so-called deflator valve, the fiscal future looks sound for at least a couple more years. It is difficult to predict if and when a fiscal crunch might ever hit.[85] No matter what the voters had in mind when they voted for Proposition 13, the result of the $7 billion tax cut has been a shift to the state of ever-greater responsibility for the financial well-being of local governments.

In addition to the legislation surrounding the issues raised by Proposition 13, the state legislature, because of mounting public pressure, adopted three proposals to reduce taxes. These measures dealt with indexing the state's income-tax brackets, refunding excess state-disability-insurance funds, and eliminating the state's business license tax. The legislature's version of income indexing will save the typical family $16 during 1980. The refunding of excess revenues from the state's Disability Insurance Fund, amounting to $500 million, will give $91 to every worker earning over $11,400 in 1980. While the business inventory tax was abolished, the state bank and corporation tax was increased from 9 to 9.6 percent to absorb this tax loss.[86] The elimination of this tax served to undermine the recent initiative efforts of Howard Jarvis, discussed in the following section of this chapter.

It was only a short time ago that Proposition 13 was adopted. The ripples of its passage continue to impact government at many levels. The effects of its implementation will be felt for some time to come. The many proposals considered attest to the complexity of California's property-tax initiative. Additional administrative, legislative, and judicial decisions will have to be made before the provisions of the Jarvis-Gann Initiative are fully in place. While citizens did receive immediate property-tax relief, the passage of time will show the real impact of this revenue loss upon local governments. History will ultimately reveal if the underlying philosophy of Proposition 13 becomes a reality.

Voters believed that they were merely getting property-tax relief and sending a message to wasteful government spenders. Without realizing it, they also set in motion some forces for profound changes in California's governmental structure and political environment. Changes in governmental structure have not yet taken place. A change in the political environment is already a reality. The changing political climate involves a sharp turn toward fiscal conservatism.

Throughout the post-Proposition 13 legislative session, many bills failed because they cost too much or created more government controls.[87] Fiscal conservatism was also exhibited by the legislature's attempt to establish some form of long-term governmental taxing and spending controls. In the long run, such a philosophy may serve to contain the growth of government. In the short run, however, it means that citizens, organizations, and special-interest groups seeking legislative solutions to particular problems will face increasing resistance. If government is to hold down spending, citizens must ultimately lower their expectations relative to public services.

The Taxpayers' Revolt Continues

California has served as the initiator of the national taxpayers' revolt. The coauthors of Proposition 13, Paul Gann and Howard Jarvis, are now advocating additional government taxing and spending limitation proposals. Gann, four months after the initiative had passed, organized the Spirit of 13 committee. Jarvis, on election night (6 June 1978) launched the American Tax Reduction Movement. Gann was angered over the state legislature's failure to place a spending limitation measure on California's November 1978 ballot. He decided to do it himself. Jarvis's organization, the American Tax Reduction Movement, Inc., is attempting to impose both taxing and spending limitations on the federal government. This organization is also trying to mandate additional tax cuts on the state of California. The continuing efforts of these pioneers of the taxpayers' revolt are discussed in the following paragraphs.

In Paul Gann's words,

> When people voted for Proposition 13, they voted for a tax cut—not a tax shift. If government can just raise taxes again, then Proposition 13 won't have accomplished anything at all.[88]

> People were mad when they passed Proposition 13. . . . The politicians didn't get the message and have pushed [the initiative] aside as a tax shift,

rather than its intended effect of being a tax cut. The only way to get the job done is to control government spending itself.[89]

When the state legislature failed to place a spending-limitation measure on the ballot, Gann decided to take matters into his own hands. He efforts proved to be very successful.

To force the issue, he founded the Spirit of Prop. 13, Inc., a political committee designed to achieve two purposes: to gather a sufficient number of signatures to qualify a new spending-limitation initiative for the state ballot and to coordinate the extensive campaign efforts to ensure the measure's passage. Many organizations volunteered their services for this effort. The five largest and most active organizations in the movement were the People's Advocate, the American Farm Bureau, the California Association of Realtors, the State Chamber of Commerce, and the National Federation of Independent Businesses.[90] These organizations also solicited the support of their respective members for this cause.

Gann refers to his new measure as an outgrowth of "one of the greatest spontaneous popular movements in recent California history."[91] He may be right. Petition signatures were filed with the secretary of state on 19 March 1979. While 553,790 signatures were needed to qualify the initiative for the ballot, more than 900,000 signatures—nearly twice the number necessary— were obtained. The number of signatures gathered is the third largest ever filed in California for an initiative.[92] On 10 April 1979, the secretary of state announced that the Gann Spending Limitation had qualified for the state's ballot.[93] It was placed on California's November 1979 special election ballot. It met with overwhelming voter approval.

While Proposition 13 was aimed at reducing taxes, the Gann initiative imposes controls on government spending. This proposal, which added a new article to the state constitution, attempts to limit the growth of state and local governments, return surplus revenues to the citizens, and require the state to fund the total costs of programs it mandates on local governments. This measure authorizes spending over the limit if approved by the voters. Governments are allowed to maintain a reasonable level of emergency reserve funds. This initiative became effective in the fiscal year following its adoption. These provisions are examined in greater detail below.[94]

Limits Growth of Government. The initiative restricts the total annual appropriations of state and local governments to changes in the U.S. consumer price index, plus changes in population. The spending limit can be adjusted when responsibility for services is transferred to another governmental entity or to the private sector. Emergency funds are permitted within the limit. Expenditures from these funds are exempted from the limit.

Surplus Revenues. State and local governments are required to return all surplus revenues to citizens within two years. This can be accomplished by a reduction in tax rates or user-fee schedules.

Exceeding the Limit. Spending in excess of the annual appropriation limit can be authorized by the electors of a governmental entity, subject to and in conformity with constitutional and statutory voting requirements. This provision has an automatic "sunset clause" in order to assess the continued need for appropriation changes.

Base Year. The initiative established fiscal year 1978–1979 appropriations as the year upon which the spending limits are based. This base year is intended to reflect the expenditure reductions resulting from the passage of Proposition 13.

State Mandates. The initiative requires the state to fund the costs of all programs it mandates upon local governments. This provision was retroactive to 1 January 1975. Such programs can only be financed from funds within the state's authorized buget-appropriation limit.

State Subventions. State subventions are included in the appropriation limits of recipient local governments. Subventions are excluded from the state's appropriation limit. This permits the state to meet unforeseen revenue losses due to Proposition 13. Local governments may not use the aid to spend in excess of their established appropriation limits.

Exemptions from the Limit. The initiative exempts several items from the spending limits imposed on state and local governments. These exemptions include (1) expenditures of federal funds; (2) appropriations required to comply with mandates of courts and of the federal government; (3) service of existing debt and future bonded-debt approved by the voters; and (4) nontax-supported government services.

Included in the Limit. The initiative covers all state and local government taxes including, but not limited to, state income taxes, property taxes, state and local business taxes, revenue from regulatory licenses, and user charges and fees to the extent that such charges and fees exceed the actual cost of providing the service, product, or regulation.

Interestingly, Howard Jarvis did not endorse Paul Gann's spending limitation. In fact, he accused Gann of promoting it for personal gain which, of course, Gann denied.[95] It appears that this onetime "dynamic duo" of the tax-revolt movement have gone their separate ways. Gann stated that he has not talked with Jarvis since the election of 6 June 1978.[96]

While Gann has chosen to limit his activities to his home state, Jarvis has gone nationwide with his American Tax Reduction Movement.

Jarvis, immediately after the overwhelming approval of Proposition 13, stated that "the job has just begun. The biggest problem is the bloated federal budget."[97] To organize citizens on a national scale to force federal spending and taxing restrictions, he founded the American Tax Reduction Movement, Inc. This organization, headquartered in Los Angeles, is large—and powerful. It has close to 150,000 members, each of whom gave a contribution between $25 and $1,000 for the privilege of membership.[98] Simple multiplication reveals that this organization is also well financed. In fact, it recently opened a Washington office, complete with a full-time paid lobbyist.[99] This is the largest and most powerful taxpayers' organization in the nation's history.

The goals of the American Tax Reduction Movement are fourfold: (1) to organize citizens' tax-reduction drives throughout the nation; (2) to finance a permanent taxpayers' legislative action committee to fight special-interest lobbyists in Washington and the state capitals; (3) to educate leaders in business, government, and the media about the need for tax reform; and (4) to oppose big government and free-spending politicians by exposing their records to the public.[100] These goals set the long-term agenda of Jarvis' movement. The current taxpayers' revolt, Jarvis states, is "the most important movement since the Boston Tea Party."[101]

The primary emphasis of the American Tax Reduction Movement is focused on the federal government. Jarvis hopes to force "big spending cuts, huge tax reductions, and the elimination of inflation caused by government's irresponsible fiscal policies."[102] Legislation sponsored by this group has already been introduced into Congress.[103] This legislation, if adopted, would reduce the federal income tax, reduce federal spending, impose limits on the capital-gains tax, index the federal income-tax structure, and use excess revenues to balance the federal budget. This mandate would be phased in over a four-year period. This phased implementation, Jarvis notes, will enable "Washington to have plenty of time to get used to its new, tighter, purse strings."[104] This bill has already gathered wide, bipartisan support from many members of Congress. The major provisions of this legislation are described below.[105]

Reduce Federal Taxes. A $50 billion annual tax cut would be phased in over a four-year period at a rate of $12.5 billion per year. This plan would be financed by an across-the-board tax reduction of 20 percent and a lowering of the capital-gains tax from its current level of up to 28 percent to a maximum ceiling of 15 percent.

Reduce Federal Spending. A $100 billion annual reduction in spending would also be phased in over a four-year period at a rate of $25 billion annually. This action is intended to ease the current level of deficit spending and arrest the trend of spiraling inflation. Deficit spending is held to be the single major cause of inflation. This proposal is projected to reduce the annual level of deficit spending by 2 percent. The national debt, in theory, would be eliminated in fifty years.

Indexing the Income Tax. Presently, personal-income-tax rates increase as a result of salary increases based on the cost of living. Hence, the taxpayers' purchasing power is greatly diminished by inflated income and higher-tax brackets. This provision would index the federal income-tax brackets to increases in real income only. This would enable taxpayers to maintain much of their purchasing power. It would also reduce federal taxes and government spending.

Jarvis also attempted to mandate a government spending and taxing limitation in his home state—California. To achieve this objective, he organized the Save Prop. 13 Committee, a permanent project of his larger organization. Like Gann, he was also upset over the state's implementation of Proposition 13. He has stated that

> Assembly Speaker Leo McCarthy, a band of politicians, ultraliberal social planners, bureaucrats, welfare workers' organizations, government employee unions and other tax-spending special interests want to "improve" Prop. 13. They want to achieve their own goals in the name of Prop. 13—and throw away [the citizens'] property tax and state income tax savings in the process.[106]

Jarvis was also repulsed by the continued accumulation of state-surplus revenues.[107]

Motivated by these factors, Jarvis planned a new initiative drive to force additional taxing and spending restrictions on California's state government. This measure attempted to reduce the state's personal-income tax, index the state-income-tax system, eliminate the business inventory tax, and freeze the state's sales and use tax at its present level. These provisions, if implemented, would have become effective on 1 January 1981. The details of these provisions are examined below.[108]

Reduce the Personal-Income Tax. The state's personal-income tax would have been reduced by 50 percent. The income tax—the state's second largest revenue source—currently produces $4.8 billion annually. Revenue from this source would have been reduced by one-half, to about $2.4 billion per year. Jarvis noted that between 1974 and 1978 tax collections on personal income increased by 89 percent, while personal income itself increased by only 54 percent.

Indexing the Income Tax. The state's income-tax structure would have been fully indexed and linked to the California consumer price index. This would have reduced the existing taxable income rates by one-half and eliminated paying additional taxes on inflated incomes. Taxes on personal income would have been based on increases in real income. Cost-of-living salary increases would not force workers into higher-tax brackets. This would have represented a tax cut of slightly over 18 percent.

Reduce State Taxes. The state's business inventory tax would have been eliminated. This tax, a varying percentage applied annually to the assessed valuation of a business' inventory, presently yields about $225 million annually. The sales and use tax—the state's largest revenue source—would have been frozen at its present level of 4.75 percent. This tax currently generates about $5 billion annually. Since these revenue sources represent existing taxes, they are exempt from the restrictions imposed by Proposition 13.

The Save Prop. 13 Committee started its signature-gathering drive during the summer of 1979. To qualify its proposal for the state's ballot, nearly 554,000 valid signatures were required.[109] The Spirit of 13, Inc., obtained twice the number of signatures needed to qualify its initiative for the ballot. Jarvis' initiative efforts did not prove to be equally successful. The political climate in California, however, appears to be highly favorable for additional taxing and spending controls, especially in light of the state legislature's implementation of Proposition 13.

There were two somewhat similar initiatives on the state's November 1979 special election and June 1980 general election ballots. While Gann hoped to limit government spending by imposing restrictions on annual budget appropriations, Jarvis attempted to further reduce taxes. This strategy would have also lead to a reduction in government spending. The major difference between the two proposals was in their scope. Gann's measure affected both state and local governments. Jarvis's proposal, on the other hand, would have only affected the state government.

The taxpayers' revolt started with the passage of Proposition 13. This mandate has served as a model for similar taxing and spending limitation measures in other states. Now the federal government is the focus of a new taxpayers' revolt. Jarvis and Gann are at the forefront of this new populist movement. Since June 1978, these gentlemen have been very busy. Both have given speeches almost daily on how to organize taxpayers' revolts. Jarvis is gaining national attention for his fiscal attack on the federal government. He even authors a nationally syndicated column titled "At the Grass Roots," published by over sixty newspapers in many states.[110]

The taxpayers' revolt is spreading nationwide. Citizen interest in controlling government is at an all-time high. Taxpayers have found they have power—the power to limit taxes and control growth of government. This newly found power is likely to be exercised in many states across the nation. It may even be used to control the federal government. The next few years will reveal if the national taxpayers' movement can sustain its initial momentum, a momentum started in California.

Notes

1. California, Assembly, Revenue and Taxation Committee, Willie L. Brown, Jr., chairman, *Summary of Legislation Implementing Proposition 13 for Fiscal Year 1978–79*, (Sacramento, 2 October 1978), p. 87.

2. "Local Government Profile," *Cal-Tax Research Bulletin* (November 1978):4.

3. Richard P. Simpson, "Spotlight on Proposition 13," *Western City Magazine* 53 (April 1978):10.

4. California, State Department of Finance, *A Study of the Local Government Impacts of Propostion 13,* 3 vols. (Sacramento: State Department of Finance, January 1979), vol. 3. p. 16.

5. "Local Government Profile," p. 3. The actual figure was 43 percent.

6. Ibid., p. 9.

7. California, Senate, *Senate Bill 154,* sec. 16250(a) (Sacramento, 24 June 1978), pp. 11–12.

8. Samuel E. Wood, "The 'Sleeper' in Proposition 13: Statewide Planning's Chance to Work," *Cry California*, 3 (Fall 1978):8.

9. Ibid.

10. Ibid.

11. Ibid.

12. California, Governor, *Executive Order No. B–45–78,* Executive Department, Sacramento, Calif., 23 June 1978.

13. Ibid., p. 1.

14. A. Alan Post, chairman, Commission on Government Reform, *Commission on Government Reform—Final Report,* State of California, Sacramento, 5 February 1979.

15. California, Governor, *Executive Order No. B–45–78.*

16. Wood, "The 'Sleeper' in Prop. 13," p. 9.

17. Ibid.

18. California, Governor, *Executive Order No. B–45–78.*

19. Francis Viscount, "Task Force Takes Close Look at Effects of Proposition 13," *Nation's Cities Weekly* 2 (12 February 1979):1.

20. California, Governor, *Executive Order No. B–45–78.*

21. A. Alan Post, chairman, Commission on Government Reform, *Individuals Serving as Task Force Members for the Commission on Govern-*

ment Reform, State of California, Sacramento, 30 August 1978, pp. 1–5; idem, *Organizations Represented on Task Forces of the Commission on Government Reform,* State of California, Sacramento, 30 August 1978, pp. 1–10.

22. A. Alan Post, *Commission on Government Reform—Final Report,* p. 1.

23. Ibid., p. 9.
24. Ibid., pp. 10–12.
25. Ibid., pp. 12–14.
26. Ibid., pp. 14–19.
27. Ibid., pp. 19–24.
28. Ibid., pp. 24–27.
29. Ibid., pp. 27–29.
30. Ibid., 29–31.
31. Ibid., p. 32.
32. Ibid., pp. 33–34.
33. Ibid., pp. 34–35.
34. Ibid., p. 45.
35. Ibid., pp. 45–46.
36. Ibid., p. 47.
37. Ibid., p. 51.
38. Ibid.
39. Ibid.
40. Ibid., p. 52.
41. Ibid.
42. Ibid.
43. Ibid., p. 60.
44. Ibid., pp. 60–61.
45. Ibid., pp. 61–62.
46. Ibid., p. 62.
47. Ibid., pp. 62–63.
48. Ibid., p. 63.
49. Ibid.
50. Ibid., p. 64.
51. Ibid., pp. 64–65.
52. Ibid., p. 65.
53. Ibid., pp. 65–66.
54. Ibid., pp. 68–70.
55. *Legislative Bulletin,* 17 November 1978, p. 6.
56. *Legislative Bulletin,* 18 August 1978, p. 2.
57. *Legislative Bulletin,* 18 July 1978, p. 8.
58. *Legislative Bulletin,* 5 September 1978, p. 2.
59. *Legislative Bulletin,* 13 September 1978, p. 13.

60. Ibid.

61. *Legislative Bulletin,* 23 February 1979, p. 2.

62. Legislation was introduced dealing with the allocation of property taxes (League of California Cities, *Digest of 1979–80 Assembly Bills Affecting Cities,* Report No. 3, League of California Cities, Sacramento, 1979, p. 11); the modifications of assessment practices (League of California Cities, *Digest of 1979–80 Senate Bills Affecting Cities,* Report No. 2, League of California Cities, Sacramento, 1979, p. 4); correcting property-tax inequities ("Property Tax Shift Proposals," Lynn M. Suter, legislative consultant, to Oakland Mayor and City Council, 30 January 1979, files of Oakland City Council, Oakland, Calif., pp. 1–3); and changes of property ownerships (League of California Cities, *Digest of 1979–80 Senate Bills Affecting Cities,* Report No. 3, p. 14).

63. Legislation was introduced to modify Proposition 13 assessment practices (League of California Cities, *Digest of 1979–80 Senate Bills Affecting Cities,* Report No. 3, p. 13); implement special assessments (Ibid., p. 12); use industrial development bonding (*Legislative Bulletin,* 6 April 1979, p. 3).

64. Legislation was introduced to continue the bail out with surplus revenues ("Report on Current Legislative Activities," Lynn M. Suter, legislative consultant, to Oakland Mayor and City Council, 6 April 1979, files of Oakland City Council, Oakland, Calif.,); redistribute a portion of the state sales tax to local governments (Ibid., p. 2); and allocate additional property taxes to local governments (*Legislative Bulletin,* 13 April 1979, pp. 1–2).

65. Five pieces of legislation were introduced dealing with limiting governmental taxation and spending (*Legislative Bulletin,* 16 February 1979, pp. 2, 4, 5, 6, and 7).

66. Several bills were introduced to restrict the ability of local governments to levy user fees and charges (*Legislative Bulletin,* 23 February 1979, p. 1).

67. League of California Cities, *Digest of 1979–80 Assembly Bills Affecting Cities,* Report No. 3, p. 11.

68. John Balzar and Jerry Roberts, "Legislature Approves 5 Tax Breaks," *San Francisco Chronicle,* 15 September 1979, p. 14.

69. "$210-Million State Tax Cut—Big Boost in Renter Credit also Enacted," *Oakland Tribune,* 15 September 1979, sec. A, p. 1.

70. Ibid.

71. Ed Salzman, editor, "California Adopts Long-Term Bailout," *Tax Revolt Digest* 1 (August 1979):3.

72. California, Assembly, *Assembly Bill No. 8* (Sacramento, 24 July 1979).

73. Salzman, "California Adopts Long-Term Bailout," p. 3.

74. California, Assembly, *Assembly Bill No. 8*, secs. 47.3 through 47.7.

75. Ibid., pp. 5–13.

76. *Legislative Bulletin,* 20 July 1979, p. 1.

77. Salzman, "California Adopts Long-Term Bailout," p. 4.

78. Leo T. McCarthy, speaker of the assembly, *Letter to Educators and Civic Leaders,* Office of Assemblyman Leo McCarthy, Sacramento, Calif., 12 June 1979, p. 3 of enclosure 1.

79. Ibid., p. 2 of enclosure 1.

80. Salzman, "California Adopts Long-Term Bailout," p. 3.

81. McCarthy, p. 3 of enclosure 1.

82. California, Assembly, *Assembly Bill No. 8,* secs. 44, 45, and 46.

83. Salzman, "California Adopts Long-Term Bailout Plan," p. 1.

84. Ibid., p. 5.

85. Ibid.

86. Balzar and Roberts, "Legislature Approves 5 Tax Breaks," p. 14.

87. Edward R. Gerber, "Life after Jarvis: The New Political Climate and the Changing Government Structure," *California Journal* 9 (September 1978):292.

88. Paul Gann, *Spirit of 13 Fact Sheet* (Los Angeles: Spirit of 13, Inc., n.d.), p. 1.

89. "Gann Says Initiative on Spending Lid Has Made It," *San Francisco Chronicle,* 17 March 1979, p. 5. Reprinted with permission.

90. Paul Gann, founder of Spirit of 13, Inc., interview held in Oakland, Calif., 23 April 1979.

91. "Gann Says Initiative on Spending Lid Has Made It," p. 5.

92. "'Spirit of 13' Qualifies for State Ballot," *Oakland Tribune,* 11 April 1979, sec. A, p. 7.

93. Ibid.

94. Paul Gann, *Signature Campaign Underway to Limit Government Spending* (Sacramento, Calif.: Spirit of 13, Inc., n.d.), p. 1.

95. "'Spirit of 13' Qualifies for State Ballot," p. 7.

96. Paul Gann, interview, 23 April 1979.

97. Howard Jarvis, *Howard Jarvis' American Tax Reduction Movement* (Los Angeles: American Tax Reduction Movement, Inc., n.d.), p. 1.

98. Peggy Kolkey, administrative assistant to Howard Jarvis, interview held in Oakland, Calif., 23 April 1979.

99. Howard Jarvis, "History in the Making," *Taxing Times* (Los Angeles: American Tax Reduction Movement, Inc., n.d.), p. 2.

100. Howard Jarvis, *Cut Taxes and Reduce Government Spending— American Tax Reduction Movement* (Los Angeles: American Tax Reduction Movement, Inc., n.d.), p. 3.

101. Howard Jarvis, *Letter to "Dear Fellow Taxfighter"* (Los Angeles: American Tax Reduction Movement, Inc., n.d.), p. 4.

102. Jarvis, *Howard Jarvis' American Tax Reduction Movement,* p. 1.

103. American Tax Reduction Movement, Inc.; legislation has been introduced by Congressman Robert K. Dornan, a California Republican, and Senator Thomas Luken, an Ohio Republican, as *H.R. 1000,* United States Congress, Washington, D.C., 1979 Legislative Session.

104. Howard Jarvis, "T.V. Special Kicks Off A.T.R.M. Tax Cut Plan," *Taxing Times* (Los Angeles: American Tax Reduction Movement, Inc., n. d.), p. 1.

105. American Tax Reduction Movement, *A Summary of H.R. 1000— The American Tax Reduction Act of 1979* (Los Angeles: American Tax Reduction Movement, Inc., n.d.), p. 1.

106. Jarvis, *Letter to "Dear Fellow Taxfighter,"* p. 2. Reprinted with permission.

107. "Jarvis Considering Drive against State Income Tax," *Oakland Tribune,* 16 March 1979, sec. C, p. 6.

108. Harvey A. Englander, "Howard Jarvis Announces New Tax Cut Initiative," *Butcher-Forde Consulting News,* 16 April 1979, pp. 1–4.

109. "Jarvis Takes Aim at State Income Tax," *Oakland Tribune* 17 April 1979, sec. A, p. 3.

110. John Kearns, sales manager, Inter-Continental Press Syndicate, interview held in Oakland, Calif., 21 April 1979.

7 Conclusion

Proposition 13 in Retrospect

It was not long ago that the political battles over the merits of Proposition 13 were being fought. Proponents of the initiative were attempting to convince California voters that the measure, in addition to reducing property taxes, would sharply curtail waste in government and eliminate the so-called fat contained in many local government budgets. Virtually the entire political establishment, from the governor on down as well as various vested-interest groups, attempted to persuade citizens otherwise. Opponents of the measure alleged that it was fiscally irresponsible, would produce economic and governmental chaos, and would reduce much-needed and vital public services. While the proponents of the Jarvis-Gann Initiative appear to have won the battle, they face the possibility of losing the war.

Proposition 13 has fulfilled few of the dire predictions made by its opponents. While the initiative was poorly drafted, it withstood the California Supreme Court's test of its constitutionality. It has achieved its intended purpose of reducing existing property taxes, limiting future increases in property taxes, and placing constraints on the ability of the state and local governments to implement new taxes. The state's many homeowners have already reaped the substantial property-tax savings mandated by the initiative. The revenue loss created by Proposition 13, however, has been substantially replaced by the allocation of state-surplus revenues and by increases in local taxes, fees, and user charges. The predictions of severe reductions in public services never became a reality. While many local governments were forced to reduce their budgets, these reductions, for the most part, have had only a marginal impact on prevailing public services.

The impact of Proposition 13 on Oakland's finances and public services was typical of the effect of this measure on other California municipalities. Prior to the election, city politicians claimed that the initiative would have a drastic impact on the city's finances, requiring massive reductions in public services. Police and fire services, public works, and many culture and recreational programs were scheduled to be severely curtailed. Through a combination of state aid, the use of one-time savings, and increases in local taxes, Oakland's city officials restored most of those public services planned to be reduced. The fiscal impact of this measure on the city's finances, though definitely measurable, had only a marginal effect on prevailing public services. The hiring freeze imposed by the city manager greatly reduced the magnitude of required employee terminations.

Oakland's elected officials managed to cope successfully with the passage of Proposition 13. While the political and administrative response of the city's elected and appointed officials contained several shortcomings, the process undertaken proved to be fairly successful. This response commenced almost immediately after the initiative had qualified for the state ballot. The prompt action by city officials provided several months time in which to plan for the eventual adoption of the Jarvis-Gann Initiative. During these months, city staff provided the council with several reports concerning the anticipated consequences of the initiative. These reports prompted the city council to plan for and ultimately adopt a contingency budget which met the expected revenue reductions imposed by the intitiative. More importantly, Oakland's citizens had the opportunity to become involved in the political process. The many public meetings, the budget hearings, and the posting of notices on city facilities served to enhance public awareness of the potential impact of the initiative on the city of Oakland.

Most local government officials in California waited for election day to determine the fate of the initiative before taking any action. By this time, only three weeks remained before the requirements of the initiative became effective. Prior to the election, the status of the state's surplus revenues was uncertain. Therefore, the predicted revenue reduction would require severe cuts in the many services provided by local governments. The wait-and-see approach taken by most local governments left little time to properly plan and implement strategies for coping with the various restrictions mandated by the initiative. Consequently, the citizens of most municipalities were never made aware of the anticipated impact of the initiative. This default of leadership on the part of local elected officials left an informational vacuum. Lacking information to the contrary, citizens generally believed that the initiative would only "reduce the fat" in local governments. The predictions provided by the proponents of the initiative were, in most cities, the only source of information available.

State aid served to delay the real impact of the Jarvis-Gann Initiative for an additional year. In Oakland these funds reduced the magnitude of the city's Propostion 13 revenue loss by nearly one-third. The state legislature has continued aid for yet another year, further postponing the real fiscal impact of the initiative. Additionally, several legislative proposals were considered to provide permanent fiscal relief to California's local governments. If this occurs, the citizens will be angry. What Jarvis and Gann are saying will become a reality. The intent of the initiative—fewer taxes and public services—will have been politically subverted. The tax cut mandated by Proposition 13 will have almost entirely been offset by replacement revenues. This means that the initiative will have resulted in, using Jarvis and Gann's phrase, a tax shift instead of a tax cut.

So far, the major effects of the Jarvis-Gann Initiative have been more political than fiscal or structural. For the most part, local governments are still fiscally alive and operationally well. There have been no major attempts to change or reorganize the structure of California's local governments. The findings of the Commission on Government Reform, while comprehensive and commendable, are only advisory in nature. A long-term political solution to the implementation of Proposition 13 is still pending. The real aftermath of the initiative will not be realized until the state treasury runs out of bailout funds. Time will tell if this day ever comes.

In the meantime, people are waiting and watching. If a suitable political solution to Proposition 13 is not adopted, additional taxing and spending limitation initiatives may loom on the horizon. The mere fact that these alternatives exist may serve to deter the state's politicians from providing permanent replacement revenues. Citizens are also aware that the conditions leading to the accumulation of state-surplus revenues still exist. State taxes have not been lowered. Inflated incomes are still pushing citizens into higher-tax brackets. The vicious circle—more taxes and reduced purchasing power—continues unchanged. The people of California are presently looking to Sacramento to see what action, if any, the state legislature will take to ameliorate these conditions.

Equally as important as the immediate financial impact of Proposition 13 on local governments are its long-term ramifications. By imposing restrictions on increases in assessed valuations, and by limiting property-tax rates levied by local governments, the growth of property-tax revenues has been sharply curtailed. Prior to the mandate, local governments could simply adjust their respective property-tax rates to offset potential budget deficits. This political option for balancing local-government budgets has now been eliminated. What has traditionally been a fairly flexible revenue source has become inelastic. These factors will ultimately serve to restrict the growth of local-government programs and services.

While the real fiscal impact of the initiative has not yet been felt, the revenue reductions mandated by the measure required local governments to reduce their budgets by varying degrees, depending upon the extent of their reliance on property-tax revenues. Statewide, local governments had to reduce their budgets an average of about 10 percent. Although these amounts might not seem significant, the political and administrative effects of reducing governmental operations are the same, regardless of the magnitude of the service cut. It is easy to add on new programs and services in response to the demands of special interests. It is a very difficult and tedious process, however, to decide which programs and services to reduce. Political and administrative strategies for coping with revenue-reducing mandates are likely to become increasingly important. At present, such political and administrative tools do not exist. Lacking more comprehensive and sound approaches to reducing programs and services, local governments are doomed to disjointed and incremental responses to such mandates.

The conditions leading to Proposition 13—high taxes and a general distrust of government—exist in many other states. The popularity of the tax-revolt movement is spreading to many other areas of the nation. Several states are now being forced to cope with successful initiative drives to reduce government taxing and spending. Citizens' initiative drives are alive and well in many other states. In some states, politicians are taking the lead by adopting self-imposed taxing and spending controls. Because of increasing citizen pressure, the political climate in many states is slowly changing. This changing political climate is spreading nationwide. Additionally, many states have already called for a constitutional convention to balance the federal budget. Only a few more states are needed to mandate a constitutional convention on this important issue. Political observers feel that the likelihood of this phenomenon is great.

By analyzing the response taken by Oakland's city officials and learning from their mistakes, a model, or paradigm, can be developed for managing the political and administrative process necessary to cope successfully with revenue-reducing mandates. The following section of this chapter examines Oakland's shortcomings and sets forth a logical and methodically sound approach for managing governmental responses to similar revenue-reducing legislation. It is hoped that this paradigm can be used by both elected and appointed officials in other states and cities that are forced to grapple with similar taxing and spending limitation measures. By utilizing this approach, state and local governments nationwide can effect an orderly transition to a reduced revenue base.

Coping with Revenue-Reducing Mandates

Oakland's city officials simply reacted, sometimes overreacted, to the impending Proposition 13 mandate. Once the initiative had passed, the process of approving replacement revenues was much more deliberately planned. The few key discretionary revenue sources available were increased, by varying degrees, to help ease the mandated property-tax-revenue loss. The entire political and administrative response undertaken in Oakland contained several advantageous aspects worthy of emulation. These included the quick response by city officials to assess the potential impact of the initiative, the timely information provided by the staff reports, the many public meetings and hearings held on this important issue, the adoption of a contingency budget, and the city's extensive public-informational campaign.

On the other hand, Oakland's response contained several inherent weaknesses. These shortcomings included the improper sequence of staff reports, the subjective information contained in these reports, the lack of political leadership and administrative direction in the budget-reduction process, the nature of the budget-reduction strategy itself, the process undertaken to notify the work force of impending terminations, and the lack of a follow-up public-information effort to bridge the gap between the anticipated and actual impact of Proposition 13 on the city. Several factors, including time constraints, lack of previous experience in dealing with revenue-reducing mandates, and the heterogeneous nature of Oakland's body politic, contributed to these faults.

By analyzing Oakland's response to the initiative and correcting these weaknesses, a comprehensive approach can be developed for managing governmental responses to similar revenue-reducing mandates. This approach will enable other elected and appointed officials to efficiently and effectively plan and manage the political and administrative process necessary to deal successfully with potential revenue-reducing mandates. This strategy, which is illustrated sequentially in figure 7-1, is discussed in detail in the following paragraphs.

A great deal of publicity usually surrounds any initiative process, particularly a successful one. Many information sources exist for both elected and appointed officials to become aware of impending initiative movements. Legislative advocacy organizations, professional societies, paid lobbyists, as well as the news media, are all available to keep officials informed on such issues. If a revenue-reducing initiative qualifies for the ballot, a legal interpretation of the measure should be obtained immediately. If the initiative does not qualify for the ballot, a governmental entity can proceed with the preparation of its normal budget. The prevailing political climate usually determines the nature of this process.

The legal opinion should analyze all provisions of the initiative and set forth reasonable assumptions upon which to base relevant revenue projections. Any operational constraints in the initiative, such as mandated deadlines, should also be analyzed. The possible ramifications of the initiative on the city's revenue sources should then be fully examined and analyzed. The opinions contained in the legal analysis should be used as the basis for determining the potential impact of the initiative on a government's revenues.

A financial assessment of the anticipated effect of the initiative on a government's revenue sources should then be undertaken. All possible sources of revenue influenced by the initiative should be examined. Secondary effects on other revenue sources, if any, should also be explored. For example, while Proposition 13 directly affected property taxes, it indirectly influenced the real estate transfer tax since fewer properties are now sold because of increased taxes. Once all relevant revenue sources have been properly assessed, the magnitude of the possible revenue loss should then be determined. Once this has been accomplished, the potential impact of the revenue loss on prevailing public services should be objectively determined.

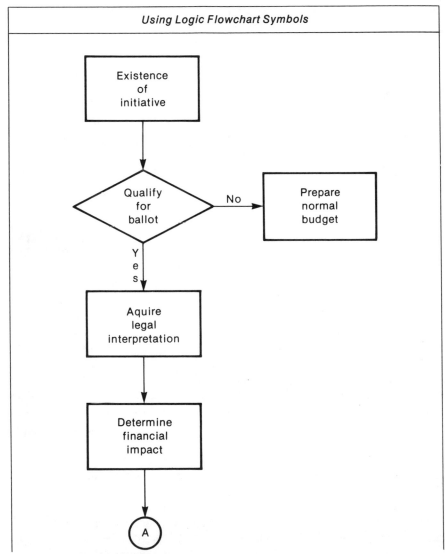

Figure 7-1. Strategy for Managing the Impact of Revenue-Reducing Initiatives

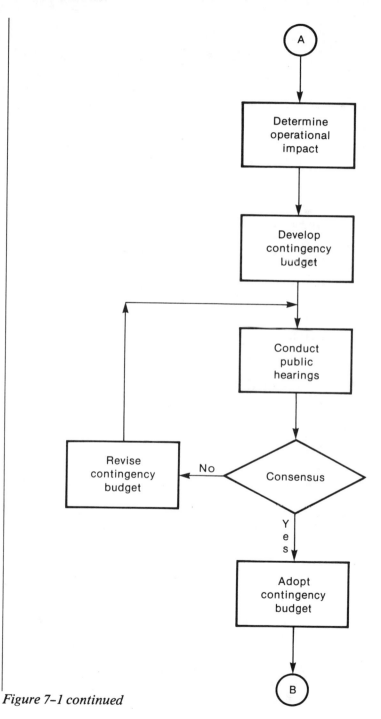

Figure 7-1 continued

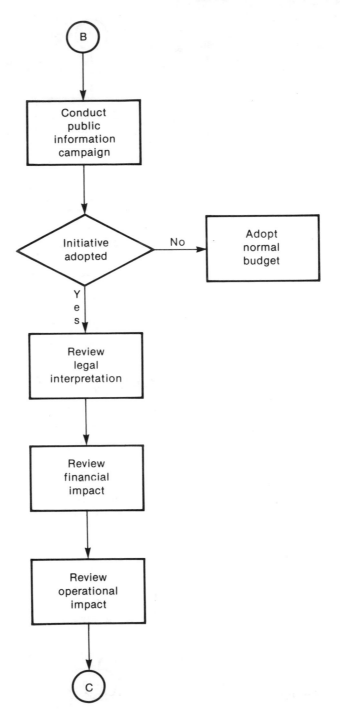

Figure 7-1 continued

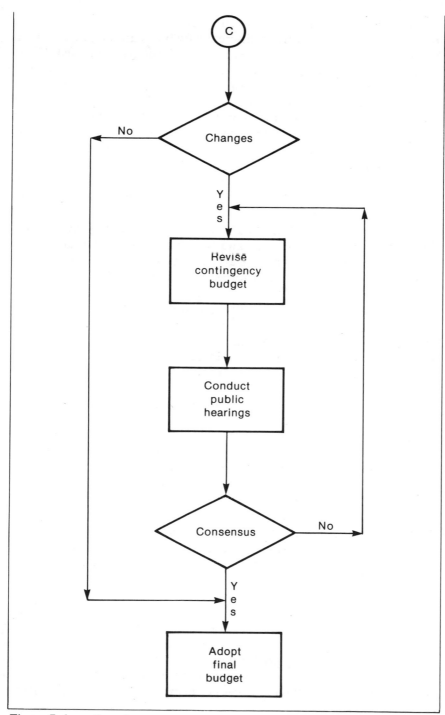

Figure 7–1 continued

The initial operational assessment should examine several factors. If the potential revenue loss affects discretionary funds, the majority of public services provided by a governmental entity will be directly impacted. If non-discretionary revenue sources are reduced, such as specific taxes used to finance selected public services, the analysis need only address the influence of the revenue loss on these services. If other funds can be diverted to pay for these services, however, the impact of diverting such funds away from other public services should be examined. In any event, the operational analysis should be thorough and should assess the anticipated impact of the initiative on appropriate public services. Assessing the impact of the revenue loss on public services, in addition to educating elected officials and creating public awareness, should lead to the next step: the development of a contingency budget.

The contingency budget should be based on the projected level of limited resources—both revenues and fund balances—should the initiative be adopted. Fund balances may be affected due to the implementation of a hiring freeze or administratively forced budgetary savings. The leadership for the development of this budget should normally come from elected officials since they alone are directly responsible to the citizens. When no such leadership exists, it is up to appointed administrative officials to propose a definitive and comprehensive budget-reduction strategy. The strategy selected is the main factor in undertaking a successful budget-reduction plan. Such a strategy is set forth and examined in the subsequent section of this chapter. Once this budget is developed and reductions in public services have been determined and presented to the elected officials, appropriate public hearings and meetings should be scheduled and conducted. The purpose of this is to permit citizens to review the proposed budgetary and service reductions and to provide for proper public input into the political decision-making process. Needless to say, the contingency budget will have to be modified until a consensus is reached by the elected body as to the desirability of service reductions. Once this has been accomplished, the alternative budget should be adopted. Its implementation would be contingent, naturally, upon the passage of the initiative.

As soon as the alternative budget is adopted, citizens should be made aware of the potential impact of the proposed budget reductions on their public services. Any of a combination of several vehicles can be used for this purpose. Additional public meetings, or workshops, can be scheduled to review this impact; press releases can be prepared and disseminated to appropriate members of the news media; a public-service impact statement can be prepared and made available to the public; and notices can be prepared and placed on appropriate public facilities and programs that would either be reduced or eliminated should the contingency budget become a reality. The purpose of this exercise is not to campaign against the initiative, but merely to inform citizens of the possible effect of the anticipated revenue loss on their public services. This effort should be designed to relate projected revenue losses to real reductions in public services. Once the public is informed, it can more intelligently weigh the merits of the initiative based on more objective information. This entire process serves to counteract the reduce-the-fat mentality that prevails in the absence of information to the contrary.

If the initiative is not approved by the voters, the governmental entity can proceed with the adoption of its regular budget. This budget would have assumed the availability of normal funding levels. As previously noted, the prevailing political environment would have determined the nature of this budgetary undertaking. If the initiative is approved, the legal interpretation should immediately be reviewed in light of currently available information. Additional judicial, legislative, or administrative decisions may have been adopted or implemented that would affect the previous legal opinion.

After the legal analysis has been reviewed and modified, as necessary, the financial impact of the mesure should then be appropriately reassessed. Once this has been completed, the impact of the revenue loss on public services should be reevaluated. If changes are required, the contingency budget would have to be revised accordingly. This process should involve a series of additional public hearings in order to achieve a new consensus concerning the revised budget and its impact on public services. Discretionary actions may be taken by elected officials during this period to mitigate the anticipated revenue loss, thereby minimizing the impact of the initiative on public services. Once this process has been completed, the governmental entity's final budget can be adopted. At this point, the contingency budget becomes the normal budget for the ensuing fiscal year. The contingency would have been eliminated with the passage of the initiative.

There are basically two types of revenue-reducing mandates: those implemented through the initiative process and those that are self-imposed by a legislative body. This latter approach to reducing governmental taxing and spending is becoming increasingly popular as use of the initiative process grows. Legislative action in this area is usually taken in reaction to an initiative movement and in order to dissipate support for same. This was the case with Senate Bill 1, the unsuccessful attempt by the California Legislature to provide an alternative to the Jarvis-Gann Initiative.

The previous strategy for managing the impact of revenue-reducing intitiatives can be adapted to legislative mandates. Simply by relabeling a couple of steps, the methodology previously described can be successfully used to accomodate revenue-reducing legislative mandates. The same process undertaken to cope with voter-approved revenue constraints can be used for similar legislatively induced mandates. Figure 7-2 examines the steps that can be taken by public officials to manage this process. Managing the impact of revenue constraints, regardless of their source or magnitude, must be accompanied by a well-thought-out strategy for developing appropriate and logically defensible budget reductions. This brings us to our next topic of discussion.

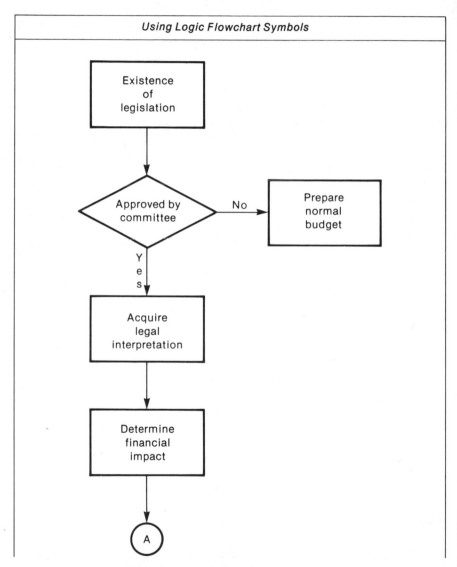

Figure 7–2. Strategy for Managing the Impact of Revenue-Reducing Legislation

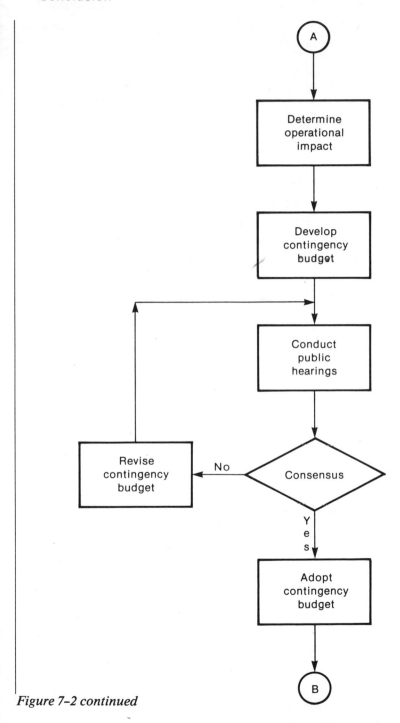

Figure 7–2 continued

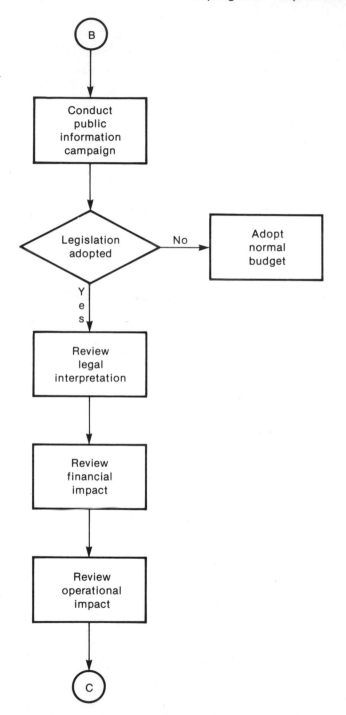

Figure 7–2 continued

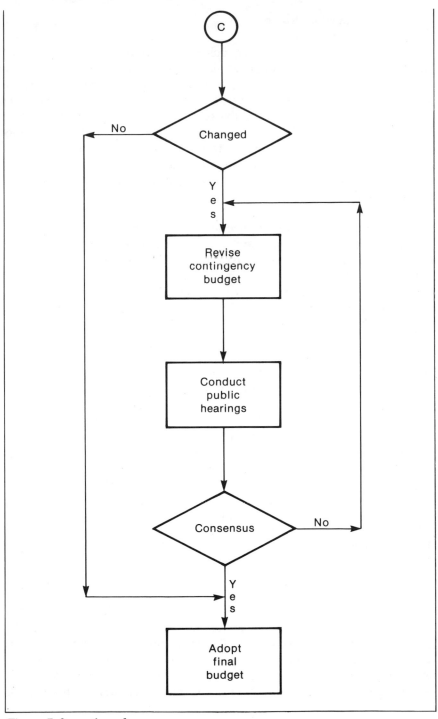

Figure 7–2 continued

The Budget-Reduction Process

One of the greatest problems in reducing any governments's budget is the highly political question of the relative value of public services. All public services are valuable to some extent, at least to those citizens who utilize the service. Elected officials who have tried to reduce public services benefiting only a selected segment of the population can attest to this fact. The people benefiting from the service under consideration for reduction invariably desire, out of their own self-interest, to participate in the political process. Even if the service in question benefits only a few, these citizens jamming the hall of a public meeting can apply a great amount of pressure to the political decision-making process. Hence, it is difficult, sometimes impossible from a political perspective, for elected officials to reduce public services. This phenomenon is a rudimentary fact of political life.

The services that are easiest and most politically expedient to reduce are those provided by staff departments. Such services primarily benefit other line departments and, therefore, have no existing public constituency. Lacking a public advocacy base, the programs offered by these departments fall easy prey to the highly political budget-cutting process. Staff services, unfortunately, usually only consume a relatively small portion of a government's total annual budget. Because of this factor, while reductions in these services can easily be implemented, the magnitude of savings is not great. Such budget reductions only serve to sidestep the question of the relative value of public services. The question of what public services to cut still remains.

It is incumbent upon elected officials to ensure that any budget-reduction process be as objective as possible, taking into consideration the relative value of services to the entire population served. Such a process should be comprehensively planned and methodically sound, containing valid criteria for proposing reductions. Everyone will agree that there are varying levels of public services: some more important than others, some benefiting many, others serving only a few. The relative importance of specific services is the overriding question. To solve this perennial problem, public services should be hierarchically divided into categories based on their relative importance to the entire community.

The continuum of public services ranges from mandated programs that cannot under any circumstances be reduced to public services that have merely evolved because of pressure from special-interest groups. The former programs include basic services and those services mandated by other higher levels of government. The latter programs encompass those services that are nice to have but do not promote the overall safety, health, or welfare of the entire community. Any budget-reduction process must take into consideration the relative value of public services. Such a process will serve to benefit the entire community, rather than selected special-interest groups benefiting from specific public programs.

In an effort to overcome this problem, four separate categories with different criteria have been developed for prioritizing, or placing values on, specific public services. These groupings span the entire continuum of public services, ranging from those programs operating beyond a government's discretionary power to programs that should be reduced, notwithstanding a government's particular financial situation. Prior to undertaking any budget-reduction process, the services provided by a governmental entity should be divided into these categories. This effort will ensure that proposed program reductions take into consideration communitywide interests rather than the narrow interests of special groups. These groupings of public services are further explained below.

Service Level 1. This level encompasses essential public services. These programs, because of their nature, cannot or should not be reduced under any circumstances. Basic minimal levels of police, fire, and public-works services would fall into this category. Public services that are mandated by the federal or state government, those that are necessary to meet debt-service obligations, or those whose net cost to a government's discretionary funds is zero or negative are also included in this category. This latter classification is usually due to the existence of state and federal funding. Programs in this category include services that a government cannot reduce because of legal requirements, programs that provide a minimal level of services to ensure public safety, and programs that are not economically feasible to cut for one reason or another. Programs entirely financed out of user fees should also be included in this category since it would serve no purpose to reduce such programs.

Service Level 2. These programs include those that are highly desirable, but not absolutely essential. The public services provided in this category usually fall into four groupings. One, the particular public service is mandated by the government's elected officials. Two, the services provided make an important and measurable contribution to the safety, health, and general welfare of the entire community. Three, the service in question results in the receipt of substantial funding from another level of government (state or federal). Four, the program generates substantial volunteer services which noticeably contribute to the overall level of services provided to the community. Such volunteer services provide leverage in the form of unpaid personnel. It would be counterproductive to eliminate these programs.

Service Level 3. This is referred to as the nice-but-not-necessary category. Programs in this level have significant value but do not provide essential or necessary public services. These programs do not contribute to the overall health, safety, or general welfare of the entire community. Such programs usually only benefit a specific client group or generate volunteer services which contribute to the level of services provided to only a portion of the community. Such programs usually only generate a portion, if any, of their costs through user fees and receive no outside funding from other governmental agencies. These services are usually initiated at the request of special-interest groups and only benefit the group seeking the service. These groups normally only represent a small portion of the community and do not represent the interests of the majority of citizens.

Service Level 4. Services that fall into this level can be described as the first-to-go programs. If funds are restricted for whatever reasons, these programs would be the first to be eliminated or reduced. Public services provided by such programs contribute to enhance the health, safety, or general welfare of only a minor portion of the community. These services usually augment or increase the basic level of services, and not funding the service would have no great impact on the prevailing level of public services. Outdated, impractical, and frivolous programs providing little benefit to the community would fall into this category. Oftentimes, such programs should be eliminated regardless of financial constraints.

The above criteria are only suggestive. It would lend greater political legitimacy to the budget-reduction process if the criteria used to rank public services were determined by elected officials in a public-forum setting where citizen input could be solicited. Once agreement has been reached on how to place value on different public services, a framework exists upon which to objectively evaluate and group all services provided by a governmental entity. Once this step has been completed, all the programs offered by all departments can be examined, analyzed, and ranked according to predetermined criteria.

Once this important step has been completed and all programs provided by a governmental entity have been properly grouped, proposed budget reductions can then be made. This entire process leads to a more orderly assessment of public services and provides an easy measure upon which to analyze reductions in those public services. Additionally, since programs are usually not eliminated in their entirety, another set of criteria is needed to determine the severity of incremental reductions on prevailing public services.

Generally speaking, governments usually increase their annual budgets by varying increments. Occasionally new programs are added, but the majority of additional funds are usually a result of increases in personnel, inflationary increases in operation and maintenance costs, and increases in the level of existing services. Since budgets are usually formulated in incremental amounts, it stands to reason that when they are cut they are reduced in decremental amounts. It is politically more desirable to merely reduce the level of services provided by a program than to reduce the program entirely. This is an agreeable solution that is mutually advantageous; both elected officials and citizens benefit from such service reductions when cuts must be implemented. This process of reducing a government's budget is referred to as "decremental budgeting." The public services offered by programs are not eliminated but are merely scaled down to meet dwindling resource requirements.

To properly assess proposed budget reductions, their relative impact on prevailing public services must be determined. Many program reductions, due to existing personnel vacancies, may have no substantial impact on public services, while other program reductions may have a measurable influence. Within each of the four service levels, a further breakdown is needed to adequately assess the actual impact of proposed budget reductions on public services. Four categories, or levels of service reductions, have been developed for this purpose.

Reduction Level 1. Program reductions in this category would reduce a substantial portion of a program or eliminate the program entirely. Such reductions would impact essential public services. These program reductions would affect the health, safety, and general welfare of the citizens of the community.

Reduction Level 2. Program reductions in this level would reduce a sizable portion of a program. Essential services, however, would not be affected. The impact of this program reduction would definitely be felt by those citizens using the public service provided by the program being reduced. Such reductions would only marginally influence the health, safety, and general welfare of the community.

Reduction Level 3. These reductions would only reduce a portion of a program. Essential public services would not be altered. This ranking would be given when staff reductions are necessary, but only result in a marginal impact on prevailing public services. Reductions in this category would not substantially affect the safety, health, or welfare of citizens in the community.

Reduction Level 4. Reductions in this grouping would have little or no impact on prevailing public services. They should be implemented regardless of a government's financial condition. This category includes program reductions resulting from reorganizations, planned economies, or simply reductions in operation and maintenance costs that do not affect the services being provided. Such reductions do not influence the safety, health, or general welfare of citizens in any way.

Once the relative importance of public services has been properly determined and the impact of particular budget reductions categorized, program cuts can be implemented. Governments, regardless of their level, will probably never have to eliminate those programs in service levels 1 and 2. Most budget reductions will fall into service levels 3 and 4. Likewise, all budget reductions should be implemented commencing with those reductions in level 4. All budget reductions should be implemented, in ascending order of their severity on public services, to the level desired to balance the budget. This process of undergoing budget reductions—grouping levels of services and the severity of budget reductions—would prove to be both politically and administratively logical from a number of different perspectives.

While this process can be undertaken administratively, the leadership and direction for such an endeavor should come initially from elected officials. Such initiative serves to legitimize the highly political budget-reduction process. If such leadership is not provided, it is incumbent upon appointed administrative officials to propose the use of similar ranking criteria. Regardless of the source, it is necessary to undergo such a process in an era of dwindling resources. Public services must be properly assessed and the severity of budget decrements determined before mandating reductions in public services.

Prior to eliminating any public services for reasons of economy, consideration should first be given to financing the program on a user-fee basis. The willingness of people to pay the cost of a service demonstrates the existence of citizen demand for that service. Financing a program on a user-fee basis enables government to provide a level of service that meets the demand. All fees should be realistically developed to reimburse government for the full expense of providing the service, including applicable overhead costs. Every effort should be made to preserve equity in the delivery of public services. Special consideration should be given to those individuals who may find that a charge for services creates an undue economic hardship.

Taxes and Public Services

The evolution of local governments is analogous to the development of a product on an assembly line. These governments started out as simple models, offering basic services to all citizens at an equitable cost. It is now nearing the end of the assembly-line process, and some people do not like the final product. What has emerged is sometimes perceived as too large, too costly, and containing too many services that most people do not need or utilize. Many people now want to lower the cost, as well as change the product. They want a more affordable model, one without all the "extra" options. They want a government that provides services for their more basic needs. This is the essence of the national taxpayers' movement.

This philosophy raises several important questions relative to the future role of government. These questions apply particularly to state and local governments since they can be easily altered through the use of the increasingly popular initiative process. It is commonly believed that taxes are the price the individual pays for the governmental services he uses. Throughout history, most Americans have agreed with this belief. This premise assumes that all taxes are applied equitably, that governments are responsible and accountable for their spending priorities, and that people are getting that for which they pay.

The current taxpayers' movement places the very essence of this philosophy in question. This is not necessarily a symptom of discontent with taxes per se, but rather with the benefits that taxpayers think they are receiving for their hard-earned money. For elected officials to run for political cover in the face of this discontent or to emerge as born-again Howard Jarvises is an abdication of responsible political leadership. This would be particularly unfortunate to the extent that the cost for such political metamorphoses is borne by those citizens who are least able to bear it.

Citizens voted for Proposition 13 out of their own self-interests. That is to say, people calculated the trade-off between the prospective gain from paying fewer taxes to government and the anticipated loss of their public services. Since most citizens stood to realize an immediate financial benefit from the property-tax relief provided by this initiative, they overwhelmingly supported it. Most people believed that their basic services would not be reduced. For the most part, this belief has held true. Similarly, because many minorities, renters, and poor citizens stood to lose most in the form of government services, they generally voted against the initiative. The California voting pattern reflected this political dichotomy. It all boils down to the fact that many citizens were tired of subsidizing many governmental programs that they do not directly consume.

The public sentiments that led to the landslide victory of the Jarvis-Gann Initiative are increasing, both within and outside California's political boundaries. As these sentiments manifest themselves at voting booths throughout the nation, the political arena is bound to become more turbulent. This change in public attitude is likely to lead to a gradual change in public policy, as politicians are forced to move to the forefront of this "populist" movement. This is bound to lead to more government belt-tightening, a thorough review and evaluation of existing public programs, and closer scrutiny of new public programs. As governmental resources become increasingly scarce, selected public programs will have to be reduced in order to balance budgets. The era of unlimited revenues, brought about by ever-higher taxes, is now coming to an end. This is becoming a political fact of life.

Increasingly, the budget-cutting process will be hard-fought as conflicting values are debated and priorities are established. As the purse strings become tighter, special-interest groups will attempt to influence elected officials in order to maintain their programs. For this effort they are likely to form coalitions. Elected officials cannot merely yield to the pressures brought to bear by these special interests. They must, instead, devise practicable strategies that enable budget reductions to proceed in a logical and defensible manner. This process must take into consideration community-wide interests, as opposed to the narrow concerns of these vested-interest groups. If this does not happen, citizens are likely to continue to vent their frustrations at the polls by mandating additional government taxing and spending controls.

This sorting, prioritizing, and rationally reducing government spending is the most pressing challenge facing public officials today. By analyzing the political and administrative process undertaken by one municipality to cope with such a mandate and by setting forth an orderly and sound strategy for budget reductions, it is hoped that this study has provided insight and clarity to this arduous challenge. A strategy that shows responsibility not only to the beneficiaries of special services, but also to those who always foot the bill, must ultimately prevail.

During the process of coping with Proposition 13, Oakland's city council became intimately familiar with the pressures brought to bear by revenue and expenditure adjustments. The extensive involvement by council members in the budgetary process provided unprecedented insights into city finances and operations. Nearly a decade ago, Arnold Meltsner, in *The Politics of City Revenue,* stated that Oakland's city council merely rubber-stamped staff recommendations concerning revenues and expenditures. The many alternative budgets, staff meetings, work sessions, and public hearings held during the preparation of the city's Proposition 13 budget attest to the fact that Oakland's council has definitely taken a more assertive role in city finances. Times have changed in Oakland. Elected officials elsewhere will increasingly, out of necessity, have to become more involved in their government's budgetary process and the difficult task of sorting out the relative value of public services.

Bibliography

Chapter 2

Amador Valley Joint Union High School District et al. v. *State Board of Equalization et al.* 22 Cal., 3d Series (1978).

"Analysis of SB 1 (Behr) Property Tax Relief and Proposition 8." Oakland Director of Finance, to Oakland City Manager, 10 March 1978. Files of Office of Budget and Management Services, Oakland, Calif.

Benninghoven, Don. *Proposed Jarvis/Gann Constitutional Amendment on June 6, 1978 Ballot.* Sacramento: League of California Cities, 15 February 1978.

California Assembly. Revenue and Taxation Committee. Willie L. Brown, Jr., chairman. *Facts about Proposition 13—the Jarvis-Gann Initiative.* Sacramento, 15 February 1978.

"California Journal Ballot Proposition Analysis." *California Journal* 9 (May 1978): 3–8.

California Senate. *Senate Bills 1* (effective 3 March 1978); *154* (24 June 1978); and *2212* (30 June 1978).

Cool, Shirley, CPA, Greenstein, DeMarta & Rogoff, Certified Public Accountants, Fremont, Calif. Interview, 12 December 1978.

Eu, March Fong. *Statement of Vote: Primary Election, June 6, 1978.* Sacramento, Calif.: Office of Secretary of State, July 1978.

Eu, March Fong, and Hamm, William G. *California Voters Pamphlet: Primary Election, June 6, 1978.* Sacramento, Calif.: Office of Secretary of State, June 1978.

Garretson, Fred. "Bay's Core Cities Voted 'No' on Proposition 13." *Oakland Tribune,* 18 June 1978, sec. A, p. 9.

Goode, John G. *Jarvis-Gann: Implications for Holders of State of California Municipal Issues.* San Francisco: Davis, Skaggs & Co., 8 March 1978.

Hall, Kenneth, and Gerber, Edward R. "Supreme Court Upholds Complete Text of Proposition 13." *Prop. 13 Impact Reporter,* no. 6 (26 September 1978): 13.

Hovey, Juan. "Hottest Election Items—Jarvis-Gann, Behr Bill." *Oakland Tribune,* 25 May 1978, sec. B, p. 21.

League of California Cities. *Summary Analysis of "Jarvis" Initiative.* Sacramento: League of California Cities, January 1978.

People's Advocate and United Organization of Taxpayers. *Statewide: People's Petition to Control Taxation.* Los Angeles: People's Advocate and United Organization of Taxpayers, 1977.

Salzman, Ed. "Jarvis in the High Court: How Much (if any) Will Survive?" *California Journal* 9 (July 1978): 212, 215, and 216.

―――. "The Court Ruling: Constitutional on All Counts." *Tax Revolt Digest* 1 (November 1978): 2.

Simpson, Richard P. "Spotlight on Proposition 13." *Western City Magazine* 53 (April 1978): 9–12.

"Special Bulletin Regarding Property Tax Relief." *Legislative Bulletin* (3 March 1978): 1–2.

Chapter 3

"Analysis of SB 1 (Behr) Property Tax Relief and Proposition 8." Oakland Director of Finance, to Oakland City Manager, 10 March 1978. Files of Office of Budget and Management Services, Oakland, Calif.

California Assembly. Revenue and Taxation Committee. Willie L. Brown, Jr., chairman. *A Brief Analysis of a Proposed Initiative Relating to Property Taxation and Legislative Voting Requirements of Certain Bills by People's Advocate and United Organization of Taxpayers.* Sacramento, 6 December 1977.

City Clerk. *City Council Meeting Minutes.* Oakland, Calif.: Office of City Clerk. 24 January, 14 March, and 28 March 1978.

City Manager. *City of Oakland Adopted Budget: Fiscal Year 1978–79.* Oakland, Calif.: Office of City Manager, November 1978.

Helmke, Martin. *Jarvis-Gann Initiative.* Sacramento: California Senate Office of Research, 13 December 1977.

"Jarvis-Gann Budget Reductions." Oakland Director of Budget and Management Services, to Oakland Department Managers, 15 March 1978. Files of Office of Budget and Management Services, Oakland, Calif.

"Jarvis-Gann Initiative." Oakland City Attorney, to Oakland City Council, 23 February 1978. Files of Office of Budget and Management Services, Oakland, Calif.

"Jarvis-Gann Initiative." Oakland Director of Finance, to Oakland City Manager, 24 January, and 28 February 1978. Files of Office of Budget and Management Services, Oakland, Calif.

League of California Cities. *Summary Analysis of "Jarvis" Initiative.* Sacramento: League of California Cities, January 1978.

People's Advocate and United Organization of Taxpayers. *Statewide: People's Petition to Control Taxation.* Los Angeles: People's Advocate and United Organization of Taxpayers, 1977.

Soennichsen, Sue. "City Run by Old Whites if Proposition 13 Passes?" *The Montclarion,* 5 April 1978, p. 7.

——. "Proposition 13 Warning—Council: 'They'll Get What They Vote for.'" *The Montclarion,* 22 March 1978, p. 1.

Suter, Lynn M. *The Jarvis-Gann Initiative.* Sacramento, Calif.: Office of Lynn Suter, legislative consultant, January 1978.

Chapter 4

Ayres, Gene. "Barbs Fly as Speakers Debate Property-Tax Cut Pros and Cons." *Oakland Tribune,* 2 April 1978, sec. A, p. 1.

——. "Ax Is Set to Fall on City Facilities." *Oakland Tribune,* 10 May 1978, sec. A, p. 4.

City Clerk. *City Council Meeting Minutes.* Oakland, Calif.: Office of City Clerk. 18 April, 27 April, and 9 May 1978.

City Council. *Resolution No. 57201 C.M.S.* Oakland, Calif., 9 May 1978.

City Manager. "Proposition 13—Posters Announcing Possible Closure and/or Service Reductions." *Administrative Bulletin* (Office of City Manager, Oakland, Calif.), 2 May, and 1 June 1978.

——. *Recommended Budget for Fiscal Year 1978-79.* Oakland, Calif.: Office of City Manager, May 1978.

Cox, Ernie. "City Jarvis Notices Irk Cop." *Oakland Tribune,* 5 May 1978, sec. D, p. 27.

——. "City Tightens Purse Strings." *Oakland Tribune,* 16 May 1978, sec. D, p. 27.

——. "Wilson Attacks Trib on Jarvis Coverage." *Oakland Tribune,* 10 May 1978, sec. A, p. 5.

Director of Budget and Management Services. *Contingency Budgets B and C—Jarvis-Gann Emergency Budget: Fiscal Year 1978-79.* Oakland, Calif.: Office of Budget and Management Services, April 1978.

——. *Issue Paper, Jarvis-Gann Alternative Budgets, Fiscal Year 1978-79.* Oakland, Calif.: Office of Budget and Management Services, 25 April 1978.

——. *Jarvis-Gann Emergency Budget: Fiscal Year 1978-79.* Oakland, Calif.: Office of Budget and Management Services, April 1978.

——. *Public Service Impact Statement—Jarvis Gann Emergency Budget: FY 1978-79.* Oakland, Calif.: Office of Budget and Management Services, May 1978.

Foucault, Suzanne, special projects director, League of California Cities, Berkeley, Calif. Interview, 11 January 1979.

"Jarvis-Gann Alternative Budgets." Oakland City Manager, to Oakland City Council, 25 April 1978. Files of Office of Budget and Management Services, Oakland, Calif.

"Jarvis-Gann Budget Reductions." Oakland Director of Budget and Management Services, to Oakland Department Managers, 15 March 1978. Files of Office of Budget and Management Services, Oakland, Calif.

"Jarvis-Gann Emergency Budget—Fiscal Year 1978–79." Oakland Director of Budget and Management Services, to Oakland City Manager, 4 May 1978. Files of Office of Budget and Management Services, Oakland, Calif.

"Jarvis-Gann Emergency Budget—FY 1978–79." Oakland Director of Budget and Management Services, to Oakland City Manager, 14 April 1978. Files of Office of Budget and Management Services, Oakland, Calif.

Jones, Will. "Mayor Wilson's Warning: Jarvis Means City Chaos." *Oakland Tribune,* 2 April 1978, sec. A, p. 1.

Soennichsen, Sue. "Jarvis-Gannized Budget Refined by City Council." *The Montclarion,* 26 April 1978, p. 1.

——. "Prop. 13 Budget Cut 35%, Closing Signs to be Posted." *The Montclarion,* 3 May 1978, p. 1.

——. "Proposition 13 Shadow on Lease." *The Montclarion,* 10 May 1978, p. 5.

Chapter 5

Abernathy, Walter A., executive director, Port of Oakland. Letter to Board of Port Commissioners, Oakland, Calif., 23 June 1978.

Bierman, Donald L., budget director, city of Oakland. Interview, 13 March 1979.

"Budget Reduction Alternatives for FY 1979–80 (Nonrestricted Funds)." Oakland City Manager, to Oakland City Council, 4 June 1978.

Burgardt, James R., data-processing manager, city of Oakland. Interview, 6 March 1979.

California Assembly. Revenue and Taxation Committee. Willie L. Brown, Jr., chairman. *Summary of Legislation Implementing Proposition 13 for Fiscal Year 1978–79.* Sacramento, 2 October 1978.

California Senate. *Senate Bills 154* (effective 24 June 1978), and *2212* (30 June 1978).

City Clerk. *City Council Meeting Minutes.* Oakland, Calif.: Office of City Clerk. 13, 15, 23, 27, and 29 June 1978; 6, 13, 20, and 27 July 1978; 10 August 1978; 19 September 1978; 17 October 1978; and 12 December 1978.

City Council. Resolutions No. 57201 C.M.S. (9 May 1978); No. 57298 C.M.S. (13 June 1978); No. 57317 C.M.S. (27 June 1978); No. 57602

C.M.S. (17 October 1978); and No. 57691 C.M.S. (21 November 1978). Oakland, Calif.

City Manager. *Additional Revenue Projected.* Oakland, Calif.: Office of City Manager, 15 June 1978.

———. *Adopted Budget for Fiscal Year 1978–79.* Oakland, Calif.: Office of City Manager, October 1978.

———. *Budget Restoration Projection.* Oakland, Calif.: Office of City Manager, 27 June 1978.

———. *Effects of Proposition 13 on Property Tax Related Revenue.* Oakland, Calif.: Office of City Manager, 13 June 1978.

———. "Financial Planning for FY 1978–79." *Administrative Bulletin* (Office of City Manager, Oakland, Calif.), 27 October 1978.

———. *Four-Million Dollar Hold Back in Ratio to Original Cut.* Oakland, Calif.: Office of City Manager, 29 June 1978.

———. *Jarvis-Gann Budget.* Oakland, Calif.: Office of City Manager, 29 June 1978.

———. *Layoffs 6/28/78.* Oakland, Calif.: Office of City Manager, 28 June 1978.

———. *Policy Matters for Specific Council Attention.* Oakland, Calif.: Office of City Manager, 13 June 1978.

———. *Priority Decisions for Consideration.* Oakland, Calif.: Office of City Manager, 15 June 1978.

———. *Recommended Budget for Fiscal Year 1978–79.* Oakland, Calif.: Office of City Manager, May 1978.

City Manager and Vice President, International Fire Fighters Association, Local 55. *Letter of Understanding.* Oakland, Calif., August 15, 1978.

Cox, Ernie. "City Council Looks at Future Budgets—Reorganized City Government Seen." *Oakland Tribune,* 5 July 1978, sec. E, p. 47.

———. "City Council Trims Own Sails." *Oakland Tribune,* 3 August 1978, sec. B, p. 17.

———. "City Cuts Could Start Tomorrow." *Oakland Tribune,* 26 June 1978, sec. C, p. 21.

———. "Council Pushes Through New Business Taxes." *Oakland Tribune,* 24 June 1978, sec. A, p. 1.

———. "Council Stalled on Budget Cuts." *Oakland Tribune,* 14 June 1978, sec. C, p. 31.

———. "'Error' Gives City Extra $5.6 Million." *Oakland Tribune,* 15 June 1978, sec. A, p. 1.

———. "Fire Boxes Get Ax from '13'." *Oakland Tribune,* 7 July 1978, sec. A, p. 1.

———. "Hiring Freeze to Cut 200, Save $4 Million Annually." *Oakland Tribune,* 7 July 1978, sec. D, p. 25.

————. "'Walk' Lights to be Discontinued." *Oakland Tribune,* 14 July 1978, sec. E, p. 27.

Curtis, David, senior consultant, Arthur Andersen & Co., San Francisco. Interview, Oakland, Calif., 28 February 1979.

Data-processing Manager, city of Oakland. *Meet and Confer Monthly Salary Report.* Computer Report No. MC84LBYP, data-processing department, Oakland, Calif., 23 June 1978.

Director of Budget and Management Services. *Contingency Budgets B and C—Jarvis-Gann Emergency Budget: Fiscal Year 1978-79.* Oakland, Calif.: Office of Budget and Management Services, April 1978.

————. *Jarvis-Gann Budget—Fiscal Year 1978-79.* Oakland, Calif.: Office of Budget and Management Services, 5 July 1978.

————. *Jarvis-Gann Emergency Budget: Fiscal Year 1978-79.* Oakland, Calif.: Office of Budget and Management Services, April 1978.

————. *Public Service Impact Statement—Jarvis-Gann Emergency Budget: Fiscal Year 1978-79.* Oakland, Calif.: Office of Budget and Management Services, September 1978.

English, James L., management assistant, Office of Finance, city of Oakland. Interview, 13 February 1979.

Eu, March Fong. *Statement of Vote: Primary Election, June 6, 1978.* Sacramento, Calif.: Office of Secretary of State, July 1978.

Garretson, Fred. "Bay's Core Cities Voted 'No' on Proposition 13." *Oakland Tribune,* 18 June 1978, sec. A, p. 9.

"Impact of Proposition 13 on General Government Department—FY 1978-79." Oakland Planning Director, to Oakland City Manager, 16 November 1978. Files of Office of City Manager, Oakland Calif.

"Impact of Proposition 13 on the Office of Finance." Oakland Acting Director of Finance, to Oakland City Manager's Office, 21 November 1978. Files of Office of City Manager, Oakland, Calif.

"Impact of Proposition 13 Reductions on Retirement Administration." Oakland Retirement Administration Manager, to Oakland City Manager's Office, 21 November 1978. Files of Office of City Manager, Oakland, Calif.

Jameson, Arrece, city clerk, city of Oakland. Interview, 6 March 1979.

"Jarvis-Gann Emergency Buget—Fiscal Year 1978-79." Oakland Director of Budget and Management Services, to Oakland City Manager, 4 May 1978. Files of Office of Budget and Management Services, Oakland, Calif.

Johnson, Walter, retirement administration manager, city of Oakland. Interview, 28 February 1979.

Kennedy, Carl, contract compliance officer, Office of Public Works, city of Oakland. Interview, 15 February 1978.

Kuchler, Ralph, assistant to the city attorney, city of Oakland. Interview, 13 March 1979.

Legislative Bulletin (League of California Cities). 9 June 1978.

Oakland Assistant City Attorney, to Oakland City Manager, 21 November 1978. Files of Office of Budget and Management Services, Oakland, Calif.

Oakland City Charter. Arts. 14 and 20; 5 November 1968.

Oakland Police Officers' Association et al. v. *City of Oakland et al. Superior Court Case No. 512463-1,* Oakland, Calif., 29 December 1978.

Piccardo, Lino D. "Lies about Proposition 13." Editorial, *Oakland Tribune,* 19 July 1978, sec. B, p. 23.

"Recommendation to Approve an Ordinance Amending Ordinance Number 9336 C.M.S. (Master Fee Schedule) to Amend Fees Assessed by the City Clerk." Oakland Director of Budget and Management Services, to Oakland City Manager, 17 August 1978. Files of Office of Budget and Management Services, Oakland, Calif.

"Recommendation to Approve an Ordinance Amending Ordinance Number 9336 C.M.S. (Master Fee Schedule) to Amend Fees Assessed by the City Planning Department." Oakland Director of Budget and Management Services, to Oakland City Manager, 31 August 1978. Files of Office of Budget and Management Services, Oakland, Calif.

"Recommendation to Approve an Ordinance Amending Ordinance Number 9336 C.M.S. (Master Fee Schedule) to Amend Fees Assessed by the Fire Prevention Bureau." Oakland Management Assistant, to Oakland City Manager, 19 October 1978. Files of Office of Budget and Management Services, Oakland, Calif.

"Recommendation to Pass an Ordinance Amending Ordinance No. 9336 C.M.S. (Master Fee Schedule) to Amend Fees Assessed by the Office of General Services." Oakland Management Assistant, to Oakland City Manager, 6 December 1978. Files of Office of Finance, Oakland, Calif.

"Recommendation to Approve an Ordinance Amending Ordinance Number 9336 C.M.S. (Master Fee Schedule) to Amend Fees Assessed by the Office of Parks and Recreation." Oakland Management Assistant, to Oakland City Manager, 21 November 1978. Files of Office of Finance, Oakland, Calif.

"Recommendation to Approve an Ordinance Amending Ordinance Number 9336 C.M.S. (Master Fee Schedule) to Amend Fees Assessed by the Police Department." Oakland Management Assistant, to Oakland City Manager, 21 December 1978. Files of Office of Finance, Oakland, Calif.

"Recommendation to Pass an Amendment to Ordinance No. 9336, Master Fee Schedule, in Order to Increase Certain Parking Fees under the

Jurisdiction of the Off-Street Parking Commission.'' Oakland Management Assistant, to Oakland City Manager, 10 October 1978. Files of Office of Budget and Management Services, Oakland, Calif.

"Recommendation to Pass an Ordinance Amending Ordinance No. 9336 C.M.S. (Master Fee Schedule) to Add Fees Assessed by the Office of Finance.'' Oakland Director of Finance, to Oakland City Manager, 14 February 1979. Files of Office of the City Manager, Oakland, Calif.

"Recommendation to Pass a Resolution Adopting a Final Budget Plan and Appropriating Additional Nonrestricted Funds to Carry Out Said Final Budget Plan for Fiscal Year 1978-79.'' Oakland Budget Director, to Oakland City Manager, 10 October 1978. Files of Office of Budget and Management Services, Oakland, Calif.

"Revenue Alternatives.'' Oakland Assistant to Director of Finance, to Oakland City Manager, 22 June 1978. Files of Office of Budget and Management Services, Oakland, Calif.

Schneider, George S., purchasing manager, Office of General Services, city of Oakland. Interview, 15 February 1978.

Soennichsen, Sue. "Budget Review.'' *The Montclarion,* 19 July 1978, p. 4.

————. "Budget Sessions Scheduled.'' *The Montclarion,* 12 July 1978, p. 1.

————. "Business Taxes Are Increased.'' *The Montclarion,* 28 June 1978, p. 1.

————. "City Budget Tally.'' *The Montclarion,* 28 June 1978, p. 4.

————. "City Car Allowance Scrutinized.'' *The Montclarion,* 16 August 1978, p. 1.

————. "City Setup to Receive Hard Review, Overhaul.'' *The Montclarion,* 16 August 1978, p. 1.

————. "City's New Lights Nearly Done.'' *The Montclarion,* 27 September 1978, p. 5.

————. "Employee License Fee Puts Council in Quandary.'' *The Montclarion,* 7 July 1978, p. 1.

————. "Entertainment Tax Repealed by Council.'' *The Montclarion,* 27 September 1978, p. 1.

————. "Gloom and Rumors in Oakland's City Hall.'' *The Montclarion,* 14 June 1978, p. 1.

————. "Oakland's Vote on Jarvis: A Plus in Sacramento.'' *The Montclarion,* 21 June 1978, p. 1.

————. "Reductions in Proposition 13 Cutbacks.'' *The Montclarion,* 21 June 1978, p. 1.

————. "To Junket or Not to Junket.'' *The Montclarion,* 14 June 1978, p. 1.

Spencer, Richard. "Oakland Employee Fee Upheld.'' *Oakland Tribune,* 30 May 1978, sec. A, p. 1.

"State OK's '13' Bailout Funds." *Oakland Tribune,* 8 March 1979, sec. B, p. 5.

Suter, Lynn M. *Legislative Committee Report.* Sacramento, Calif.: Office of Lynn Suter, legislative consultant, 13 February 1979.

Taylor, Marla. "Proposition 13 Pay Limitation Unconstitutional, Rules State Supreme Court." *California Public Employee Relations Special Reporting Series,* no. 8 (20 February 1979): 1–2.

Williams, Jayne, acting personnel director, city of Oakland. Interviews, 28 February 1979 and 6 March 1979.

Wilson, Lionel J., mayor, city of Oakland, to Oakland City Council, 27 June 1978. Files of Office of Budget and Management Services, Oakland, Calif.

Wood, Barbara. "Two More Taxes Okayed by Council." *The Montclarion,* 5 July 1978, p. 1.

Wood, Samuel E. "The 'Sleeper' in Proposition 13: Statewide Planning's Chance to Work." *Cry California* 3 (Fall 1978): 7–13.

Chapter 6

American Tax Reduction Movement. *A Summary of H.R. 1000—The American Tax Reduction Act of 1979.* Los Angeles: American Tax Reduction Movement, Inc., n.d.

Balzar, John, and Roberts, Jerry. "Legislature Approves 5 Tax Breaks." *San Francisco Chronicle,* 15 September 1979, p. 14.

California Assembly. *Assembly Bill 8* (effective 24 July 1978).

———. Revenue and Taxation Committee. Willie L. Brown, Jr., chairman. *Summary of Legislation Implementing Proposition 13 for Fiscal Year 1978–79.* Sacramento, 2 October 1978.

California Governor. *Executive Order No. B-45-78.* Executive Department, Sacramento, 23 June 1978.

California Senate. *Senate Bill 154* (effective 24 June 1978).

California State Department of Finance. *A Study of the Local Government Impacts of Proposition 13,* 3 vols. Sacramento: State Department of Finance, January 1979.

Englander, Harvey A. "Howard Jarvis Announces New Tax Cut Initiative." *Butcher-Forde Consulting News,* 16 April 1979.

Gann, Paul, founder of Spirit of 13, Inc. Interview, Oakland, Calif., 23 April 1979.

———. *Signature Campaign Underway to Limit Government Spending.* Sacramento, Calif.: Spirit of 13, Inc., n.d.

———. *Spirit of 13 Fact Sheet.* Los Angeles: Spirit of 13, Inc., n.d.

"Gann Says Initiative on Spending Lid Has Made It." *San Francisco Chronicle,* 17 March 1979, p. 5.

Gerber, Edward R. "Life after Jarvis: The New Political Climate and the Changing Government Structure." *California Journal* 9 (September 1978): 291–293.

Jarvis, Howard. *Cut Taxes and Reduce Government Spending—American Tax Reduction Movement.* Los Angeles: American Tax Reduction Movement, Inc., n.d.

———. "History in the Making." *Taxing Times.* Los Angeles: American Tax Reduction Movement, Inc., n.d.

———. *Howard Jarvis' American Tax Reduction Movement.* Los Angeles: American Tax Reduction Movement, Inc., n.d.

———. *Letter to "Dear Fellow Taxfighters."* Los Angeles: American Tax Reduction Movement, Inc., n.d.

———. "T.V. Special Kicks Off A.T.R.M. Tax Cut Plan." *Taxing Times.* Los Angeles: American Tax Reduction Movement, Inc., n.d.

"Jarvis Considering Drive against State Income Tax." *Oakland Tribune,* 16 March 1979, sec. C, p. 6.

"Jarvis Takes Aim at State Income Tax." *Oakland Tribune,* 17 April 1979, sec. A, p. 3.

Kearns, John, sales manager, Inter-Continental Press Syndicate. Interview, Oakland, Calif., 21 April 1979.

Kolkey, Peggy, administrative assistant to Howard Jarvis. Interview, Oakland, Calif., 23 April 1979.

League of California Cities. *Digest of 1979–80 Assembly Bills Affecting Cities.* Report no. 3, League of California Cities, Sacramento, 1979.

———. *Digest of 1979–80 Senate Bills Affecting Cities.* Reports no. 2 and 3, League of California Cities, Sacramento, 1979.

Legislative Bulletin (League of California Cities). 18 July, 18 August, 5 September, 13 September, 17 November 1978; 16 February, 23 February, 6 April, 13 April, and 20 July 1979.

"Local Government Profile." *Cal-Tax Research Bulletin.* November 1978.

McCarthy, Leo T., speaker of the California assembly. *Letter to Educators and Civic Leaders.* Sacramento: Office of Assemblyman Leo McCarthy, 12 June 1979.

Post, A. Alan. *Commission on Government Reform—Final Report.* Sacramento: State of California, 5 February 1979.

———. *Individuals Serving as Task Force Members for the Commission on Government Reform.* Sacramento: State of California, 30 August 1978.

———. *Organizations Represented on Task Forces of the Commission on Government Reform.* Sacramento: State of California, 30 August 1978.

"Property Tax Shift Proposals." Lynn M. Suter, legislative consultant, to Oakland Mayor and City Council, 30 January 1979. Files of Oakland City Council, Oakland, Calif.

"Report on Current Legislative Activities." Lynn M. Suter, legislative consultant, to Oakland Mayor and City Council, 6 April 1979. Files of Oakland City Council, Oakland, Calif.

Salzman, Ed, editor. "California Adopts Long-Term Bailout." *Tax Revolt Digest* 1 (August 1979): 3–4.

Simpson, Richard P. "Spotlight on Proposition 13." *Western City Magazine* 53 (April 1978): 9–12.

"'Spirit of 13' Qualifies for State Ballot." *Oakland Tribune,* 11 April 1979, sec. A, p. 7.

"$210-Million State Tax Cut—Big Boost in Renter Credit also Enacted." *Oakland Tribune,* 15 September 1979, sec. A, p. 1.

Viscount, Francis. "Task Force Takes Close Look at Effects of Proposition 13." *Nation's Cities Weekly* 2 (12 February 1979): 1 and 8.

Wood, Samuel E. "The 'Sleeper' in Proposition 13: Statewide Planning's Chance to Work." *Cry California* 3 (Fall 1978): 7–13.

Index

216

About the Author

Roger L. Kemp is presently city manager of Seaside, California. He is also a lecturer at the Graduate School of Public Administration, Golden Gate University, Monterey Campus. Dr. Kemp formerly held positions in Oakland's Office of Budget and Management Services and the Office of the City Manager. He received the Bachelor of Science degree in business administration and the Master of Public Administration degree from San Diego State University and the Doctor of Public Administration degree from Golden Gate University. Dr. Kemp has published numerous articles in the fields of public administration, municipal finance, and taxation. Most recently he was contributing author to *Managing with Less*.